# GARDNER'S *guide to*

# Audio
# POST PRODUCTION

## Mark Scetta

GARTH GARDNER COMPANY

*GGC publishing*

Washington DC, USA · London, UK

Publisher: Garth Gardner, Ph.D.
Editor: Chris Edwards
Cover Designer: Desiree Rappa
Concept Designer: Nic Banks
Illustrator: Holly Wach
Layout Designer: Rachelle Painchaud-Nash

Editorial inquiries concerning this book should be mailed to:
The Editor, Garth Gardner Company, 5107 13th Street N.W., Washington DC
20011 or emailed to: info@ggcinc.com.
http://www.gogardner.com

Library of Congress Cataloging-in-Publication Data

Scetta, Mark.
  Gardner's guide to audio post production / by Mark Scetta.
     p. cm.
  ISBN 1-58965-028-X
  1.  Sound motion pictures. 2.  Sound--Recording and reproducing. 3.
Video tapes--Editing. 4.  Motion pictures--Editing.  I. Title.
  TR897.S415 2007
  778.5'344--dc22

                                    2007014484

Printed in Canada

# Table of Contents

**Acknowledgments** ix

## Chapter 1

**Pre Post: Establishing Shot** 1
Why you need this book 2
Plan of attack 3
What exactly is a soundtrack? 4
There are at least two ways to use this book 7

## Chapter 2

**Pre Post: The Enchanting Illusion of Sight and Sound** 9
The vision: your favorite films 10
Behold the magic: when sound and picture come together 10
Listening to the world 11
Watching the picture–and only the picture 14

## Chapter 3

**Pre Post: Visualizing Sound** 19
Pure imagination 20
Dialogue first 22
Sound design: Foley and sound effects 24
Making your bed: ambient environments 27
Music: sweet emotion 30
In the mix: bringing it to life 33

## Chapter 4

**Setup: The Audio Studio: Wiring and the Workstation** 37
Can't I just mix the sound in my non-linear video editor (NLE)? 38
Video versus audio editing platforms 40
Platform choices 41
Sound cards, audio interfaces, and mixers 43
Signals 44
Things to know about digital gear 47
Cables 49

Specifying the right cables for your needs     50
The power and the buzz     52
Your monitors, your friends     56
Plug-ins     58
DAW tips     59
Comfort and ergonomics     61

## Chapter 5

**Setup: The Accurate Listening Environment**     **63**

Workflow: Getting set for mixing     64
Tips for creating a more accurate listening environment     64
Proper positioning     65
Acoustical treatment – overlooked and underestimated     69
Sound smear     71
DIY: other options for a great sounding room     74
Calibrating the monitoring environment     76

## Chapter 6

**Setup: Prepare to Make the Jump to Light Speed**     **83**

First, lock picture     84
Everything you ever wanted to know about sync
but were afraid to ask     87
Application translation: OMF and AAF     89
What to do if you can't OMF/AAF     94
Rendering the video file     95

## Chapter 7

**Setup: The Audio Session**     **99**

The sequencer environment     101
Check out the view…and the pool!     102
The track     104
Insert effects     106
Offline processing     107
Auxiliary channels     108
Group channels     109
The Master Bus     110
Stereo or surround?     111

Rudiments of digital audio ....................................... 112
Looking ahead: Templates ...................................... 121
Looking ahead: Key commands .............................. 124

## Chapter 8

### Elements: Dialogue, Most Importantly ........... 127

Dialogue editing workflow ...................................... 128
Setting up ................................................................. 129
Emergency ward: Noise ........................................... 132
Removing crackle ..................................................... 137
Removing hums and buzzes .................................... 139
Noise we like, noise we don't .................................. 141
Airplanes and air conditioners: removing broadband noise ... 143
Rumble: EQ to the rescue ......................................... 149
Level control ............................................................. 149

## Chapter 9

### Elements: Replacement Dialogue (ADR) and Narration ... 153

ADR: Do I have to? .................................................. 153
Recording techniques for ADR ................................ 154
Syncing dialogue ..................................................... 161
Mic choice and recording techniques for narration ... 162
Narration editing ..................................................... 165
Edit and clean up the narration ............................. 166
Getting the best take .............................................. 167

## Chapter 10

### Elements: Sound Effects and Foley ............... 169

Where to find Foley and SFX libraries .................... 172
Getting organized ................................................... 175
Foley: The pits, the props, and the pain ................ 177
Footsteps first ......................................................... 178
Beyond footsteps .................................................... 181
Off-camera sound effects: interpreting emotion, creating tension ... 186
Can't find it? Make it: Recording SFX and Foley ... 187
Bodyfalls and fireballs: Creative SFX .................... 191

## Chapter 11

**Elements: Ambience and Room Tone**      **193**

What's in an ambience?      194
Pouring the foundation      196
More ideas for ambience and tone      200
Room tone: Good noise      200
Where to find room tone      203
How to lay in ambiences and RT      204
Excess ambience      211
Looking ahead: some extra thought in production saves headaches in post      214

## Chapter 12

**Elements: Music**      **215**

Temp tracks      216
Licensing pre-existing music      219
Budgeting and fees      222
Finding music for your film      225
Custom scores and working with composers      233
Music editing      237
Music-editing basics      238
Looping and extending musical passages      239
More ideas for using music      242

## Chapter 13

**Home Stretch: Special Effects**      **243**

Tiny speakers: put it through a telephone      244
Massive ambience: put it in a huge room      245
The muffle: put it in the room next door      246
Dream weaving      248
An approach to narration      249
Creative panning      250
Doubling      251
More sound design, please      252
Working methods for special processing      253

## Chapter 14

**Home Stretch: The Mix**                                         **255**

Ready to mix                                                       256

Loudness, dynamics, and compression                               257

Crash course in equalization                                      260

Mastering music                                                    264

The soundstage: Creating an effective sonic panorama              266

Everything in its right place: Reverb                             274

The master channel                                                276

Metering                                                          277

Mixing and levels                                                 279

Checking the mix                                                  286

## Chapter 15

**Home Stretch: Output, Layback, and Archiving**                  **291**

Exporting the final mix                                           292

Laying the sound back into the video                              295

Backing up, going forward                                         295

## Chapter 16

**Post Mortem: Looking Ahead**                                    **297**

Tips for location recording                                       297

Make time for sound                                               299

**Glossary**                                                      **301**

**Index**                                                         **307**

# Acknowledgments

The author would like to extend his deepest thanks to:

- Anthony Mason & Chris Edwards at the Garth Gardner Company, for initiating the idea for this book and seeing it through, Holly Wach at HollyWach.com for her tireless devotion in bringing the pages to life with her talents of pen and ink, his parents for their unrelenting support, all of his former indie film clients, whose production sound recordings made this book absolutely necessary, and to everyone below. You have all contributed to this work in some way to benefit filmmakers everywhere. My sincerest thanks for lending your time and expertise.

- Dominick Tavella at Sound One NYC

- Alex Holz at The Orchard

- Andy Potvin at Dolby Labs

- Brian Nimens at Sound Ideas.com

- Bryon Rickerson at UglyMusicProductions.com

- Stephanie Kantorski at stephoto.us for a literary hand hold

- Jacob Waxler at IndieFlavor.com

- Stephen Unger at FeeFyeFoeFilms.com

- Raza Sufi for diode crimp rods and a mic closet

- Hannah Nackson for quantization ditherings

- Harry Bissell, guru's guru

- Aneikit Bonnel

- Dr. Faye Mandell

- Bill Gladstone of Waterside

- Robert Larow

Additional technical consulting:

- Alan Silverman
- Bob Ohlsson
- Jeff Levison
- Jeff Straw at InGrooves.com/ZoomLicense.com
- Ethan Winer, RealTraps.com, and the MusicPlayer.com acoustics forum
- Larry Hathaway and Bill Whitlock at Jensen-Transformers.com

# Chapter 1

# Establishing Shot

The explosion of digital editing technology since the 1990s has made it possible to edit your film and create a high-quality soundtrack using commonly available computer equipment. These blessings have their drawbacks, however, and the "technical overload" of hardware, software, file formats, and working methods can easily discourage a new filmmaker's dreams. This book will help you solve your film's audio problems while creating a dynamic soundtrack using practical, hands-on audio engineering techniques. You can make a great-sounding mix with patience, careful listening, some basic computer and audio gear, and a strong desire to get it done.

This book takes a practical and holistic approach to post-production sound, guiding you through creative exercises and clear procedures toward the goal of a clean, dynamic, emotionally moving, and broadcast quality mix for your picture. We're assuming that you have an existing soundtrack that needs heavy work in every way, riddled with problems – such as crunchy dialogue and an empty mix. We're also assuming you have at least a small amount of previous experience editing video or audio on a computer.

There is no longer any reason to shy away from noise problems and other sound troubles because the mystical art of audio seemed overwhelming. Most of the audio issues that plague new ~~audio engineers~~ filmmakers are quite solvable by anyone with some technical aptitude and a little patience.

## Why you need this book

Anyone who can edit video can create the 'magic' that happens when picture and sound are working together and the thrill of a movie comes alive. This book is a good place to start if:

- Your film has sound problems that need attention.
- You want to take a decent sound mix – or your digital audio skills – to the next level.
- You are curious about how the soundtrack for any genre of film is created.

This book is for the hands-on filmmaker or video editor who is finally ready to brave the audio jungle. This person is comfortable with using an audio or video sequencing program and finally wants to build a quality soundtrack. This person is willing to get their hands dirty with some studio setup, listening exercises, and technical procedures. By the end of this book, this filmmaker's desire and dedication will result in a rich learning experience and a soundtrack to be proud of.

An old adage says to first plan the work, then work the plan. First, we'll mentally prepare the sonic canvas by dreaming up a vision for your soundtrack. Then we will paint the soundtrack you're dreaming of. We'll minimize the technical hurdles on the way to your masterpiece with a results oriented approach.

# Plan of attack

We're going to build a complete soundtrack from the ground up. We begin with a couple of planning and setup chapters to transition you from video editing to the audio equivalent. Before getting into a lot of technical procedures these **Pre post** chapters first help you define the vision for your soundtrack. You will compose your soundtrack on paper as you jot down ideas and trouble spots to work on. These notes will be your breadcrumbs through the forest of your first post-production audio adventure.

The middle **Setup** chapters lead you through the dense jungle of audio cabling, studio acoustics, computer setup, and audio sequencers. This section gives you a hand to hold through the transition from a video editing platform to an audio workstation and gets right into editing audio in an audio sequencer. These chapters explain the tough technical stuff such as the OMF (Open Media Framework) and AAF (Advanced Authoring Format) cross sequencer translation tools, analog and digital signals, decibel scales, and both hardware and software are tackled in the **Setup** chapters. Once we've roughed out your studio and computer framework, we begin construction on the soundtrack.

These **Elements** chapters make up Act II of the book and work through each sonic layer of your new mix, one feature at a time. We begin the **Elements** section with a full-service treatment of dialogue. The magic act of that most ubiquitous of production sound concerns – noise – will be revealed. You'll see that there is *good* noise, noise that is your friend, noise that you can take home to mom, noise used for smoothing dialogue transitions.

Like editing picture, sound sculpting often involves scrapping some perfectly good footage. Even precious dialogue can take away from a scene sometimes. You might find yourself replacing weak dialogue, or muting it into oblivion, choosing instead to charm audiences through your new souped up music and sound effects tracks.

After working out the dilemmas of dialogue you'll learn how to create and enhance the other layers of a soundtrack. You'll combine music, ambience beds, sound effects, and Foley to create rich, believable sound environments. It doesn't stop there: you'll learn tips and techniques for voiceover (VO) recording, putting special effects on dialogue, and finding music for your film.

After making it through the **Elements** you'll come to the **Home Stretch**: making the final mix. Bringing it all together can be overwhelming not only aesthetically but also in staying organized among hundreds or thousands of audio clips. It's a challenge just to maintain consistent volume levels across all scenes–no small feat for a full length feature. The interesting, full, exciting mix we're shooting for requires much more than just setting fader levels. By the end of this section you will also have learned how to properly use reverb, compression, EQ, and other audio effects to put the final sheen on your new soundtrack. Then you'll deliver the mix to the video platform, confident that it's ready for the screen–whether television, cinema, or computer.

We'll wrap with a **Post Mortem** discussion about what your biggest challenges were in audio post. From this we'll come up with some ideas for your next shoot to ensure that your next sound mix goes more smoothly.

## What exactly is a soundtrack?

If you're interested enough in film production to be holding this book you have probably at some point listened carefully to a movie soundtrack and picked out the various elements of the sound mix. Where and when is music best used? What are the best volume levels for background ambience tracks? Where do we find unusual sounds that we can't record ourselves? How do we make sound effects sound believable yet immense–like they do in big budget films?

Let's introduce a few of the elements of a successful soundtrack. Maybe you've heard one of the unsung heroes of a soundtrack, **ambience tracks**, working its subliminal magic in a scene. These low-level sonic environments assure us that our actors are actually *in* that large restaurant, or 1950s small town, or space station. Sometimes these ambiences are simply the very low-level noise that defines a room or space. We call this **room tone** – a very quiet audio track made of the appliances, machinery, lights, or distant traffic in a scene. Both of these kinds of ambiences turn a sterile sounding, lifeless scene into one that draws the viewer in and keeps their attention. These tracks give your film an edge over other low budget films that often lack that extra layer of believability and immersion. We'll learn how to build these crucial environments, where to find them, and how to fit them into a mix.

## SOUND EDITORIAL ON A BIG BUDGET

Digital technology continues to increase the possibilities and lighten the workload of post-production film sound departments. Even after digital editing software and hardware exploded independent filmmaking, we continued to see innovations that improved our workflow. LCD monitors show us greater detail and clarity than ever. Sound effects libraries can now be conveniently delivered on devices such as hard drives and portable media players. We are fortunate that we can realize our own filmic vision in as much detail and realism as we want today, even on modest budgets. Throughout the last 80 years, however, it has taken the work of a whole team of post-production audio specialists–over many weeks or even months–to bring a soundtrack together. This team is generally built around the following specialists:

- 🎧 The **Supervising Sound Editor** oversees the post-sound department, creates schedules, budgets, and timelines for the crew, and works directly with the director and producer to realize their vision of the soundtrack.

- 🎧 **Dialogue Editors** report to a **Dialogue Supervisor**. They cut up and line up production dialogue to match actors' lips. They work at a level of precision that lets them substitute words and even syllables in lines of dialogue.

- **ADR Mixers** and **Editors** report to the **ADR Supervisor** and deliver re-recorded dialogue lines to the dialogue editors. The **ADR Mixer** and **ADR Recordist** hold recording sessions with the actors, working from a cue sheet of production dialogue that either needs to be replaced or was never recorded in the first place, due to an unfavorable recording environment on set. *(Note: Automatic Dialogue Replacement refers to studio recorded dialogue (in post) that replaces location (production) dialogue.)*

- **Foley Artists** are the sound department's unsung heroes and get to work with all kinds of fun and dangerous props to recreate the natural sound effects you expect to hear when watching the action. They create the actors' footsteps, punches and bodyfalls, and make you believe that the slow crrrrack of a piece of celery is the crushing of some actor's skull. The **Foley Mixer** records the **Foley Artist** in session, and **Foley Editors** cut up this work and prepare the files for the **Foley Supervisor.**

- The **Sound Effects Mixer** reports to a **SFX Supervisor** and goes out to record live sound effects, while the **SFX Editor** digs up and designs new whooshes, bangs, killer sharks, light sabers…

- **Sound Designer** is a generic term sometimes used to describe the single, or more senior, sound mixer/editor on a lower budget or independent film. On a large budget film, this title refers to a sound effects specialist who provides particularly creative sound effects that are not easily recorded, synthesized, or otherwise obtained by the SFX Editors.

- **Re-Recording Mixers** build the final soundtrack from the work of Sound Editorial by matching and sweetening tracks into a final mix. We'll do this, too, in the section called **The Home Stretch**.

- And finally, though it's kind of vague, the title of **Sound Mixer** refers to the person who recorded the sound on set during production, and took holiday in Aruba during post.

It can be overwhelming to think that there are entire careers behind each of these areas of expertise. But after all, low-budget filmmaking is all about giving a film a high production value on a much smaller budget. To that end you may find yourself wearing the hats of every one of these people–especially if your shoot lacked the time or experience to make high-quality recordings. While this is typical of independent filmmaking, by the end of the book we'll see that budgeting for better sound recording on set can save a lot of time, money, and frustration in post.

Perhaps you've felt that there is another element of realism missing from your film's world. It might be what we call **Foley** (after Jack Foley, M.P.S.E., 1891 1967)–the everyday sounds of footsteps, clothing movement, car doors, creaky floors, fight scenes, and more – that most pictures do not record during shooting. The integrity of your actors' performances depends on these sounds, and their quality will take your film's believability and professionalism to the next level.

Finally, amid all of these supporting layers is the **dialogue**, and dialogue, as they say, is king. But what if your dialogue is riddled with hums, noise, and distortion? Even the production dialogue of high-budget films sometimes comes out noisy or even unusable. So we clean up the production dialogue that can be saved, and we re-record noisy, distorted and unnatural sounding dialogue in the studio as ADR. Then we get it all sounding clean, natural, warm, dynamic, and at the right level in the mix. It sounds daunting, and dialogue makes up a fairly significant amount of the workload of audio post. Large budget pictures may have up to five people all working on various aspects of just the dialogue tracks. However, you may be surprised at the quality that can be achieved from today's digital audio tools, some patience, and a good set of ears.

## There are at least two ways to use this book

We want to make a compelling soundtrack with all of the elements of a professional mix. But how do we get there? The chapters of the book are arranged in workflow order, from the basics of setting up the work environment all the way to outputting a full-featured mix. The most comprehensive approach is to pursue them in order, letting them infuse you with sound engineering skills and insights as you compose your first full-featured soundtrack.

Alternately you may have specific problems you need to research and solve right away. Since the chapters treat the building blocks of a sound mix one element at a time, it's easy to jump around in a non-linear fashion and work out what needs attention. But also be sure to check out the **Setup** section, especially the chapters on audio studio wiring and setting up an accurate listening environment. Improper gear setup can lead to hums, buzzes, and other problems. And poor studio acoustics always translate into poor sound mixes. These topics have some secrets that might make or break all of the work you're about to put into your mix.

First, let's talk about why you're doing this in the first place.

## Chapter 2

# Pre Post: The Enchanting Illusion of Sight and Sound

Even lower-budget independent film soundtracks can be developed into much more than just a cleaned up version of their production sound. Now that you are familiar with the other elements that can be added in post, you can start to visualize a more robust soundscape for your picture. Use the exercises in this chapter to get the juices flowing.

## The vision: your favorite films

What is it about the films in your Top 10 that fascinate you? The thrill of suspense, the wild creative world of animation, the drama of reality TV, the impact of action that appears to jump out of the screen… films are emotional sculptures that strive to be memorable experiences. They require more than good writing, shooting, and editing, an attention to technical details across many disciplines is needed. Good filmmakers spare the viewer from distractions like unflattering lighting, flawed continuity, and noisy dialogue.

Great stories are only as powerful as how well they are told, and this year's viewer assumes better sound and picture than last year's. The successful filmmaker knows that it takes a lot of stamina to make it to post production, and that the quality of her editing team will make or break the film. It's a given that she has to overcome a huge number of technical challenges to achieve the highest quality she can in post. In this quick chapter we'll learn what it is about the medium of film that reaches around the viewer and really grabs hold of him.

## Behold the magic: when sound and picture come together

Seeing a film for the first time you feel the dramatic impact when sound and picture collide and take over your senses. Watch a movie you love for the third, fourth, or fifth time and you can really start to see how it's sewn together. You'll notice that there is real magic in the dynamic punch when sound meets picture. These moments of dramatic impact overload our senses and bring the picture to life. This is quantum filmmaking: the whole emotional impact is much more than sum of the audio and video. This is what makes moviemaking worth the effort.

Great sound meets inspired, creative shots and emotional acting, and a movie comes alive. The excitement of a battle is a direct result of the believability and complexity of the Foley sound effects: gunshots that are well timed and match the type of gun, footsteps that match the person and place and aren't distracting, wooden wheels rolling across the loud, rough texture of gravel. Even the most delicate moments in a picture have the potential to make this magic. An extreme close up of a destitute, forlorn main character can be made quite intimate with clean dialogue and a howling desert wind mixed in at just the right level.

Making these moments requires technical and artistic attention to *both* sound and picture. It requires patience to learn new procedures but it pays off in the satisfaction of having created something of quality. Taking the extra time in post to create a slick soundtrack can mean the difference between a movie that was 'OK' and one that makes memorable impact.

## Listening to the world

People skills and project management notwithstanding, very little prepares a person to become a great filmmaker more than a strong imagination. Those steeped in a fine arts education have the opportunity to develop their senses of sight and sound to a high degree. And just as technical ability can be learned with patience, aesthetic sensitivity can be enhanced with practical exercises.

## Exercise: Going blind

When one of our senses goes deprived, another will come around and play double-time to compensate. This is an eye opening exercise for which you'll need a friend and, interestingly enough, a blindfold.

Find a safe and quiet location with some natural obstacles but without hazards like stairs or traffic, perhaps somewhere outside in a park or in a very large room. Put on the blindfold and walk around, and try to find your way around. Have your sighted friend guide you, keeping an eye out for obstacles. After a short time you should find that your hearing has perked up to a sensitivity you didn't know you had. In a reasonably quiet location, you begin to hear your own footsteps and those of your friend. Your aural perception escalates until after 20 or 30 minutes you may begin to 'sense' where obstacles are, as if you could feel their locations by their density in the space around you.

What is particularly interesting about the blindfold walk is that our ears suddenly become very prescient and valuable. Rather quickly we are tuned in to the ambience around us: things like traffic or birds become very clear—you can follow the trajectory of a particular car or of a single bird. Footsteps, in particular, become very present, taken for granted as almost useless information before. They reveal something about character and help us interpret what's going on with a person we cannot see. We can learn a lot from the way a person walks: what kind of mood they are in, what they wear on their feet, what kind of room they are in, how loud that room is—heavy steps or fast, clumsy steps? Boots or barefoot? Hard, cold frozen ground or creaky wood flooring? Are the footsteps barely audible or are they the only major sound in the room? We don't realize how acute our own hearing actually is until we use it for study or safety.

The blind lady in the train station taps her way around because the reflections of that sound cue her in to how close or far objects, especially objects with hard surfaces, are in space. The louder the tap, the denser the echoes of that tap, and the closer she is to something. The more high frequencies in that tap, the closer a hard surface is. A loud tap with no echoes and more bass suggests perhaps people, fabric, or other absorptive material is in close range.

Most sighted people have more immediate means of finding their way around and so do not develop this level of sonar, but sound cues can still help build a mental picture of a place never seen before. In film, detailed and relevant sonic textures help build a more interesting and richer world that commands more from the viewer's senses—exactly what every director wants.

## Watching the picture–and only the picture

A lot of filmmakers today are enthralled with the wonders of cinematography and film and video editing. They are crazy about the latest CGI techniques, compositing, cloning, body motion sensors, and how the visual aspect of film can take the viewer beyond the real world. What they often don't realize is that the same care taken in post sound can enhance a film on even the tightest of budgets such that its quality and message make people stand up and take notice.

Deep within the soundtrack lies the emotion that the filmmaker is ultimately trying to convey. The talents of cinematographers and VFX designers notwithstanding, it is no wonder that great picture without great sound can easily leave the viewer unmoved.

### Exercise: Turn it down

This exercise is simple but valuable. Watch a TV show or a movie you don't know with the sound turned down. Before boredom completely sets in, imagine a fresh, new, detailed soundtrack for the picture.

Let's take an example scene. Dream up a sound that might work with a close up, wide angle shot of an obese man eating a very substantial Italian meal. How could you interpret the scene sonically? You could simply present him through the natural, location sound of

him and the
restaurant. Or
you could bring
the viewer into
his intimate world
by muting the
production sound,
re-recording all of
the knife and
fork Foley, and
minimizing the

restaurant ambience. This artistic decision requires
more work in post, and creates a more intimate, and
perhaps paranoid effect. Another soundtrack might
accompany this shot with slowed down, time-stretched
or echoed sound effects, creating a dream-like, ethereal world that picks up off of the strangeness created
by the wide angle lens. This character and filmic
moment can be made casual, intimate, proper and
reserved, gluttonous, just plain funny, or a number of
other interpretations. Sound designers for cartoons
and animated films know this inherently and always
seek to enhance drama through unusual or interpre-
tive sound effects.

## Exercise: Watching the sound

Here's the opposite of 'watch the picture.' Put on a
movie you've seen before and watch it without the

picture...turn off the TV and just listen to what's going on in the soundtrack. Are the sonic events and environments creating images in your head that tell a story? Follow the actor's footsteps; is she walking away from us or toward us? Listen to that punch that the lead actor just took – did he get hit in the head, stomach, or somewhere else? How natural was the impact, or how stylized/hyped? Was there a lot of heavy bass in it? (Does that happen with real punches in real life? Does it matter?) Did he fall hard, hit something soft, or roll to the ground?

This exercise is particularly fun and challenging with an animated picture, since there is no natural production sound and all of the sound is designed in the studio. Sometimes sound effects can  imply any of a number of different types of motion and action.

## Exercise: Listening in other languages

Here's another exercise you can do to get your ears used to separating the sonic layers of a mix. Put in a foreign film, turn off the subtitles, and grab some popcorn. You quickly lose interest in the dialogue and the ear tries to grasp the things it can understand. The sound effects and music cues pop right out.

When you're not focused on the story, layers of the soundtrack fall apart like a warm croissant. Your ears are more able to pick apart the various soundtrack elements.

This also works great on foreign language radio stations. Check out the cheesy sound effects they add between lines of voiceover in the commercials. Listen for the ambience beds of traffic or restaurants that try to instill some realism.

Hopefully, your family will understand why you're suddenly tuning into Spanish radio....

# Chapter 3

# Pre Post: Visualizing Sound

Y ou need a vision of your soundtrack before doing any sound design or actual mixing. The clearer and more detailed you are about what you might like to hear in your film, the easier the whole post-sound process will be. As you dissect your film and create the vision for your soundtrack, your notes – both mental and written – will be your road map. In this chapter we're all about opening up new doors to give your film a comprehensive sound treatment. When it comes time to produce your new intricate soundtrack you will need a clear idea of what needs to be done.

But first let's talk about what CAN be done.

## Pure imagination

Creating a film can be an endless process. Once in post, we discover that there were things we wish had been shot differently or even written differently. Post production means making the best product out of available footage, improving existing scenes, and even creating additional shots. Film and video editors add establishing shots, close ups, B roll, and animation that stretches the visual dynamic range of the film, using stock libraries and custom artistry completely in post. *Audio* post is no different: we make the best of the recorded production sound. But like video editing, the production tapes are just the beginning of your new, multilayered soundtrack.

Do you wish more location sound was recorded on set for some of your scenes? Perhaps you have *no* sound at all for certain scenes. Not to worry. We'll be learning how to build a soundtrack from the bottom up, including how to replace lost dialogue. Audio post is about getting the most out of the sound you do have, and it's also about bringing average – or problem – scenes to life with new sonic layers.

Luckily, a lot of sound *can* be created in post. The only limits are your imagination and sonic resources. Existing dialogue can be cleaned up, cut and spliced, re-recorded and creatively altered. Vast libraries of sound effects and ambiences offer the resourceful filmmaker the ability to create worlds from other countries or other planets. And the filmmaker does not have to go it alone. The internet makes it easy to find talented composers, engineers, voiceover artists, and other sound enthusiasts eager to be part of a film.

### Brainstorm

The first ingredient of a successful soundtrack is a solid plan of attack. Let's build yours in the most creative way possible. Whenever you are thinking about your picture, say, during video editing, keep a notebook (or notebook computer) of good ideas for your soundtrack. Anytime something comes to mind that may improve the sound of the picture, make a note of it right there and then. Writing down your ideas every time will eventually develop into an organized plan of attack that will keep you on track throughout the long and complex post-sound journey.

As you brainstorm about what you would like to hear in your own film, watch other movies in the same genre – and keep your notebook with you. Write down what you like about that film's soundtrack. Narrow it down to specific things to the best of your technical vocabulary. Use the ideas in this chapter and comb over the table of contents to jog your mind.

Writing it down will make all the difference in how many of your ideas get accomplished. Work like a pro: keep your notes clear, organized, readable, and in linear order as much as possible. In later chapters, when even more ideas and tasks are whirling around, this basic task list will help you turn your most important ideas into reality.

## Dialogue first

When characters in a movie speak, viewers listen. The viewer needs to be able to understand them with relative ease on any decent playback system. It is the job of the post-sound engineer to be sure the dialogue is comfortable to hear on a variety of playback systems. That engineer, in this case, is you.

We want dialogue to sound clean and easily intelligible for every kind of speech, from a whisper to a shout, in both sparse and busy backgrounds, for voices light and bold. Furthermore, dialogue must have a consistent tone between shots and scenes, whether it was recorded during the scene, after the scene on set (wild), or in post (ADR). Lastly, our dialogue must be believable by sounding like it exists in a real world location, be it a factory, field, wine cellar, or well.

## Taking note(s)

What do you feel needs to be done to improve your dialogue? How noisy is it? What kind of noise is it? Is there too much background in the recording? If you're not sure if a portion of dialogue is usable, make notes about what the trouble is. If you're working on a long running film, give these notes specific time references. Jot the approximate time in the picture and describe the general issue. Later you can decide to clean up the dialogue or re-record (ADR) it.

Specifically describe the noise issues: listen for hiss, clipping (distortion due to volume levels that got too loud for the recorder to handle), dropouts (*either* moments of missing sound or unnatural 'jump cuts' in the audio), clothing and mic rustle, radio interference (from wireless mics), and any other problems. Does the dialogue sound thin or boomy in places? Are there special effects (like telephone voices) that need to be applied for realism?

Your notes might look something like this:

Scene 8 – Val and Betty arguing

– Betty's dialogue very low throughout scene. –

00:04:24:18* (Note: This is SMPTE timecode referring to 0 hours, 4 minutes, 24 seconds, and 18 frames from picture start. Use a normal time reference if you are more comfortable with it, or just keep your notes in order to make it easy to find your way through the list later.) – Val's voice sounds thin

00:04:25:10 – plosive (harsh 'pop' on the letter 'P') in Val's line 'Put the gun down'

00:05:35:20 – airplane passing overhead, masking Val's line

00:05:40:24 – loud thump (Val hits chest mic)

00:05:48:00 – Betty sibilance (loud whistling 'ssss' sound) on phrase 'a little silence in here'

00:05:53:00 – Distortion/clipping as Val shouts at Betty

Etc....

A great sounding dialogue track is the number one sonic concern of most filmmakers and with good reason. Clean, pleasing, and believable dialogue can make or break both the impact of the story and the patience level of the viewer. In the *Elements* chapter on dialogue we will solve each of the issues of dialogue one at a time.

## Sound design: Foley and sound effects

Dialogue is king. In big budget pictures, sound effects are usually the next of kin. While music may be the queen of emotion, in a feature it

plays a backseat to the action, filling in around dialogue and events. Documentaries may take a different approach, but for narratives we need to enhance the *action* in order to bring out the story.

Production Sound Mixers and their microphones are not to blame for a lack of sound effects in your film. They need to be concerned primarily with the dialogue while recording. It's not necessarily the Sound Mixer's job to capture all of the essential incidentals – the footsteps, doors opening and closing, clothing movement, vehicles, etc. – it is up to the post-audio engineer to obtain and place these sounds to give the film the believability of natural action and movement. A good Sound Mixer will, however, provide the audio-post department with as many extra 'wild sound' recordings of sound effects as possible, but these are done separate from the dialogue. Clean dialogue is their priority.

It can be a fine line that separates Foley from sound effects. Think of Foley as the natural sounds the viewer expects to match the action on screen. As mentioned in the introduction, these pertain to footsteps, vehicles, doors, clothing movement, equipment handling, and other sounds that are normally performed live by a Foley Artist in a studio with hundreds of special props.

Foley for fight scenes, car chases, and other moments of excitement quickly becomes full-on sound effects design when the director wants to take a scene up a notch. The impact of a punch, kick, slap, fall, skid, or explosion can sound dull if left natural or it can be greatly enhanced with sound effects from stock libraries – whatever best suits the feel of the film. Likewise, you might not have a car chase in your film, but there are probably plenty of actions that can be enhanced with sound effects. It's a matter of watching a film with an ear turned toward the motions of the people and props on screen.

Sound effects can go way beyond layering basic Foley (like a punch) with larger impact effects. They can make an almost musical score out of drones and strange noises for dream sequences and ethereal shots. They can smooth or intensify transitions between cuts with whooshes and sweeps to animate fun moments and keep the film moving. The uses of a quality sound effect collections are limitless.

## Exercise: Get fresh

After some time away from the picture, try to watch your film as if for the first time. Be acutely aware of every actor's movement including the brushing of clothes and any other moving objects in the scene. As you discover new actions that don't seem to have associated sound, write down the action that needs aural illustration. For example 'Robert getting up from kitchen chair,' 'April walking barefoot across tile floor,' 'placing spoon in metal sink.'

If your scene is particularly thin or was recorded MOS (without any production sound) focus now on making an exhaustive list of sounds that are lacking in the scene. Find every action that deserves a sound. Think in layers, where many sounds get combined to create a larger, more believable environment. Later, we'll find these sound effects and learn how to integrate them into the mix. Do this for every scene and you will be on your way to a realistic, detailed, and stimulating soundtrack.

For scenes that have usable production soundtracks, identify where the existing sounds could use a little boost – perhaps some impact in the bass region of a certain sound, something to improve its clarity, or an overlaid sound to make it more interesting. An example of this might be fireworks – you can often layer multiple fireworks explosions over each other for a stronger impact. It's up to you to decide how natural, brute, comical, etc., you want your sound effects to be.

Even sound effects and ambiences have a certain amount of crossover. Look for places to enhance the meaning of a scene with additional, off camera sound. Radios, TVs, machinery, airplanes, traffic, and people are all possibilities. 'Idea for ambience track – add children playing outside the kitchen window.' Make notes for any sound you imagine would enhance the scene and later we will find, place, and mix these enhancements to the drama.

## Making your bed: ambient environments

The other unsung hero of a convincing soundtrack is the ambience track. The ambience track may actually be made up of several environmental sounds, constant textures, and unique incidents putting your foreground action or dialogue in the context you desire. Often these layers are very low in the mix, but without them there is a sense of a picture sounding empty, sterile, unnatural, or unfinished.

Interestingly enough most low-budget narratives and documentaries end up with *too much* ambience in the dialogue track. And often these background levels vary greatly, jumping from soft to loud between shots. We'll learn how to solve these and other issues in the *Elements* chapter on Ambiences.

### Background work

Consider the background environments for each scene in your film. For some scenes, there may be a general feeling that something is missing – it sounds empty, like the action is happening in a vacuum. For these scenes, imagine what you might hear in that set location in real life. Also imagine the general feeling you are trying to get across in the scene so that you can engineer this feeling later.

For scenes with overly noisy backgrounds, is the noise constant, or dynamic and changing? Might noise reduction help, or is there so much background that you're hoping to re-record (ADR) the dialogue and build new ambience tracks from scratch? (Note: If this sounds daunting, don't be deterred. We're going to learn how to do all of this and more in step-by-step fashion as we proceed through the book.) Begin to make notes about each scene's ambience and background noise.

Additionally, follow the actors' every motion – are there uncomfortable holes between dialogue phrases that could be filled with off camera events like passing cars, planes, machines, or animals? Take note.

Begin to think in terms of *layers* of ambiences and individual sound events. Many scenes won't require such complex layering but an interesting, custom background might be just the thing for tension filled or slow moving scenes. A busy ambience track might include:

- 🎧 immediate surroundings or room tone (constant sounds of the immediate locale like refrigerator hum, crowds, machinery, etc.)
- 🎧 distant, low-level ambience (faraway traffic, crickets, industry, desert wind, etc.)
- 🎧 specific ambient events: birds, dogs, specific vehicle pass-bys, airplanes, etc.

Though you want to give the scene all of the realism it deserves, you might be at a loss about what is missing. Scenes with too little ambience can be remedied by layering in new ambience recordings or stock

library tracks, which we'll learn to do later. For now, jot down the feeling you are trying to create in the scene. For each scene, express your ultimate ambient aspiration: tense, romantic, estranged, industrial, busy, disturbing, shocking, pleasing, disorienting, etc.

If you're particularly curious, you can skip ahead and ruffle your imagination with the list of common background textures located in the *Elements* chapter on Ambiences. Start planning how you want to build environments for your scenes, and note places where the background is so loud that re-recording the dialogue and adding new ambience might be best. For quiet scenes, listen for shifting levels in the background room tone. Determine where "room tone" is actually hum from the camera, mixer, or recorder. Aspire toward clean, interesting, subtle, and realistic backgrounds and we'll make it happen.

## Music: sweet emotion

Some kinds of films are really all about the music. For silent films, music videos, and pictures driven by a strong soundtrack, it's vital to carefully choose the right music and even cut picture to the music. Other times music is a subliminal interpreter of the action, subtly steering the audience to feel comfortable, anxious, or some other emotion. Whether composed or layered in from stock libraries, how music is used depends on the genre and intentions of film.

From a production standpoint, music can help mask or distract the viewer from problematic dialogue. By muting the other tracks, music can *become* the mix. When carefully chosen and edited it can assume all of the action and the emotion, carrying a scene for minutes at a time. Where, why, and for what effect you want music are questions that call for careful contemplation.

A custom film score of any genre, be it electronic, ambient, orchestral, or pop, naturally improves a film's sense of emotional depth and pacing. However, the independent filmmaker does not always have the luxuries of time and budget to hire a composer. We'll explore all options for obtaining music later.

# MUSIC FOR ALL GENRES

Music in film is used for a variety of reasons. Not only does it personify and underscore the emotion of the players but it can also give the viewer a break from scenes of long dialogue. It can be subtly relaxing or suggestive in a scene, it can create meaning through its lyrics, or it can contradict the action, turning it satirical or sardonic. The style of music used is a personal choice but often subscribes to some standard conventions.

**Documentaries** often need music in the background to keep things moving. Depending on the neutrality versus biased approach to the subject, they will also give screen time to music that describes, through the lyrics of a song, an insight or attitude the filmmaker is trying to get across. Docs also borrow from any of the other conventions below.

**Reality genre** pictures keep things exciting with instrumental loops and pop music beds underneath the dialogue or action. Royalty free, loop-based instrumental music is often widely available (we will cover this and other options in the later chapter on music acquisition).

**Horror** and **suspense** films are often enhanced with creative uses of bass drones, low-level whines, and other steady, threatening tones and noise layers. Orchestral and electronic/synthesized film scoring and sound design brings the suspense of a thriller alive.

**Action** scenes most often use orchestral scores with lots of strong hits and builds from the string and percussion sections, but anything that creates tension will do well, including drones, rock music, or synthesized scores.

**Family** or **children's** films and TV shows stick to the orchestral or electronic musical score and original pop songs. Sometimes they use songs like a musical does – for a fun release or a sing along – and often to teach through the lyrics. Beds of friendly music often underscore the dialogue as well.

**Comedy** tells its tale with pop songs between segments of dialogue and instrumental versions of these tunes under dialogue. A custom electronic, popular, or orchestral score might be used in dramatic or suspenseful scenes. Like animation, comedy music might spice up the action with tracks that poke fun at the actors' performance.

**Drama** is a general term, borrowing from all the other conventions, but as a genre usually calls for custom musical scores that follow the action or tracks by musical artists (as foreground music or a background bed).

**Science fiction** indies are rare, due to production costs. When they do get made they rely on the many libraries of electronic sound beds that were-created for the genre, employing drones, machine noises, and other artificial ambience beds in conjunction with a film score. They are a natural fit for electronic musicians/keyboard synthesists.

**Animation** has traditionally relied on custom orchestral music that closely follows the drama, dramatically punctuating the characters' actions. But anything goes with animation. It might be cut to a pop song, or rely entirely on creative sound design without music.

### Music spotting

Make notes of where you want to use music. Consider what a scene would sound like *with* music and *without*. If you're in the planning stage, liberally jot down any styles, bands, or songs that you know that might work in a scene.

Consider where you want music to take center stage in your scenes and where you might want it at a low-level underneath the action. Where is it instrumental and where would vocal music be best? Should it make up the whole soundtrack for a particular scene or will it be layered with sound effects, ambiences, and/or production sound? When should it start, how hard or softly should it come in, how long should it play for, should it stop or should it continue low (or *duck*) under the dialogue at some point? Will you need to re-cut video to the rhythm of a specific piece of music at any point?

Have you identified what styles of music you want for your picture? Perhaps you or your editor has already placed temporary music tracks in your video sequence. If you intend on any kind of public performance or distribution for your film, these tracks will need either replacement or licensing. Later, we'll cover both of these options in detail.

### Temp tracks

During the editing process, lay in temporary music to each scene. Choose music that reflects the emotion or meaning you want to enhance in the scene. Search your own music collections, the internet, and ask friends for help in finding that track for that bar scene that sounds like Manfred Mann meets Marilyn Manson. Carefully consider the music's tempo and overall mood. Place the music accurately in the timeline according to where you want it to start and end.

These temporary tracks provide a starting point for your future composer or music editor (you…?) to get the general mood and feel of each scene. Later if you choose to hire a composer or replace these tracks with other music you will at least have something to work from. These temp tracks will also speak a thousand words to musicians and friends who can help you find songs or compositions later.

## In the mix: bringing it to life

During the final mixing process we not only tweak volume levels but also put sounds in their appropriate spaces. 'Space' refers to the diegetic, or filmic, world of the actors or action. Reverberation and other effects change the timbre, dynamics, or character of a sound and create this final stage of believability.

In the mix, Foley, sound effects, and even dialogue can undergo serious changes in character. The engineer uses echo, reverb, equalization (EQ), and other effects to put a sound in its on-screen setting. Running water, added from a stock library, has to sound like it's happening in a bathroom. Reverb and other effects make it so. A car horn in a tunnel wouldn't sound right without applying the unique character of a tunnel echo (or reverb) to it. Even living rooms have a warm quality that makes dialogue and SFX appear intimate and actually in a real living room. Stock library sounds don't always sound natural or appropriate when 'dry' (without some sort of processing).

Oftentimes layered production and effects tracks build up too much bass, or an overly busy and harsh midrange. When mixing in a reasonably good sounding studio it's easier to see this coming before it becomes a problem. We'll see how to clean up the mud and smooth out the mids to make an easily intelligible, higher fidelity sound.

Mixdown is also the time to adjust the relative volume levels of every sound on every track. There are rough industry conventions for these levels that you'll learn about in the chapter on mixing. Other more challenging aspects of the mix will also emerge over the next few chapters: dialogue matching and EQ, compression (controlling volume levels, not encoding/decoding), metering, panning, and other more advanced mix practices.

### Special treatment

Identify the settings or locations in each of your scenes. Unless you are taking a plain documentary or reality genre approach you'll notice many places where the dialogue and SFX (especially those added in post) lack clarity, punch, or realism. Do the car passbys pan across the speakers to follow the car? Are voices on the telephone sounding like they come through a tiny speaker? Does the scene have the appropriate reverb: does it sound like the actors are in a living room, bathroom, limo, tunnel, cathedral or wherever they actually are? For now, make notes about each sound event that you notice needs special treatment.

## STORYBOARDING THE SOUND

If you've been developing a comprehensive list of things to do to every layer of your soundtrack, and if those notes are arranged logically in some kind of order, then you have a laundry list of to-dos to finish your soundtrack. You've been developing a plan of what you would at least like to hear in your soundtrack. Some of your notes may require techniques out of the scope of your time or abilities, but most of them and more will be achievable by the end of this book.

Continue to make notes as you work through the *Setup* and *Elements* chapters. Whenever you watch a film with great sound effects, or a certain quality of dialogue that you can't quite put your finger on, or that uses music in a creative way, make a note of it. Trying to describe it in words often helps you discover the essence of what you find appealing about that scene. And you'll build an organized plan of attack for later, when things get increasingly complicated. Better to go forward with the peace of mind that you'll remember those precious ideas when it comes time to work on the audio. Write it down!

At this point you have broken down just about every layer of a film's soundtrack. Fully layered soundscapes have the potential to get pretty deep, considering some layers (such as sound effects) can alone require dozens of tracks:

Dialogue/production sound

ADR

Foley

Sound effects

Room tone and ambience

Music

Narration

You can probably see why now is the time to start thinking about mixing and delivery formats. It's important to know now the type of multichannel mix you want and in what venue(s) the film will be playing.

Are you making a stereo or surround mix, or both? This decision not only affects the mixing techniques, but also the audio software you need, and perhaps any sound effects libraries you intend to buy.

Likewise, it's important to plan for the intended broadcast format. Are you mixing for large cinemas, small cinemas, DVD, TV broadcast, or the web? Each requires different mix techniques. If you're not sure, or if you have multiple formats to mix toward, you'll need to budget some time for rebalancing the mix for several formats.

Will you also need a M&E (music and sound effects, a mix without dialogue or narration) mix for foreign (dubbed) versions of the picture? In this case, it's vital that dialogue be kept clean and separate, with no Foley, room tone, or ambiences on the dialogue track.

The key thing with all of these various output considerations is to be prepared *now* so that the session is organized for easy adaptation from one delivery format to another.

The most important asset a filmmaker can have in post production is patience. Or perhaps it's caffeine and patience. If recordings came out unsatisfactory, or if some dialogue wasn't even captured, no worries: you restore the sound you have and create what you don't, as you learn the techniques needed and create an interesting and dynamic mix. It all starts with a solid studio setup, which we focus on next.

## Chapter 4

# Setup:
# The Audio Studio:
# Wiring and the Workstation

Before we begin restoring your production sound and building a full mix, we'll cover some of the more technical stuff first. In this chapter we'll get you wired for sound. We'll talk about types of audio signals, studio cabling, the digital audio workstation (DAW) including the computer, audio sequencer, digital audio interface (or soundcard), and studio monitors (speakers). We'll also solve some common problems with audio hardware and signal flow.

Soundtrack issues with independent films often relate back to deficiencies in studio acoustics — which help you hear the work accurately — or improper wiring. Good studio setup is also essential to a productive work environment and will free you up to create an audio tour de force with no distractions.

A comfortable work environment and a detailed, organized workflow are two keys to keeping you on target when distractions could sidetrack you. Some of the principles of optimizing the DAW also apply to video editing; perhaps you will recognize some of them.

After some basics on creating an effective audio room and making a comfortable work environment, we'll address some computer setup questions. We'll talk about how to set up your hard drives, how much space you're going to need, and some optimization tips.

The importance of staying organized both in the studio and in the sequencer is also paramount. No one wants to realize half-way into mixing a soundtrack that they don't have all the audio clips they need, or enough hard drive space, or a comfortable environment that lets them work for long hours at a time.

Once we bring in your audio files from your video editing software we'll arrange your tracks in the audio sequencer in order for easy editing and mixing. We'll set up a large, powerful session in an easy to navigate, logical way, which is very important when you're dealing with hundreds of clips in a sequence.

Toward the end we'll share some pointers on working with your digital audio workstation taking your work environment to the next level of comfort, efficiency, and sonic accuracy.

## Can't I just mix the sound in my non-linear video editor (NLE)?

You can certainly try. But expect to encounter severe limitations in the number of available audio tracks, the quality and availability of plug-ins, long rendering times, the extent to which you can edit audio clips, and other issues that make mixing anything but the simplest short film soundtrack pretty much a nightmare.

If you have been frustrated when dealing with audio in an NLE you are not alone. There should be a government warning label on video sequencer packaging: 'Attempting to edit audio in a video sequencer,

especially for narrative films and animation, can lead to pain, pain, pain.' The video workflow was not optimized for mixing audio and often results in serious workflow limitations.

Working with the dozens of audio tracks needed to make an exciting sound mix would be clumsy in an NLE. Audio sequencers, however, are designed to work with tracks into the double and triple digits. The timelines of NLEs usually do not offer the precise editing functionalities (such as different types of crossfades) of an audio sequencer. In addition NLE audio plug-ins like compression and equalization aren't as friendly or even as available as those on an audio editor's workstation. Furthermore, there are usually better sounding and more intuitive audio editing and measurement tools at our disposal in applications specially designed to work with audio.

Working your audio mix separate from your video sequence also allows you to concentrate solely on the soundtrack of your film without being distracted by more video editing. The audio sequencer is designed to help you get around and do fast, detailed work with dozens of audio tracks. For example, the ability to zoom in on and edit waveforms in minute detail is a must when fixing digital clicks and dropouts in a recording.

Porting over to an audio sequencer is not an extra ordeal; it's a blessing in disguise that allows you to give your film the soundtrack it deserves.

## Video versus audio editing platforms

| NLEs | DAWs |
|---|---|
| Multiple video tracks | Video tracks sometimes limited to just one |
| Limited number of audio tracks | Unlimited audio tracks (most applications) |
| Cryptic, inaccurate, and inferior sounding plug-in effects | Huge variety of great sounding plug-ins |
| Sometimes takes time for audio rendering | Real-time audio mixing |
| Limited choice of fade types | Precision control of fades and crossfades |
| Lack of audio driver features (sample rate, buffer size, and other controls) | Better integration with audio hardware (soundcards) and drivers |
| Inability to hear effects before applying them | Easy offline effects processing such as time stretching and pitch shifting with preview |
| Small track heights with lack of detail | Detailed waveform viewing for easy editing |
| Lack of visual organization and audio signal routing options | Ability to group tracks, colorize events, etc., to organize large sessions |

Today's NLE platforms such as Apple's Final Cut Pro, Avid Xpress and Media Composer, Sony Vegas, and Adobe Premiere allow us to do some pretty amazing things to video. For the independent filmmaker, the days of flatbed reel to reel editing and splicing are mostly in the past. Film, of course, has its own beauty and benefits – though this is not a book about mag stock. Digital technology allows us to edit and try new things more or less instantaneously. With the effort freed from running bulky machinery the digital artist can spend more time playing with creative possibilities.

Working with audio is a lot like working with video: the audio sequencer horizontal timeline uses event clips that will look familiar to anyone who has used a video editing application. Like video, there are audio effects we can render to individual sound clips or to an entire mix, and our familiar tools of cutting, pasting, splicing, stretching, and crossfading are also at our disposal.

So then, if you've edited video you're half way there. You're already familiar with moving clips around in a sequence. You know how to stay organized amongst hundreds of clips from many different sources. You are used to rendering effects, which is called offline processing in audio language. Later, we'll see where to use online processing versus offline processing in one of the more technical chapters.

## Platform choices

When the filmmaker is also the editor and sound designer, the natural choice is to use the same system for both video and audio editing. Some applications are bundled with both Mac and PC versions, making it easy to use the platform that is most familiar. If you have the budget, however, it is worth considering a new computer, audio sequencer, and a compatible audio interface for your chosen platform.

These days both the Mac and PC are reasonably reliable machines that offer quality audio editing software. If you're deciding between the two platforms, you might consider the audio sequencer that suits you best and build the workstation (computer and audio interface) around that.

# PROTOOLS AND BEYOND: A PLETHORA OF SEQUENCERS

If there is one audio term that filmmakers love to toss around it's 'ProTools.' While Digidesign's ProTools (www.digidesign.com) is the most famous name in professional audio editing, the full-featured ProTools HD setup that most professionals use is very costly and has a steeper learning curve than its competition. The next step down, ProTools LE, also requires Digidesign hardware and also has the ability to run their aftermarket 'DV Toolkit' (which you'll need for OMF/AAF importing and exporting, SMPTE support, and other film-oriented features). The lowest grade of ProTools, called M Powered, works with budget M Audio audio interfaces and does not have the ability to add the DV Toolkit features. Note that the latter two systems have limited track counts (32 or 48).

The independent filmmaker or editor on a budget should also consider the wide variety of other sequencers that do not rely on specific hardware. Most of them import and export OMF without requiring additional software and do not have track count restrictions. The more popular full-featured audio editing applications include:

| Sequencer | OMF/AFF | Surround | Mac | PC |
|---|---|---|---|---|
| Digidesign ProTools HD/LE/M Powered | * / * /No | * /No/No | X | X |
| Steinberg Nuendo | Yes | Yes | X | X |
| Steinberg Cubase/Cubase Studio | OMF/Neither | Yes/No | X | X |
| Apple Logic/Logic Express | Yes/No | Yes/No | X | |
| Apple Soundtrack Pro | *** | No | X | |
| MOTU Digital Performer | Yes | Yes | X | |

| Sequencer | OMF/AAF | Surround | Mac | PC |
|---|---|---|---|---|
| Bias Deck | OMF | Yes | X | |
| Cakewalk Sonar Producer/ Sonar Studio | Yes/Yes | Yes/No | | X |
| Sony Vegas | Yes | Yes | | X |
| Adobe Premiere Pro/ Premiere Elements | * / No | Yes/No | | X |
| Adobe Audition | No | ** | | X |

*possible via aftermarket plug-ins or additional purchase
**limited functionality
***no OMF/AAF; integrates with Final Cut Studio only

Comparing features can be less important than the user interface (the look and feel of a program). Look for demo versions at the manufacturers' websites. Give them a spin and just uninstall the demo from the computer when you're finished. An hour or two test run of getting around the software will either leave you feeling fluent or frustrated with its dialect. In addition, many hardware audio interfaces include full featured software in the purchase price, so if you're in the market for an audio interface you might also get a free application out of it.

## Sound cards, audio interfaces, and mixers

The job of a sound card (or, more professionally, 'audio interface') is foremost to get signals into and out of the computer. They have the analog to digital (AD) and digital to analog (DA) converters and often a plethora of related features, like headphone outputs, level controls, and even mic preamps. Some, like the consumer/budget SoundBlaster series from Creative Labs, are no-nonsense cards that install inside the computer, albeit with sonic compromises. Others are outboard hardware boxes like those from M Audio or MOTU that take analog inputs and send them into the computer via USB or firewire. These are often portable and built to use with either laptops or desktops.

Still others, like the Digidesign Digi 003 and the Tascam FW series, are more robust, with control surfaces (faders and knobs for controlling on screen levels in an audio sequencer). They also include connections for analog gear and high quality AD/DA converters.

The differences between these devices mostly come down to features and build quality. Features like built-in mic preamps, balanced connections, instrument level inputs, and included software influence the cost and buying decision.

Outboard audio mixers aren't always necessary anymore but they do provide a convenient, hands-on hub for the signals in the studio. A full-featured mixer makes light work of controlling and routing a variety of signal levels, providing inputs for many types of connectors. It also provides a volume level control for the signals it hosts, including those going in and out of a computer, headphone and monitor outputs, and other signal routings. Audio interfaces can often do the same jobs, however.

Some mixers have built-in analog to digital converters to translate signals from studio gear (like CD players, microphones, and instruments) into bits and bytes that the computer can understand. These kind of mixers double as a computer audio interface, putting it all in one convenient package. On the flip side, digital to analog converters allow us to hear computer or DAT machine outputs by converting them into analog signals for playback.

## Signals

Navigating the audio equipment world can be overwhelming but starts with the type of signal. Line level is the most common signal level in studio gear. Analog and digital mixers are optimized for use with line-level equipment. This includes CD players and signal processing gear like equalizers, compressors, and reverbs. Microphones, however, produce such low-level signals that they require special preamps to boost their signals up to line level. Many mixers and audio interfaces have built-in mic preamps so it's not necessary to splurge on expensive mic preamps unless you seek a certain tone quality in the preamp.

Let's step back a bit. There are several types of signals being carried over similar cables, just to make things confusing for a new audio engineer. Let's keep these straight. All audio cables carry one of basically six different types of signal:

- Line level
- Microphone level
- Headphone level
- Instrument level (guitars)
- Digital audio signals (AES/EBU, S/PDIF, optical, TosLink, etc.)
- Word clock, SMPTE, and other sync signals/control voltages

Most signals in a project audio studio are line-level signals. Line-level signals include the outputs of a CD player or a mixer. Most rack gear in a small studio that doesn't involve microphones operates at line level. These devices generally do not have their own volume controls; the 'unity gain' setting on your mixer's input trim is the preferable setting for them.

Microphone and guitar signals are much different. They are naturally much *softer* in volume necessitating what is called a preamp to bring them up to line level. Most audio mixing consoles have mic preamps built-in to provide this extra gain. Guitars, in addition, also have special *impedance* requirements. If you will be recording guitars directly into your sequencer for some reason, you need to obtain a *direct box* (D.I.) or an audio interface that can properly bring high impedance (Hi-Z) signals into your computer.

Treat headphone signals, such as those coming out of an iPod®, as you would line-level signals but be aware that these devices have their own extra gain stage, which will introduce extra (usually minor) distortion into the signal. A digital transfer is always preferable (where possible). However, when transferring via the headphone out jack, as a rule of thumb, keep the volume on the device at its 75% mark and adjust the input level on your mixer or audio interface for a good solid signal without hitting red.

Most studio sound is voltage and current riding on any of the various types of analog cables. These are analog signals, the most common signal type, although today a completely all-digital studio is indeed possible. Analog ins and outs are connected with either *balanced* or *unbalanced* cables. Balanced signals are the professional choice and are preferred whenever gear calls for them. Balanced cables can offer much better noise rejection and often better high-end (treble) response too.

Digital audio is an entirely different type of signal than analog. It isn't even a voltage riding on digital cables. Sometimes, it is very fast pulses of light. There are several types of digital signals and each absolutely requires the proper cabling. There are plenty of references online and in other audio books about the technical ins and outs of digital signals, so let's keep this discussion as practical as possible and describe what you are likely to need.

# Things to know about digital gear

### Sample rate

The frequency-based resolution of a sampled waveform. Higher is better, to a point. Approximately half this number is the highest audio frequency that the file can store. 44.1kHz is the 'CD quality' reference, with the similar 48kHz rate being more common in film post. A sound sampled at 32kHz, for example, doesn't include any frequencies over 16kHz, and might lack an 'airy' treble response between 16kHz and 20kHz. While these frequencies can be arguably unimportant for dialogue, they are important to musical material. For purposes of this book either 44.1 or 48kHz is the desirable sample rate. What's crucial is that all of the audio clips in a DAW session be at the same exact sample rate. Normally the DAW automatically conforms all imported audio for you, but always double-check the audio pool (region list) in your sequencer to be sure every clip is at the same sample rate.

### Bit depth, or word length

The other quality measurement of a sampled waveform. The bit depth determines dynamic range and 'smoothness' or harmonic fidelity of the sound. Low resolution 8 bit and 12 bit samples have a 'crunchy' type of distortion to them; 16 bit (CD quality) files sound smooth and have more 'headroom' (i.e., room to accurately store louder dynamic peaks). 24 bit waveforms are 'professional grade,' with even more headroom and resolution.

### S/PDIF

The consumer or 'prosumer' Sony/Philips digital interface is a two channel (stereo) signal running over a cable that looks like an RCA/phono cable. Great option for project studios connecting only one or two pieces of digital gear. For accurate sync it's important to use the proper double-shielded coaxial cable, not typical RCA/phono cables or composite video cables.

### Optical (ADAT lightpipe)

Another digital format (and cable type). This one is capable of either 2 or 8 channels of digital audio moving as pulses of light through a very thin cable. Widely used on consumer, semi-pro and pro equipment. Connects up as easily as S/PDIF, above, using unique cable and connectors that can't be mistaken for any other purpose.

### Toslink

Toslink is 2-channel digital audio running over the same 'lightpipe' or optical cable as the above. Be sure that gear is set properly in 2-channel or 8-channel mode, since some audio interfaces are capable of running in either mode (this is usually set in the software driver or via a switch on the device).

### AES/EBU

A professional 2-channel digital audio format that ironically (and conveniently) runs over analog XLR audio cables.

### Word clock

A professional way of keeping several pieces of digital gear running in sync with each other. Not required when only 2 pieces of digital equipment are being connected.

Word clock and SMPTE are control voltages, or clock tones, that are (hopefully) never heard but are used for syncing equipment to other equipment, ensuring that they run concurrently over long periods of time. Confusingly, sometimes these signals run over common audio cables and sometimes they use a special cable such as coaxial cables.

This covers the majority of signals running rampant around a project studio. Most setups today, due to computers, run on a combination of both analog and digital signals. Let's talk about what kind of cables these signals require, so that you can spec out what your studio needs. Once you know the proper terminology, any music store retailer should be more than happy to find you appropriate, high quality cables.

# Cables

All audio gear has inputs and outputs of some sort. The cables in between carry your vital signals around the studio. Any compromise in the cabling department makes for a senseless loss of audio quality that you are working so hard to preserve. Any audio signal is only as clean, dynamic, and pristine as its weakest link, and in a project studio the weakest link is often the cabling.

There are two basic flavors of analog audio cables, and several types that carry digital audio. Untangling the world of audio cables can be a trying task and it's best to get advice from salespeople who are familiar with your own type of studio gear. Here's a primer to speaking the basic language of audio interconnection so that you can identify and ask for what you need.

| Signal type | Type | Level and Impedance | Connector used | |
|---|---|---|---|---|
| Mic (low impedance, professional) | balanced | Microphone level | XLR ("Cannon") | |
| Mic (high impedance, consumer) | either, depending on mic | Line level | 1/4" tip-sleeve (TS) or XLR | |
| Line level, balanced (pro studio gear) | balanced | line level | XLR or 1/4" TRS (tip-ring-sleeve) | |
| Line level, unbalanced analog studio gear (CD and DVD players, etc.) | unbalanced | Line level | 1/4" TS, RCA/phono, 1/8" mini or other | |
| Instrument level (guitars) | unbalanced | very high impedance | 1/4" TS (tip-sleeve) | |
| Headphone outputs (iPod, etc.) | unbalanced | Line level | 1/8" stereo 'mini' plug | |
| Optical | digital | Line level | ADAT lightpipe | |
| S/PDIF | digital | Line level | Gold plated RCA/phono style connector (over a digital grade cable) | |
| AES/EBU | digital | Line level | XLR ("Cannon") | |

# Specifying the right cables for your needs

You can usually count on the manufacturer to tell you the appropriate audio cables required by any piece of equipment. Often, new gear comes with the right cables. Sometimes you need to examine the connectors ('jacks') on the piece of equipment to determine the signal and connector type. Reading the manual or asking a music store salesperson are your other two valuable resources when faced with strange, new gear.

Start by examining the connector or jack type on your gear. Use the chart to narrow down the types of cables that use that connector. Look for silk screened inscriptions at the jacks that offer any information about it. Consult the manuals for the equipment if necessary. Lastly, determine cable length needed.

When buying a cable describe it by the **type of connectors** at both ends (specify male or female if applicable), the signal **type** or **purpose** of the cable, and the **length** you need. Examples:

- 3-foot unbalanced line level analog audio cable with phono (or RCA) plugs at both ends, to interconnect a CD player and a mixer

- 30-foot mic cable with XLR male at one end and XLR female at the other with gold connectors and strain relief, for studio recording with a shotgun mic

- 9-foot AES/EBU digital audio cable with female and male XLRs, for use between a DAT machine and a digital patchbay

Say we are trying to connect a soundcard's outputs to an audio mixer's inputs. Looking at the output jacks of a soundcard, the jacks are 1/4" female. So we know that they will require an analog audio cable. (At this point it is not clear if they are mono, stereo, balanced, or unbalanced.) The manual for the card lists its outputs as "balanced +4dBu." We see that there is one jack for the left channel and one for the right channel, so we determine we need two balanced cables, each with 1/4" TRS connectors at this end.

To determine the other end connectors of these cables, we need to look at where they will plug into the mixer. The jacks at the mixer have printed below them "1/4" bal/unbal." Knowing that balanced cable is always better than unbalanced, we determine that 1/4" TRS connectors will also work at this end of our two new cables.

The last thing to consider is the length needed. Specify a cable length that allows for some expansion, but keep your studio tidy by limiting lengths to just a bit more than what is actually needed. Estimate linearly, but allow extra length for the places where cables curve. The cables in our example above could be specified as (2) 9' balanced cables with 1/4" TRS connectors at all ends.

### Other important aspects of cables include:

**Flexibility** – the plastic or rubber jacket type of a cable trades off durability for flexibility. For studio use, choose flexible cables that are reasonably thin and easy to wrap and store.

**Strain relief** – a rubberized jacket, metal spring, heat shrink tubing, or other material at the end of a cable that helps keep the connector attached to the cable's wire. Particularly important where cables are hanging down by their connections, putting the strain of gravity on delicate solder joints, or for cables that get plugged and unplugged often.

**Gold pins and plugs** – the use of gold plating in audio connectors is generally accepted as a more reliable connection over the surface area of the plug. Monster Cable and others offer gold connectors. The gold connectors from Radio Shack are made to tighter tolerances and perform much better than their nickel plated counterparts.

**Cable ties** – instead of Gaffer's tape, twist ties, or string, use plastic cable ties for permanent installations, or, buy a 10 foot length of Velcro® at hardware store. Cut both the soft fuzzy side and hard loopy side into 6 or 8 inch lengths, remove their backings, and stick them back to back (adhesive to adhesive). Fold this around a cable and it will stick to itself quite firmly. A 10' roll will yield 15-20 ties that last forever for less than $10.

**Red is right** – When stereo cables have one white and one red connector, or one black and one red connector, it is customary to use the *red* for the *right* channel and the other for the left. It just helps troubleshoot and stay organized.

## The power and the buzz

There's another type of cable that we need to discuss, but this cable does not carry sound across it, at least not any sound that we want to hear. These are power cables – the kind that carries alternating current (AC) power to your equipment. What is important about alternating current is that it *is* audible, and if it gets into your audio signals, you've got trouble.

Power coming from your wall outlet isn't as pure as you might be inclined to think. The power company provides 110V and all the current you can use, but they don't guarantee the quality of that signal. Problem is, by the time the sine wave gets to your studio, it has picked up interference in the form of audible harmonics. If you could 'listen' to a power cable, you'd hear the familiar hum or buzz that perhaps has crept into your gear in the past.

With nothing playing, turn up your monitors to 'reasonably loud.' The sound should be clean with eventually a slight din of hiss. There should be no hum or buzz. If you're catching a buzz then it's troubleshooting time.

1. Perhaps you ran unbalanced cables between equipment capable of using balanced cables. Always use balanced cables instead of unbalanced where the equipment has the capability. They improve sound fidelity and just might solve your hum and buzz problems.

   Isolation transformers like those available at pro-audio retailers or www.Jensen-Transformers.com are pretty much a cure-all for these types of problems, but it's always better to find the source of the problem. You can read more in the Jensen troubleshooting guides at http://jensen-transformers.com/apps_wp.html

2. Lighting dimmers. If your studio uses dimmers to control any lighting fixtures, do the test: turn up the monitors to a reasonable level, and start playing with the dimmers. If your dimmers are a problem, you'll hear a definite correlation between where your finger is on the dimmer and the level of the buzz coming from your speakers. The alternatives here are: replace solid-state dimmers with transformer-based ones, or replace the dimmer with a conventional lightswitch.

3. Your AC power cables are too close in proximity to your analog audio cables. It's time to do some re-routing. Keep power cables at least 6–12" away from audio cables, and re arrange them so that they cross only at right angles, *never* run them in parallel with each other. S/PDIF digital audio cables are also susceptible, while cable with no ground connection, such as optical audio cables, are not. Take the time to re-route your wiring; it's the cheapest option you can try.

There's a variation on this principle – for power cables with those bulky transformers in the middle of them, like those used for laptop computers. Keep the cable that runs from the transformer to the wall – and the transformer itself – away from audio cables. However, the thinner cable that runs from the transformer to the equipment carries low voltage and won't bleed into your audio signals.

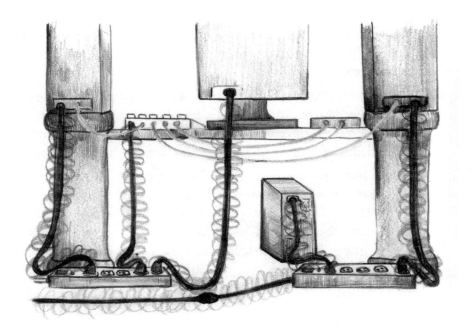

4. A piece of your gear has an outdated or wrong internal grounding method. There is no way to know this without a analyzing the inner workings of the gear, so we use process of elimination to troubleshoot. Identify the problem gear by first unplugging everything in your studio. Don't just turn everything off – unplug! This is important. Now plug in and turn on one piece of outboard gear at a time: first your audio monitors' amplifiers, then your mixer, then your computer, then video equipment and each time listen for the hum. Continue with all other gear until the hum returns and you've narrowed it down to the offending piece. Double check that the offender's power cable is routed away from any audio cables. Try physically moving the piece of gear away from other gear. If these don't help, you can 1. take that piece of gear out of service, or 2. contact a pro-audio retailer or www.Jensen-Transformers.com for the right isolation transformer.

Be aware that the way most people use those '3 to 2' (ground lift) adapters – without connecting their spade lug to ground – is downright wrong! In the event of a power surge (like lightning) a massive inrush of current will be looking for a path from the live AC wire to ground. If you're touching a piece of gear that incorrectly uses one of these adapters, you might be stepping right in that path! The proper way to lift a power ground is by connecting the ground lift adapter's spade lug to the faceplate screw of a grounded wall outlet. This restores the lifted ground connection for the equipment, providing a safe return path for power surges. The problem may not go away, however, until the gear is upgraded or the power system remedied.

5.  Cable and satellite equipment can cause ground loops in home theater environment. Since the cable or dish gets grounded outside, and the receiver inside, there can be a difference of ground potentials – an audible ground hum or buzz. This is your equipment complaining of an unclean ground. Track it down by turning up your monitors, disconnecting the coax cable, and seeing if the problem goes away. You can solve it with a cable TV isolator. Satellite is bit more problematic. Since the dish gets its power (a DC voltage) from the receiver, it's not possible to troubleshoot by disconnecting it, and an isolation transformer won't work. Instead, if you've narrowed the problem down to your satellite system, 1. be sure you've upgraded to balanced audio cables (see step 1), 2. contact your provider for a possible solution or service call, and 3. use audio and video isolation transformers to properly break the grounds.

6.  If you're hearing a buzz coming from *inside* a piece of equipment (not an audio buzz from the speakers) the cause might be dirty power. Contrary to popular belief, the AC power coming out of the wall is anything but pure, with extraneous, unwanted signals riding the power wave. Your toaster doesn't know the difference, but your sensitive audio equipment and computer prefers something cleaner.

    Plugging all of your audio and video gear into a good quality line conditioning product is the remedy. I like the ones at www.brickwall.com. They are far superior to the popular power strips that most musicians use in their equipment racks and they protect your equipment from power surges. In addition, don't plug heaters, air conditioners, or any unrelated devices into outlets that are on the same circuit as your A/V gear. Know which outlets run to which circuit breakers and plan your cable routings consciously. Don't underestimate the value of good, clean electricity. It's where your sound and video equipment gets its power.

Try each of these fixes in order and if you're still having trouble, you might have some particularly aggressive EMI (electromagnetic interference) seeping in from a local radio station, freight elevator, or other source of immense wattage. If that's the case, you have two choices: line all of the walls with tin foil, or start checking the real estate classifieds for a new studio.

In sum, route your sensitive audio cables with care. Identify problem/noisy gear by process of elimination. Keep all of your equipment plugged into clean power, and on the same circuit breaker. Spend some time laying out your audio cables, and video cables for that matter, and you will be hearing more signal, and less noise.

## Your monitors, your friends

The music store that carries cables may also have a 'pro-audio' or 'recording' department with various types of studio monitors. If you have it in your budget, now might be a good time to audition. There is a vast difference in tone quality among studio monitors and it is key to work on enjoyable monitors that inspire success. Bring audio CDs of music that you know well to a pro-audio store and test drive a few.

When setting up a surround monitoring environment, it's important to use matched speakers for the surrounds, and preferably the center channel and subwoofer as well. This may mean using smaller versions of speakers by the same manufacturer and from the same product line for the surrounds. Any pro-audio dealer can make recommendations based on your specific needs.

There aren't any 'magic frequencies' or gear or special processes that make a great film mix. In fact, most of the elements in a film mix are simply designed to sound as natural as possible, while getting them all to 'play well' together. It's the quality of the monitors – and especially of the room itself – that has far more impact on the quality of your mixes than what equalizer plug-in you use. Consider the difference between home speakers and studio monitors – studio monitors are designed to sound as neutral as possible, while home speakers are designed to color the sound in a more pleasing way (usually with enhanced bass and treble response). Obviously, you need the former for any critical listening application. Hi-fi speakers just won't give you the neutrality you need to hear to make mix decisions that translate across different playback systems.

It's also important to check your work on a variety of playback systems (monitors, headphones, TV speakers, movie theaters, whatever you have access to). Do the ambiences suddenly get too loud while listening through headphones? Does the dialogue disappear? Multiple monitoring helps ensure that your sonic intentions are making it through to every audience, especially when you don't have the luxury of an acoustically-treated room.

While monitors have the most influence on the sounds you hear, the next chapter will demonstrate how room acoustics probably have more to do with getting good sound than any piece of gear in the studio – even monitors.

## Plug-ins

Audio engineers need some basic tools in order to make magic in the mix. Beyond a capable computer setup, software plug-ins allow us to conveniently sculpt the signals in a sequence. We can change the treble and bass response (and a lot more) with equalization, reel in the loud and soft dynamics of a performance with compressors and expanders, perform noise reduction, add funky filter effects, and use reverberation to bring a sense of 'space' to our mixes.

All audio sequencers come with some basic effects, but if it's in the budget, aftermarket plug-ins are where it's at, for both sound quality and features. Variety packs are the way to go for diverse functionality. For example, the 'Waves' product line features a comprehensive suite of effects and give pro quality results with proper use. Audio interfaces are often bundled with plug-in packages, too. Some other plug-in packs, like the Universal Audio UAD-1 series and TC Electronics PowerCore, even include dedicated hardware that relieves the computer of the intense processing load of the plug-ins.

### PLUG-IN CAVEAT

Unfortunately, most new audio engineers do more harm than good with audio plug-ins while they are learning to use their new ears. It's fun to play with signals once they are in the computer and plug-ins do make for easy experimentation. But beware – some effects sound like an improvement at first but leave you in regret later. Dialogue, for example, once compressed, can't be uncompressed. The natural dynamics and 'punchiness' of the performance get squashed forever. You'd have to revert to a backup to salvage it. Some kinds of processing can also reduce the signal's potential for cleanup (like noise reduction) down the road.

Which leads us to an important working practice for using plug-ins: keep backups of *everything*. Get into the habit of duplicating the original clip or track before you take any new and interesting chances. Next week, when you decide that a telephone voice filter plug-in you applied sounds thin and noisy, you can revert back and give it another try.

If you're new to the DAW you may be wondering exactly which plug-ins you need. At the least, a parametric equalizer (EQ), noise reduction suite, and a high quality reverb will be vital for shaping most production sound into a final mix. Aftermarket plug-ins are usually more flexible and better sounding than the effects bundled with audio sequencers, but if the shoe fits (and the budget is tight) then use the stock plug-ins. There are some great freeware plug-ins, too. Try searching http://www.kvraudio.com/get.php

Most full-featured sequencers won't come with noise reduction (sometimes bundled as 'sound restoration') plug-ins. If you're curious now, check out the comprehensive list of restoration plug-ins in the Dialogue chapter. The audio quality and convenience of aftermarket plug-ins more than justifies their cost, especially when it comes to sound restoration.

## DAW tips

Here are a few extra tips for efficient session work.

🎧 Have an additional dedicated hard drive, different from the *system* drive on which the operating system is installed, for your audio projects. This is a similar rule for working with video sequencers. Audio data must be streamed (played back in real-time as it is read) – and mixed on the fly – by the audio sequencer. So it's important that this drive have plenty of free space and be different than the already busy system drive.

🎧 Create a new folder for the audio editing portion of your project and make a shortcut to it on your desktop. This is your working project folder.

🎧 Create another folder on a different hard drive (use the system drive or a large external drive) with a name like 'Film XYZ Audio Session BACKUP.' After every audio editing session, drag the entire working project folder from the audio drive to this backup folder. Today's work is done; walk away from the computer and let it over-write all of yesterday's backup files.

🎧 If you have the luxury of more than two fast hard drives in your system, use one as a system/applications drive, dedicate another to the audio session, and keep the Quicktime video file that we'll be making later on a third drive. This should make for fast parallel reading and writing and less drive hiccups.

🎧 Most sequencers have an auto backup feature whereby it saves a copy of your session to disk at a specified time interval. Be sure to set this time in your sequencer's preferences. You can also take this a step further by doing what sequencers like ProTools do automatically: get into the habit of saving new complete sessions whenever you think of it. Set up a keyboard shortcut to 'Save As...' a completely new version of your sequence. Increment file numbers as

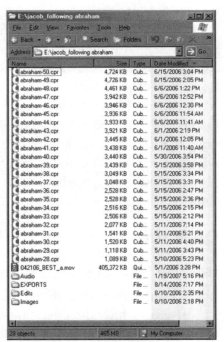

Free insurance: If your software doesn't do it for you, save new versions of your sequence every hour or so and you won't be at a total loss after a crash.

you go. Later, when the project is finished, you can delete older sessions and backup just the most recent versions.

🎧 For PC users, defragmenting is important maintenance for both system and media hard drives. It's a process that concatenates and streamlines all of the data on the drive, preparing it for fast reading and writing. Defragmenting *now* means smoother playback *later* (and less wear and tear on the drive). It can also prevent lost data, so it's important to do it regularly. Get into the habit of defragmenting your audio drives at least once a week. You can use the built-in Windows software for this (go to Start >Programs >Accessories >System Tools >Disk Defragmenter) or try a more powerful tool like O&O Defrag (http://www.oosoftware.com).

According to Apple, Mac users running OSX and later shouldn't defragment their system drives because it can worsen the file organization. However, A/V hard drives might benefit from a tune up with something like the 'Cleaning Agent' shareware from Ancodia (http://www.ancodia.com/).

## Comfort and ergonomics

Easily overlooked, ergonomics are often left to whatever studio furniture is on hand. A comfortable engineer is a productive engineer. This is not the place for an extensive discussion but let's cover some highlights:

🎧 A good chair: A good chair feels firm yet contoured to your body. Comfort, support, and proper height are key. At the right height, your feet are flat on the ground, the upper part of your legs (quadriceps) are parallel to the floor, you are sitting directly on your 'sit bones' (those two boney protrusions under the buttocks), your lower back is supported and not slouching, and your vertebrae are close to making a vertical line.

- ⌒ The workstation: organize everything so that the most important gear is within reach. Swap cables where necessary to move less used gear out of the way. Think vertically, and consider moving equipment to which you don't need easy access under the desk.

- ⌒ Monitor height: Keep your computer displays at eye level or a little above to avoid neck strain.

- ⌒ Watch out for pigeon necking: make it a point to stretch back or take a break whenever you find yourself leaning in toward the computer display.

Neck and lower back pain is common among studio engineers but can be avoided. If you're concerned, have a friend watch you work and make comments on your posture. Stopping to do some stretching a few times a day can help keep you on good terms with your back. An ounce of prevention is worth a pound of cure!

## Chapter 5

# Setup: The Accurate Listening Environment

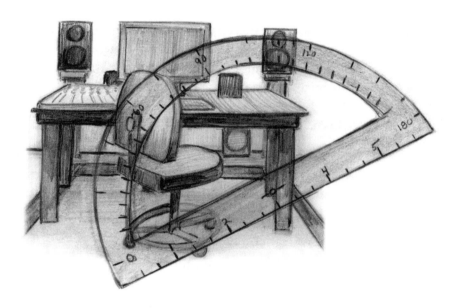

Those of us creating soundtracks to be played on other systems face the burden of making a recording that will sound good and listenable in any playback environment. After weeks of video and sound editing the film may sound great in one studio but when played back on other systems it can lack bass, clarity, punch, sparkle, balance, or consistency. A meager monitoring setup does more to harm to a mix than most gear, including choice of audio interface, cables, or studio monitors. In this chapter, we'll see why without accurate monitoring, one's audio efforts can easily result in a disappointing film screening.

Why is a calibrated listening environment important? It's how post-sound engineers create mixes that translate well to other systems. They don't do it just by watching level meters, and there isn't some magic plug-in they put on the dialogue. The truer the sound from the monitors, the more easily and clearly the engineer hears, and the more accurate she can mix. Your mix may balance just fine in the 'studio' (is it really a bedroom, basement or garage...?) but played back, say, on a friend's TV the dialogue is muddy, the sound effects are lame, and the ambiences and music are overpowering the actors. It may sound surprising, but the techniques in this chapter will probably have the most effect on the sound quality of your mix. Put the time into tweaking your room's speaker setup, calibration, and acoustical treatment. It's the only way your mixes will translate to theaters and other systems.

## Workflow: Getting set for mixing

There are a few factors working behind the scenes here. Each affects all of the little decisions you make about levels and EQ while mixing. There are three main areas we need to set up and calibrate:

- The height, position, and angle of the monitors
- The acoustics of your room
- The volume level at which you monitor

In short, 1. Use speaker stands and set your monitors up in the proper formation; 2. Get the room sounding as neutral as possible by installing acoustical treatments; and 3. Properly calibrate your listening level so you can make good mix decisions. After you do all this, mixing is less of a magic act and more a natural fact. In this chapter we'll explore each of these important aspects of room calibration.

## Tips for creating a more accurate listening environment

- Use studio monitors, preferably powered monitors – never home or hi-fi speakers.

- Get audio monitors off the desk. Use proper speaker stands and position them appropriately. In particular, never place speakers or subwoofers in corners, where bass builds up.

- Keep monitors as far from front and side walls as practical. Locate them at least that distance from the engineer's ears.

- Place yourself midway between the front speakers, forming an equilateral triangle.

- Use surround, center channel, and subwoofer monitors that are matched to your mains and position them properly as well.

- Build or buy bass traps, or at least rearrange large, soft furniture into the corners to help absorb low frequencies.

- Hang acoustical absorption panels around the mix position to tame sound reflections.

- Consider a drop ceiling, rugs, and other absorptive material to treat hard room surfaces.

- Treat the rear wall (behind the engineer's head) and if possible the front wall (behind the monitors) with acoustical diffusers.

- Calibrate your listening environment and mix at the proper listening level (SPL). (Note: dB SPL is yet another decibel scale; it measures the level of sound pressure level traveling through a medium such as air.)

## Proper positioning

The first step is to reposition your desk and equipment to get a more accurate sound from your monitors. The results are well worth the effort of shifting your room around, if necessary.

Most rooms are rectangular, with two wider walls and two narrower walls. Start by setting up the main (left and right front) studio monitors along the narrower wall of the room, facing the rear (also narrow) wall. This gives the sound a longer travel distance before hitting the reflective (and problematic) rear wall. Keep them equally away from the side walls and also keep them away from the wall behind them. Set up surround speakers at the proper angle and distance as recommended by the manufacturer.

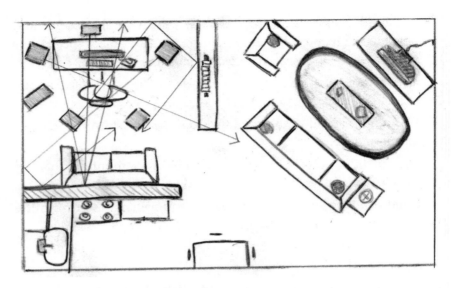

## STAND UP

Good speaker stands, like those available in the Pro-audio'or Recording departments of music equipment stores, give more than just the obvious benefit of a speaker platform. They allow you the freedom to locate speakers where they sound best in the room, and by providing a solid, sturdy platform they also tighten up the low end (bass) a bit.

Almost any tall, heavy support can make a good speaker stand. I use 30" tall decorative pillars of cast concrete like those found in home and garden shops. Since they are not adjustable, I chose pillars at a height that, based on my desk and chair setup, put my monitors' tweeters exactly at my own ear level.

While seated in your chair, measure from your ear to the ground. This is the correct tweeter height; your stands will be several inches shorter than this depending on the cabinet size of your monitors. Also, allow for a couple of inches of foam under the monitors for decoupling.

Sound coupling is the transmission of sound through materials that physically touch. It's exactly what we don't want to happen between the monitors and the stands. Place firm pieces of foam or rubber under your monitors so the sound doesn't resonate through the stands. At their worst, these resonances boost arbitrary bass frequencies enough to distract you and skew the room response. Most any firm foam will do (hockey pucks, too); be sure it is firm enough that the monitors are strongly supported. Auralex offers a popular commercial product called the MoPAD that does the job and is properly contoured for most studio monitors.

### Determine the best listening position

Determine the best listening position by locating the main monitors rather widely apart from each other (about 2/3 of the room width) and at least a foot or two from the rear, left, and right side walls.

Set the speaker stand heights so the tweeters are at ear level when you are in the mix position, whether your monitors are positioned vertically or horizontally. If vertical, the (larger) woofers should be below the tweeters.

Determine the 'sweet spot' by forming an equilateral triangle between the left and right mains and the engineers head position. Refer to the angles shown in the diagram.

Next, angle the speakers in toward the engineer's head. When looking at the mains from the mix position, you shouldn't be able to see the sides of the cabinets; that's how you know they are angled directly at the mix position. It's easier to do if a friend moves the cabinets while you watch the monitors from the mix position.

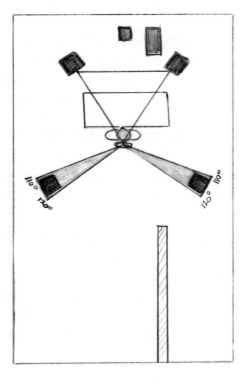

Position the surround left and right monitors at the proper height, distance, and angle according to the diagram and the recommendations in their manual.

Set up the center channel directly between the mains, perhaps under your video monitors or another convenient location.

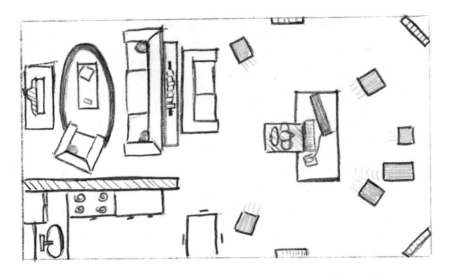

For now, position the subwoofer a bit off center between the mains, about 1/3 closer to say, the right front speaker. Getting even bass response in a room is difficult at best; we'll refine its position during the calibration process later.

Install your desk, furniture, and other equipment around this setup.

## Acoustical treatment – overlooked and under-estimated

It's the bane of audio engineers that every sound we hear adopts the sonic fingerprint of the space in which it was played. Every room has a unique sound due to variances in size, shape, and building materials. Without acoustical treatments, we would never hear anything close to an honest sonic representation of what we're working on. There is no sonic neutrality – unless your studio is outside in open air!

While it would be foolish to set up a mixing environment in a room that sounds like a YMCA pool, the same principles of out of control room resonances, bass build up, and long reverberation times affect every untreated filmmaker and editor's studio. The smaller the room, the bigger the problem. With some time put into improving your room

acoustics, your mixes – and listening enjoyment – can improve expo-
nentially.

# SOUND TREATMENT VERSUS SOUND-PROOFING

We're talking here about sound treatment and getting the sound of the room more neutral in order to hear a more
accurate playback. However, this has nothing to do with sound-
*proofing* which deals with sound transmission between rooms.
The techniques in this chapter won't help too much in that
department.

Heavy concrete, brick, sheetrock, etc., are most effective at stopping sound (like that from your neighbor's apartment). An extra
layer of sheetrock (or some of the more modern varieties of dense

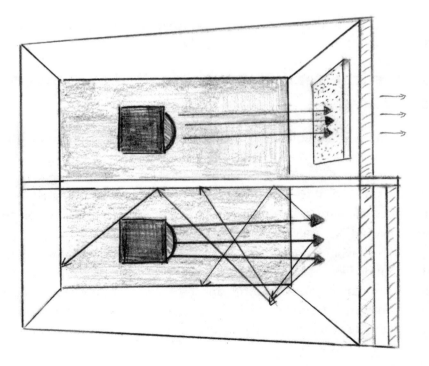

soundboard) sealed at all edges with Tempco or other acoustical sealant is your best bet for a do-it-yourself improvement to help block sound transmission.

The best soundproofing alternates *mass* and *airspace*. Professional studios build entirely new inner walls within a room, leaving 6″ of airspace from the existing walls, being careful to keep the new inner 'room' walls from touching the existing room walls. The air gap creates a decoupling effect that helps keep sound from getting out of the new inner sanctum. This, however, is a big construction job. Aside of going that route, thicker walls between you and the outside world is your best option for keeping sound out – or keeping it in.

Fortunately, improving room acoustics is easy with a little knowledge and effort. Acoustical treatment mostly comes down to three things: taming high frequency reflections, controlling bass build up, and creating random diffusion to avoid buildup of specific frequencies. Reflections like those shown in the illustration are perhaps the most troublesome yet not very difficult to manage.

## Sound smear

Like ripples in a pond, sound waves emanate out from their source (your monitors) and interact with walls and objects in the room. The ripples hit an object and fold back into themselves, creating dense, compound waves that smear the soundstage. We don't want to squander the soundtrack's clarity and frequency response with echoes and reflections that turn accurate audio into sonic soup.

These sound ripples occur because of the room's hard surfaces, especially the ones around the engineer's head. In fact, the distances between the sound source and the various walls and room obstacles do a lot to define the room's sonic character. When sound waves hit a hard, reflective surface they create build-ups of certain frequencies (standing waves) and phase cancellation, both of which create uneven frequency response that smear the audio picture. Aside of building a new room specifically designed for sound accuracy, there are plenty of things a new sound engineer can do to help an existing room.

## ATTACK OF THE 50-FOOT BASS BOOM MONSTER

Put in a favorite CD, turn up the volume, and walk around your room. Check out what it sounds like in the middle of the room, near the side walls, and then in the corners. The extra bass resonance you hear while standing in the corners might sound like free lunch, but is part of what is *wrong* with your studio. Corners skew the frequency response of the room more than anything else, so the first thing to remember is to keep studio monitors away from room corners.

How does monitoring with a little extra bass hurt your mixes? After all, it sounds ok, right? The 'boominess' – especially of small (say, less than 1500 cubic feet) mixing rooms – means A. less bass is

going into your mix (i.e., the engineer is hearing so much bass from her room that she dials too little into the mix) resulting in mixes that sound thin on other systems, and B. other frequencies in the sonic spectrum, like those required for clear dialogue, are getting masked, resulting in an inability of the engineer to clearly hear the dialogue and midrange. It can be all too easy to mix the Foley up too loud, too, in an effort to overcome the overly loud, bass heavy drones of a suspense film. It's an extreme example, but this mix might sound big and full in one room, but in actuality be an annoying, midrangey mix of footsteps and dialogue with little bass, when played in a theater!

For now, listen to and be aware of the frequency response of your room. This may mean tapping into a new aural awareness of when loud bass notes stick out of a mix. Do some research at the links listed later in this chapter. Invite musicians and other engineering friends over and get their advice on setting up your room for mixing. And look to the end of this chapter for more help in controlling runaway bass.

Contrary to popular belief, simply covering the walls in egg cartons is not going to do much to help your mixes, or your soundproofing! You need acoustical diffusers and absorption materials instead. Since the surfaces to the right, left, and above the engineer's head are the most important points of sound reflection, it's crucial to dampen these reflections with sound absorption panels. You can buy absorptive panels that do the job perfectly; they run between $500 and $1000 for four panels. Thick blankets, soft furniture, heavy fabric wall hangings, etc., can also help control sound reflections at these critical points in a pinch. Another attractive alternative is making your own custom absorptive panels. They're not hard to make and might save you money and trouble in the long run. See the next section for some advice on doing it yourself.

When sound waves travel from the monitors to the back wall (the one behind the engineer's head) and back again to the mix position, they build up by overlapping themselves many times over. This leads to gross distortions in especially the low-end frequencies, creating standing waves and null points. So it's also important to treat the *rear* wall with *diffusers*. A diffuser is an object with random surfaces that scatter sound waves, keeping them from building up and distorting the frequency response of the room. Find room furnishings with random surfaces that look like they send sound waves bouncing off in all directions. Large bookshelves make great diffusion. Position as many sources of diffusion as possible at the rear wall behind your head.

## DIY: other options for a great sounding room

The previous sections in this chapter outlined some techniques for improving the acoustics of most common rooms. This calls for soft, absorptive materials on the walls and ceiling around the mix position. One of the best and most cost-effective construction materials for this are the dense fiberglass insulation panels by Owens Corning, model 703 (lighter, for absorbers around the mix position) and model 705 (denser, for bass traps). Another is rockwool. They are all available at insulation supply stores and contractors' building supply houses (you won't find them at do-it-yourself home improvement stores). Search a phone directory or the internet for insulation suppliers. The price is right – with rigid fiberglass insulation panels, some porous fabric (like loose canvas or linen), and a glue gun, anyone can make a much more accurate and enjoyable listening environment.

There are two ways to use fiberglass or rockwool absorbers. First, you can hang them on the walls and ceiling areas in an arc around the mix position. That is: to your left, to your right, and above your head while seated in the mix position. Better yet, mount them so they are 6–8" from the wall – this improves clarity even more in the lower frequency range. The difference of sonic clarity and precision these panels can make to the soundstage can be astounding. Even four of these 2' x 4' panels, properly placed around the mix position, can open up the sound and reduce smearing reflections dramatically. After treating

your room – and yourself – to these panels, you may find you enjoy music and movies a lot more on your audio system.

You can also control bass boom by attaching these panels across the corners of the room, especially the corners behind the studio monitors, to create *bass traps*. Bass traps do just that: they invite bass in to the corners of the room – where it builds up most – and stop it from leaving. Thus, at the mix position there is less artificial boominess and a much clearer representation of the mix, encouraging you to dial a more accurate amount of bass into your mix.

Improving the acoustics of a listening room is one of the secrets to making good mixes. It's often cheaper *and* more effective than buying better studio monitors!

# Calibrating the monitoring environment

You've probably wondered how post engineers know the levels at which dialogue and other elements should sit in a mix. Well, it's not actually about specific decibel levels. We can't put a number on it because the ear behaves in a funny way: it emphasizes midrange frequencies at lower volumes. It also finds that some waveforms sound louder than others. A square wave sounds much louder than a sine wave, but according to the meters they are the same voltage. This is why your ears alone need to be the final determinate of your soundtrack's levels. Mixing remains the engineer's art, not the equipment's.

We've learned so far that you can't expect to be able to make mix decisions unless your ears are at their most unbiased. That means preparing your room according to what we've talked about so far in this chapter and crossing the final frontier: listening-level calibration.

Sounds simple enough: How loud should I be listening? There are a couple of things to be aware of when talking about levels.

First, the ear responds differently to different frequencies. Since a sound with more midrange sounds louder than a bass heavy sound, we can't rely on meters to tell us real world levels. This is reason #1 why your ears are the most valuable equipment in the studio.

Secondly, the ear responds more closely to *average* (RMS) sound levels, not the peak levels your digital meters show. Peak level indicators *are* useful, however, for making sure we're not overloading.

Lastly, the ear actually hears differently when listening at different volume levels. Later when we start to mix, your ears will be able to discriminate better and make a more dynamic mix because you're monitoring at a strong, industry-standard listening level. Apologize to your family or housemates now, because monitoring too softly will make it impossible to make a proper mix!

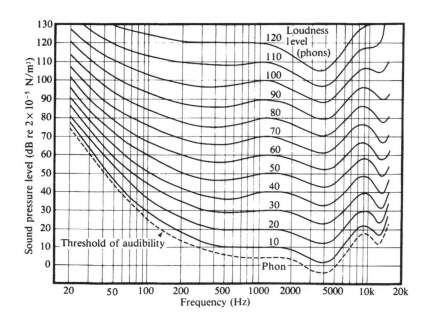

## EQUAL LOUDNESS CONTOURS

Have you ever noticed that at low listening levels the treble and (especially) the bass go seriously south? The frequency extremes disappear faster than the in-betweens as you turn down the volume of any plackback system. Try it – play back a piece of music you know well starting at a loud volume and then gradually lower it to zero. Listen as the low end increasingly evaporates and the sparkle of the treble fades away. The tune is reduced to the bulk of its clearest frequencies, the wide midrange area to which our ears are most sensitive.

Your audio system is not working any kind of voodoo with the frequency spectrum; rather it's your ears that are to blame – or credit – for this effect. At lower volumes our ears are naturally more sensitive to midrange, perhaps to make it easier to understand human speech and other critical sounds in nature at low volumes. Two scientists at Bell Labs did some probing into this phenomenon in the early 1900s, now called the Fletcher-Munson equal loudness curves.

The LOUDNESS button on consumer stereos was designed to compensate for this effect. At low listening levels, you push in the loudness button to give the low end and high end a 'smiley face' shaped EQ boost. Voilà, your music sounds nice and full again at low volumes. Helpful, but of course crude.

Anyone attempting to mix a film needs to realize that monitoring levels affect the resulting frequency spectrum of the mix. If you like to work at lower volume levels you might end up dialing in too much bass and treble into your mixes because you're not hearing enough from the monitors. Likewise, if you monitor too loudly, you're hearing lots of low end and high sizzle, dialing in little highs and lows into the mix, and when played back normally your soundtrack sounds overly harsh in the midrange. The former situation is more likely the problem.

The solution is to calibrate your room to listen at the industry standard level, and check your mixes on headphones and other systems for reference. While mixing, sometimes turn the volume down and check a few things: Is the dialogue still coming through clearly? Is it still sitting well above the ambience and Foley tracks? Did you dial in too much bass into your gunshots and explosions because you were monitoring too soft?

So what is the optimum amount of sound we want coming out of the speakers, and how do we measure this? Unfortunately no soundcard, computer, or set of monitors have any way of displaying how much sound they are pushing through the air once it leaves your gear. For that you need a little device we mentioned earlier called a sound pressure level meter. You'll need one to complete this last step of calibrating your listening environment in order to set proper mix levels. Radio Shack offers a great SPL meter (part# 33-4050) for around $45. Many professionals find that the analog version of the meter is a bit more accurate and easier to use than the digital version, but either model will work. Be sure to install a new battery in the meter, as an old battery will give incorrect readings.

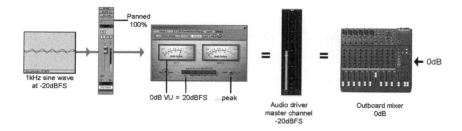

1kHz sine wave
at -20dBFS

Panned
100%

0dB VU = 20dBFS    ...peak

Audio driver
master channel
-20dBFS

Outboard mixer
0dB

← 0dB

### *Calibrate the signal chain*

Grab your SPL meter and let's calibrate your room. The first step is to get your sequencer, audio driver, and outboard mixer (if you have one) to all display the same level for a test tone.

This procedure assumes that you aren't using an outboard (hardware) mixer. If you are, check that your audio interface is going into line-level channels on the mixer (not channels with a microphone input), that the mixer channels have no EQ or auxes enabled, and that channel and master faders are at 0dB.

- 🎧 Turn off your monitors' amplifiers.

- 🎧 Download the audio clips of pink noise and the 1kHz sine wave at www.abluesky.com/asp/catalogue/download.asp?prodcode=blues kytestfiles. Import them onto a mono track in a new session.

- 🎧 In your sequencer, pan the audio channel with the test tones 100% left.

- 🎧 Set all levels – in the sequencer channels, in the audio driver, and on your monitors themselves (if applicable) to 0dB (unity gain) (Note: 'Unity gain' implies that 'the level coming in is the same level going out.' It does not mean 'no output.')

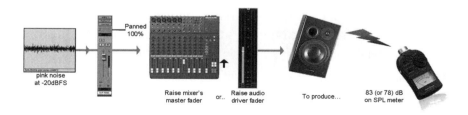

pink noise
at -20dBFS

Panned
100%

Raise mixer's
master fader

or..

Raise audio
driver fader

To produce...

83 (or 78) dB
on SPL meter

- Play the 1kHz sine wave tone through the left channel. If it doesn't read 20dBFS on your sequencer's master-channel meter, verify that your pan law is set to -6dB in both your software and audio driver.

- Pan the sequencer channel right and verify that it also produces -20dBFS on the sequencer's master channel. Only the right channel should be active.

- Check the audio driver to verify that it is also registering -20dBFS.

- If there are VU meters at any point in your signal chain, whether plug-ins (like the Bomb Factory Essential Meter Bridge, shown) or hardware meters, calibrate them so that the panned sine wave causes them to read 0dB VU.

- Stop playback. 'Set and forget' these settings: keep these settings in position anytime you are working on a film soundtrack.

### Calibrate the listening level

Now let's set the proper listening volume for mixing. You may need a friend, or a mic stand, to help hold the SPL meter.

- Turn on the monitors (including subwoofer if applicable).

- Lower the master level in your audio driver to -∞ (no output).

- Pan the sequencer channel left and play the **high frequency** (500-2500Hz) pink noise clip in loop mode.

- Turn on the SPL meter to the '80dB' setting and set it to C weighting with 'slow' response. This simply gives the meter a rough idea of the level it can expect to hear, plus or minus 10dB. Hold it at arm's length at the exact height and position of your head while in the mixing position (or you can mount it into a mic stand for convenience). Point it straight ahead to the area between the two speakers (not directly at the speaker), angled a little toward the ceiling.

  The SPL meter uses an open microphone so be sure the room is relatively free of extraneous sound, such as air conditioners or computer fans.

- Raise the level on your audio driver's master channel until the SPL meter reads 85dB (or 82dB if mixing toward television broadcast).

Verify noise output from the left monitor only.

- Pan the channel 100% right and repeat. The SPL meter should still read 85dB (or 82dB for TV).

- Likewise, for surround channels, pan the pink noise to one surround monitor at a time, including center channel, but not for the subwoofer. Still in the listening position, keep the SPL meter pointed straight ahead. Adjust the level on the surround monitor itself or in the audio driver so that the SPL meter reads 82dB (whether mixing toward cinema, DVD or broadcast TV).

- Set and forget: save these settings. This sets the proper volume level for film mixing.

### Calibrate the subwoofer

- If you have full-range monitors with a proper LFE channel, set the subwoofer's crossover frequency to 80Hz. This is pretty much a home and industry standard.

  However, if your main speakers are small and don't go as low as you would like them to, you'll want to employ something called bass management to hear all the low end in your mix. Bass management is circuitry that sends the extra bass that smaller mains can't handle to a general subwoofer that takes up the slack. This means that a bass-managed sub gets much more action than a proper LFE-only sub, and you will hear much more from a bass-managed subwoofer than you will see in the waveform of your LFE channel's mixdown (this is normal, if confusing). In this case, if possible, set your crossover frequency higher, anywhere up to one octave above the 80Hz standard (that would be 160Hz) depending on how much you can get out of your mains. Or perhaps your system has preset crossover points. In any case, the speaker manufacturer will have the best advice on properly setting up your particular system. It's worth a read of the manual or a call to the company.

- ☊ Play the **low frequency** (40-80Hz) pink noise clip in loop mode.

- ☊ Turn and re position the sub until you find a home for it that produces the most even bass response around the room and the proper SPL level. Start by placing it somewhat off center between your monitors, closer to one monitor than the other. (Note: The best position for a subwoofer is where it produces the flattest frequency response across all bass frequencies, and this is dependent on your room acoustics. Professionals use a special microphone and a real-time frequency analyzer to determine this. Adding bass traps to your room is your best bet for improving the low-end response. The references at the end of this section and at the end of the book are a good start to researching this further.)

- ☊ Pan the sequencer channel left and verify noise output in the left monitor and/or subwoofer.

- ☊ Adjust the level of just the subwoofer so that the SPL meter averages around 85dB SPL if you're using a bass-managed system, or 95dB SPL if you've got a full-range system with a dedicated LFE channel.

- ☊ Pan the channel right and check for the same results from the SPL meter.

For more details on calibration, check out what the good people at www.abluesky.com have to say about studio calibration in the 'Support' section of their website. Look for the title 'Additional Setup and Technical Information.'

Your system will now play back at the optimum level for making mix decisions. Your VU meters, if you have them, will also display industry-standard output levels. Now you can trust your ears and your intuition to guide you toward setting proper levels for the soundtrack elements. If something is too loud or soft, you will know it intuitively. Be sure to keep the faders in your audio driver at the calibrated levels at all times while working on your mix.

## Chapter 6

# Setup: Prepare to Make the Jump to Light Speed

The marriage of picture and sound creates emotional impact in a picture. Keeping these two elements in tight sync over the course of a film, however, has been the bane of post engineers for as long as movies have been made. On simple shoots, the equipment does most of the work for us. With complex productions, however, it's not always a piece of cake getting video and audio from multiple sources to stay locked both within and amongst sequencers.

It is the task of the video editor to bring in both production sound and picture into the NLE. With basic video productions where sound is recorded directly into camera, both are transferred together in one pass. With film cameras or anytime sound is *not* recorded into the camera, tracks come in individually and need to be manually synched. Usually, lining up the visual clap of a slate (sometimes called a clapper) to its audio crack at the beginning of every take ensures that audio and video runs concurrently until either the cameraperson or Sound Mixer hits 'stop,' assuming there are no equipment speed errors. Where there is no slate reference, sound gets manually synched by spotting dialogue to picture until it lines up to lips – a developed skill, and a tedious effort for any sound or video editor to do well.

## First, lock picture

Any time you're dealing with sync sound, as with dialogue that matches to lips, it is absolutely necessary that the audio engineer be working with the final edited version of the picture (the final cut). Once audio post begins, the audio sequence contains dozens, possibly hundreds of clips that must be kept in sync with the picture and each other. If the editor were to shift events around after the audio post process began, the audio engineer would have to re sync the audio clips to the new picture – a difficult and costly task.

This is obviously less important with voiceover, music, and some types of animation where exact synchronization of sound to picture isn't frame-accurate critical. In the chapter on ADR we'll deal with the evil curse of manually synching dia-logue to actor's lips.

## AVOID PAINFUL CUTS

Imagine what happens when video editor and audio engineer are working on different versions (different cuts) of the picture at the same time. Video guy outputs picture and OMF for audio girl. Audio girl imports these and starts cutting, splicing, and fading audio to the picture. Meanwhile, video guy continues editing, tightening up some scene transitions, cutting out a few frames here and there, altering the length of scenes.

Each person is now working with a slightly different version of the picture. Video guy's last few edits amounted to significant changes in length of picture and start times of later scenes, and now audio girl's dialogue doesn't line up. When it comes time to provide a sound mix to him, her audio file is off (out of sync with his new picture, enough to make dialogue scenes look like a bad kung fu movie).

The movie is a mess, nothing is in sync, and neither of our engineers is happy. Something must be done, and who is going to do it? To put this picture back together, video guy must first take the time to render a new video file for the audio engineer. Audio girl imports the new video and starts the tedious and time consuming process of lining up perhaps hundreds of audio clips manually to the new picture. If this doesn't sound hard enough, consider that there are no longer slate marks at the start of each scene. She syncs dialogue by reading lips or by visually matching up waveforms to his temp mix. It is not like starting over, it is worse than starting over: it's a frustrating process that can easily result in errors like poor sync, wrong levels, and missing audio.

To add insult to injury, this was not agreed on at the start of the project, so audio girl bills the filmmaker additional fees for the extra time. Lesson: make life easy: cut picture first, audio second.

Hopefully, your location soundperson had the foresight to record **room tone** for each scene (a recording of the environment with no action taking place, for background ambience purposes), as well as **wild sound** (special effects or other sounds unique to the action or location) and **wild dialogue** where necessary (this is non sync dialogue recorded without action on set, like ADR, perhaps because the sound recording during the scene was bad).

### *Import remaining audio files into the sequence*

- 🎧 If any of these extra audio files have not been laid into the video sequence yet, bring them in now. Label new tracks appropriately, such as 'Room Tone' or 'Wild SFX.' Bring in any and all extra material like this that may help in audio post.

- 🎧 It's a good time to also bring in any temp music that is not already present in the sequence.

## IMPORTING AND CONVERTING AUDIO

Our goal is to turn the tracks on CD or DVD into WAV files that we can use in the DAW. Fortunately, there are plenty of free and shareware applications that will import the audio for us in the right format. Your audio sequencer should do it as well. My favorite is a program called Easy CD-DA Extractor (www.poikosoft.com), which is fast, sounds great, and is easy to navigate. It also features a high quality MP3 encoder for those times when you need to make MP3s.

Import audio as 16 bit stereo WAV files. Don't bother making 24-bit files since CD audio is only 16-bit anyway. Specify the sample rate (either 44.1kHz or 48kHz) that matches the sample rate of the project, not the music file itself. This instructs the program to make any necessary format conversion to keep all audio in the project at the same sample rate.

# Everything you ever wanted to know about sync but were afraid to ask

Digital filmmaking makes sync less of an issue than it was with mechanical sound and film equipment. With some simple techniques we can easily keep our tracks locked as they move from NLE to DAW.

The audio and video need to be exported as separate file types for work in the DAW. Therefore, we need a way to ensure that they stay in sync with each other until they get re combined in the audio sequencer. The '2-pop' (or 2-beep) is simply a short (Note: The 2-pop should be about one frame in duration which is 33 milliseconds at a frame rate of 29.97 frames per second or 42ms at 24 fps.) audio blip that lets us know that the picture is going to start in exactly 2 seconds. Rendering a white flash frame in the video timeline at the exact point you place the 2-pop creates a specific reference point between the audio and video for easy re sync.

It's up to the video editor to be sure each and every audio track in the NLE has a 2-pop in the proper position. This gives the audio engineer a starting reference for lining up the sound files to each other and to the picture.

You can go one step further to ensure the audio and video stay in sync as you move from one application to another. It's an extra step, and not required in all-digital filmmaking, but it's a good practice to burn SMPTE timecode to the audio engineer's copy of the QuickTime. Normally, a timecode reader (or generator) plug-in in the NLE creates this unique sequence in the video display according to the project frame rate. You can simply remove the plug-in later when it comes time for final video export.

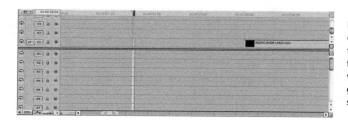

Place the 2-pops on every audio track. Line them up with a white flash frame in the video file and you've got a quick and easy sync reference.

Later, the audio engineer lines up her imported video and audio files in her DAW to the on screen timecode so that her audio sequencer's time display reads the same numbers as the timecode burn. Then, by simply comparing the timecode display (burned into the video) to the audio sequencer's running clock, she knows that both are in frame accurate sync.

While this book is no substitute for a video sequencer's manual, here's a tip that might help generate a timecode burn into your picture. Select all of the clips in your project, create a new 'nest,' and apply a 'timecode reader' video effect. (This applies to Final Cut Pro.) The burned in timecode should reflect the same time shown on the sequencer's timeline and time/transport display.

### Sync audio to picture

🎧 Place a one-frame, 1kHz audio file (2-pop) so that it starts at exactly two seconds before picture start (the first frame of the opening credits). At this point in your video track, create (or replace a frame of the existing video with) a white flash frame.

Example: If the video sequence starts at 1:00:00:00 or exactly one hour into the video timeline, copy the 2-pop audio clip to each audio track so that it starts at exactly 0:59:58:00 (59 minutes, 58 seconds, 0 frames). Create (or replace) a frame of video at this exact point with a blank white flash frame.

🎧 If you haven't worked out your opening credits yet, place the 2-pop at an arbitrary reference point such as at the first frame of the first scene. Also place a white flash frame at this point. You can always remove it later for final picture output.

🎧 Also place a 2-pop and a white flash at the end of the picture, after your last scene, as a speed reference to verify that video and audio have run concurrently from start to end.

🎧 You can also choose to burn timecode into the video to create a visual reference of every frame in the picture. This could be a particularly helpful reference later on, but does block some of the action on-screen.

## Application translation: OMF and AAF

The problem that now confronts us is how best to get the audio in the video sequencer into an audio application relatively intact. What's needed is a third-party translator to port a mini-session of the audio timeline in the NLE over to an audio sequencer. This translator must be compatible with both sequencers. Luckily, there are several solutions; the most widely used being the OMF.

If you have yet to bow down before the wonders of Avid's widely used Open Media Framework (OMF) or the newer Advanced Authoring Format (AAF), prepare to become a convert. Both formats bundle the audio from an NLE or DAW session into a format readable by most audio and video sequencers. With just a few keystrokes they zip up all of the audio clips in a sequence and create one large file containing the entire audio project for easy import into an audio sequencer. These translators allow you to port, say a Final Cut Pro session over to, say Steinberg Nuendo, retaining audio clip locations and in some cases fades and volume levels, too.

Since OMF is the current ubiquitous standard, the full procedures for using it are described in this chapter and the next. If you choose to experiment with AAF – and the Material eXchange Format (MXF) media wrapper – instead, first follow the general preparations below, and then adapt the following OMF import instructions in the next chapter to the AAF/MXF translation.

A clearly organized video sequence sets you up for easy, streamlined audio transfer into the DAW. This plays a huge part in reducing the possibility for error and can save headaches (and drive space) later on. First, prepare the video session for easy and efficient audio exporting:

### Prepare for export

- 🎧 **Achieve final cut.** Don't bother proceeding until you have locked picture. It is OK if you haven't completed the end credits, but finish editing the body of the film before beginning audio post.

- 🎧 Duplicate your video sequence for purposes of the audio export. Append the new sequence's name with something like 'for sound mix.'

- 🎧 Be sure all audio you want included in the project is in the sequence. Import last minute music choices, etc., now.

- 🎧 Organize, organize, organize: Concatenate dialogue for each actor, recorded with the same mic, onto one track. You might place everything recorded with the boom mic on Tracks 1 and 2, everything with the lavaliere mic on Tracks 3 and 4, etc, if that helps to keep similar-sounding clips on the same track.

- 🎧 Likewise, concatenate music on to perhaps just two or four tracks and keep these tracks free of other non-music sound clips.

- 🎧 Place sound effects on dedicated tracks – do not mix them with dialogue or music clips.

- 🎧 Eliminate duplicate mono clips by muting duplicate tracks. One-channel dialogue, sound effects, and other monophonic sounds are usually duplicated on to two tracks in the NLE timeline. But you don't need both of them in an audio sequencer. (Note: Since an NLE's audio tracks are by design always panned hard left or hard right, it needs two copies of a mono audio clip to create the illusion that the sound is coming from the center of the speakers. However, audio sequencers only need one mono track panned center to achieve the same effect. So delete one of the duplicates for every double-mono track in the NLE sequence, or you can plan on disabling (or deleting) every duplicate track later when we export.) If you're not sure if two clips are duplicates, leave both copies and we'll deal with them later in the audio sequencer.

    Leave true stereo files that have different left and right channels (such as music and stereo SFX) as two-channel audio. Keep these double clips locked together so they behave as one file. These

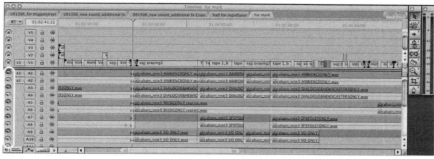
Mute unnecessary duplicate tracks to keep OMF file size down.

channels are not duplicates; they are unique lefts and rights, so leave both as they are.

🎧 Remove any inserted audio filters (plug-ins) like equalizers, compressors, or special effects. These effects might spoil the OMF export and they sound better when done in an audio sequencer anyway. However, if there are certain effects you are married to, do what you have to do to make them permanent, and then remove the filter. It's not a bad idea, too, to include the unprocessed original clip on a backup track. (Label the backup track accordingly.)

🎧 Audio fades and crossfades may help you stay sane while editing video, making things sound smooth and listenable, but it's better to draw them in the audio sequencer, for a variety of reasons that we'll learn in the 'Elements' chapters. If you have already applied fades to clips, it's ok to leave them. You will have a chance to re draw more accurate and interesting fades later in the DAW. If you haven't drawn in any fades, don't bother starting now.

🎧 The same principle applies to levels. If you haven't started, don't bother doing any mixing in the NLE except what you need in order to edit comfortably.

🎧 Be sure the one-frame, 1kHz '2-pop' sync file is on every audio track at exactly two seconds before the first frame of picture start. The procedure is described in the previous section of this chapter. Every track now is referenced to an exact point in time with the other audio tracks, and with the white video flash frame.

### Make the OMF

Prepare the session as outlined above then continue with these steps to make the OMF archive:

- 🎧 Be sure the audio 2-pop clips are the first audio events in your sequence, for easy line up to video later.

- 🎧 Pull down the *File* menu in your sequencer and select *Export Audio to OMF* (or similar). If prompted, select OMF 2.0. (Note: If you are not sure that your sequencer supports OMF v2.0, see if an upgrade is available for your sequencer. OMF 2.0 offers many advantages over v1.1.)

- 🎧 The OMF media export dialogue box will ask what size 'handles' you would like. This refers to the extra, truncated audio material before the start point and after the end point of *every* audio clip. This extra file

Specify a generous a handle size for your OMF export.

  info is one of the great benefits of the Open Media Framework and will allow us to draw longer, smoother fade ins and fade outs and fill in gaps and dropouts. Handles are very important; however, they add greatly to the file size. Specify a liberal handle length, for short or medium length films use at least 90 frames (or 3 seconds).

- 🎧 It is recommended to uncheck the box to "Include Crossfade Transitions" if prompted (Final Cut Pro) since we will draw more accurate crossfades in the audio sequencer later. Including crossfades could cause undesirable export behavior.

- 🎧 If prompted to 'Embed Audio' or 'Include Media,' select this checkbox.

- 🎧 Keep the OMF (and any other audio files coming over into the DAW) aside. Once we set up the audio session in the next chapter, we'll import the OMF into our new audio session.

## HOW BIG IS A WAV FILE?

Be sure you have enough storage space for the OMF. Let's look at how much space is needed for a CD quality, 16-bit mono file at a 44.1kHz sample rate. (Note: These numbers are intentionally rough (within a 10% tolerance) for purposes of easy remembering):

| A 16 bit mono WAV or AIF file this long… | …will take up *about* this much drive space |
|---|---|
| 1 minute | 5 MB |
| 10 minutes | 50 MB |
| 1 hour | 300 MB |
| 3 hours | 1 GB |
| 6 hours | 2 GB |

- Add 10% for 48kHz files
- Add another 50% for 24-bit files
- For stereo files, simply multiply times two

  So if you have a 30-minute picture with five mono 16-bit audio tracks at 48kHz, you can estimate: 30 minutes * 5 MB/min * 5 tracks + 10% = about 825MB (Note: The mathematic result is a little more: 843.75MB. But we were pretty close.)

  Keep in mind that this does not account for handles during an OMF export. If you have 300 audio clips in your sequence, each with an extra 3-second pre- and post handle, that's 6 seconds * 300 = 30 minutes of additional audio = about another 150MB.

*Encapsulated OMF 2.0* is the proper name of the preferred OMF export format. Note that the encapsulated specification has a 2GB file size limit. If you estimate that your audio clips will add up to more than this you will have to split your sequence into two and make two OMF exports, being careful to tightly line up the first session to the second upon import in the audio sequencer.

## What to do if you can't OMF/AAF

The benefits of OMF/AAF should be pretty apparent by this point. It retains the discrete nature and positioning of all of the audio clips in the NLE timelines, which makes for easy working with individual clips later in the DAW. It includes handles for drawing better audio fades. It allows for one-step importing of the sequence into the DAW, reducing the possibility of sync problems. For easy handling of large projects with lots of audio clips, OMF is really the way to go. If for some reason you need another way to get the audio into the DAW, the following procedure should help.

### *Export entire audio tracks from the video sequencer*

- Ready your tracks as described in the 'Prepare for export' procedure above, bringing in all remaining audio, muting unnecessary tracks, adding 2-pop cues to every track, etc.

- Set left and right locator points around all of the audio you want to appear in the DAW.

- Select *File-Export* (or similar) and choose AIF or WAV format. If asked, specify 16-bit word length at the project sample rate (usually 44.1kHz or 48kHz).

- Do this once and check the resulting WAV or AIF file by opening it in an audio editor or playing it in a media player program. If it's sounding right, duplicate the procedure for the other tracks. Be sure to label the files with some specific naming convention, like 'Dialogue Boom 1.aif' or 'Music 1 Left.wav.'

- Keep the files aside; we will import them into the audio sequencer in the next chapter.

# Rendering the video file

We'll need a video file to cut audio to picture in the audio sequencer. The quality needs to be sharp and it needs to be large enough to easily see the actors' lips moving. The most compatible and widely used format is Apple's QuickTime. Another reliable option is the Microsoft AVI (audio-video interleave) format. QuickTime (MOV) files are usually smaller and have more user-customizable options so we'll use them in the procedures below. Although Mac sequencers use QuickTime inherently, PC-based applications require downloading and installing the free QuickTime player. So if you're going to work with the audio on a PC, you can use AVI or another video format, or download QuickTime at www.apple.com.

Each audio sequencer has different video capabilities. Sometimes it takes several attempts (and some research) to produce a video of the quality, file size, and encoding method that plays back well in the audio sequencer. Aim for a file size of less than 2GB for a feature length film. Check the sidebar for some options on keeping file sizes down.

## WHAT'S A CODEC?

There are many flavors of *codecs*, the COmpression-DECompression scheme that makes small file sizes out of huge videos. They include DV (Note: DV/DVCPRO NTSC for North America, DV/DVCPRO PAL for Europe), M-JPEG (Motion JPEG), Cinepak, and others. Avid, Final Cut, Premiere, and the other video editors offer a variety of codecs to use when rendering a QuickTime from the video sequence. However, the best video encoding comes from using dedicated software designed to do the job.

Smooth video playback in an audio sequencer requires low CPU usage. This means, among other things, using a keyframe for every frame of video so the computer does not have to interpolate images. You want the video file to store each frame of the picture discretely, like an actual reel of film, so the audio sequencer will easily rewind, fast forward, and play back from any point in the file. The audio application needs to save its CPU power for what it does best – mix audio.

Creating a high quality, small-size video can be a long trial-and-error process. A foolproof way is with aftermarket programs like Sorensen Squeeze (Mac/PC) or Autodesk Cleaner (Mac only). As an example, Squeeze can get an AVI (exported from Final Cut Pro with a DV codec) down to a 2MB-per-minute, 480x360 QuickTime video that should work great in any sequencer.

Another option is to bypass some of the codec-speak and prepare an AVI instead of an MOV. However, the large file size of an AVI makes it impractical for anything but short films. Most people use the QuickTime format, selecting an encoding method on which both their video and audio applications agree.

If for some reason (web delivery perhaps) you need to make a WMV (Windows Media Video File), an application called Windows Media Encoder is available as a free download from Microsoft's website. It easily re-compresses AVIs as WMVs.

### Export the video file from the NLE

Be sure you have created a 1-frame white 'flash frame' at the same time location as your audio 2-pop clips. This flash frame should be the first video event in your sequence.

- 🎧 If possible, use the same left and right locator points you used for the OMF export. Or, set the left locator to the first video frame you want to export. Set the right locator at the approximate end point of the picture. It's not necessary to include the credit roll if there is no sync sound after your credits and you are just going to fade music out over the credits.

- 🎧 Begin the export movie process: In Final Cut, instead of choosing 'Export QuickTime movie…' from the 'File' menu, which seems to create much larger files, go to the *Browser* window and bring up the 'Export Queue' dialogue box. Choose the 'QuickTime (Custom)' format. Be sure to check the 'Use Item In/Out' which exports only between the in and out locators – not the whole timeline. Select 'Options' and specify the video compression and audio export settings.

Use Final Cut Pro's 'Export Queue' procedure for making the QuickTime video.

🎧 Export features vary by platform and codec, but look for options that allow a high-quality render, with millions of colors, at a frame size of at least 480 x 360, depending on the quality of video you will need while working with the audio mix.

Getting the right size, quality and performance may require some trial and error of the movie export settings.

🎧 Decide on a codec (such as DV) that you think will be best for your application. Check your audio sequencer's manual and its online help forums for advice. If there is a problem with importing the video into the audio program, you can try again later with a different codec.

🎧 Include audio (uncompressed, at the proper project sample rate) with the QuickTime. We may need this temp mix as a reference later.

🎧 The method is similar but different on the various Avid platforms as well as in Adobe Premiere. Consult their manuals for the video export procedure.

🎧 When it's done cooking you can test the video file in a blank audio session to see how it plays in the audio sequencer.

In the next chapter we'll have a little tour of the most important features of an audio sequencer and then we'll import the OMF and video we created in this chapter. By the end you'll have a fully featured audio session ready for editing.

# Chapter 7

# Setup: The Audio Session

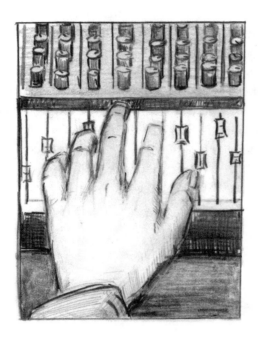

By this point your studio, no matter how crude, is ready. You have an audio sequencer that you are at least somewhat familiar with and you've readied the audio files from your video session. You've got at least one pair of audio monitors and a good set of headphones that you can count on. Your room sounds clean, clear, and quiet enough in which to mix – and at the right volume level. Music you know well sounds full and clear in the bass, midrange, and treble frequencies. Your room is properly wired, with no hum or buzz coming from the monitors (or headphones) when you turn them up. You've made some acoustical improvements to help ensure your mix will translate well when played back in other settings.

In this chapter we make the transition from NLE to DAW. If you're new to a digital audio workstation you'll find that the basic concepts are familiar to non-linear video editing. Both sessions organize clips drawn from a pool (or bin) on to a linear timeline and both have a variety of plug-ins (filters) available to modify your raw material. Audio sessions, however, use more tracks, have more complex signal routings, and output your sound sculpting results in real-time – with no rendering. We'll make use of the full potential of the audio sequencer including some lesser used capabilities of them.

We'll be making a layer cake of sound with your production tracks, adding music, voiceover, and sound effects to the recipe. Your vision may be rather straightforward and you may not think you need as much layering. In any case it will be beneficial for you to know the potential of a full soundtrack. Very often filmmakers change their minds during audio post, choosing to build a complete soundtrack when their original intention was just to clean up a few spots of dialogue.

After packing your new bag of DAW tricks we'll import the OMF you created in the last chapter and begin the hands on with your audio files. If you feel comfortable with your studio setup and have a pretty clear outline of what you want to do to your sound, you're ready to move on. If you're already familiar with audio sequencers, the end of this chapter – where we set up the audio session and import the OMF – will be the most important to you.

## The sequencer environment

DAW sequencers look rather intimidating at first. They have an abundance of ways to control, display, and analyze audio across the frequency spectrum and dynamic range of human hearing. That's a way of saying that the audio engineer has precise control of the timbre (tone quality) and volume of the precious signal at every point of its journey toward final mix.

An audio sequencer is a video sequencer flipped on its head. Hence, its video options are very restricted (sometimes to just one video track) but its audio options are virtually unlimited. It mixes multiple audio streams – processing them through plug-ins and routing them through many channels – eventually to the speaker and headphone outputs. It's easy to lose track of your tracks because signal routing in a DAW is not visually obvious. We use meters to keep an eye on our signals as they find their way to the main outputs.

Consider this section of the book as a complement to the software's user manual. If you're new to an audio sequencer, look to your manual for the basics and here we'll cover some of the creative ways that an experienced engineer might use the program. You'll want to already be familiar with things like importing audio, cutting up and moving clips around, muting and soloing tracks, and controlling basic levels. If you've worked with a DAW before, you might skip some of the following explanations but scan this chapter for tips on things like staying organized and creative signal routing.

# Check out the view…and the pool!

Let's look at some of the vitals of the audio sequencer from the top down. All reasonably powerful audio sequencers split themselves into two main views (or windows): the *sequence* (or *edit*) view and the *mixer* view. The sequencer is the arena for the dirty work like cutting up and moving around audio clips, and also some volume automation. Controlling volume levels, effects assignments, and signal routings – what is usually thought of as 'mixing' – mostly gets done in the mixer view.

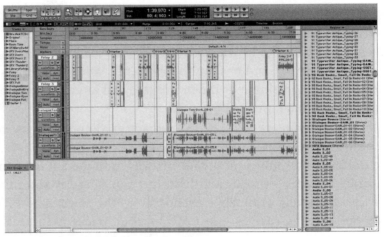

The Edit view's tracks look similar to those in the NLE.

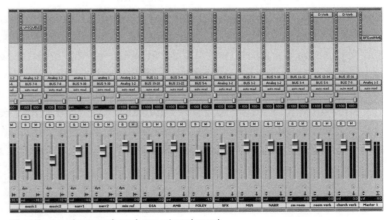

The Mix view shows each track as a mixer channel.

In addition, a sequencer needs to know how to get the audio to and from your soundcard. Inputs and outputs get set up in the I/O section. It's important to check this area before starting a new project. Verify that the sequencer is set up to record and playback on the input and output busses that you desire, and you won't ever have to wonder why it's playing back, but nothing is coming out of the speakers.

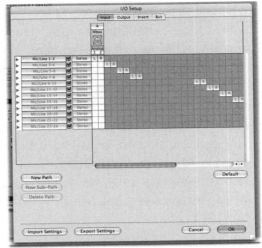

Customize the sequencer's audio ins and outs for your audio interface and working style.

Particulars to the project are set up in a 'project setup' window or the 'new session' dialogue box. The important settings are the sample rate of the audio files (usually 44.1kHz or 48kHz), the ruler reference

(Is it set to timecode or real-time? Be careful – these look similar at first.) and the frame rate (usually 24fps or 29.97 (non drop) for digital video in the U.S.).

It's important to set (or at least check) these particulars with every new project. Even if you're working from a template you created yourself, it only takes a minute to double-check the project's frame rate and other setup particulars, which can prevent synchronization and other troubles later.

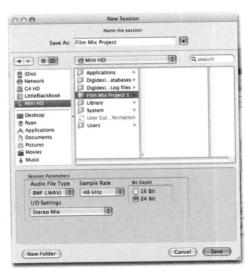

Set the sample rate and other options when you start a new project.

Also be sure to set up the project for surround or stereo mixing, as appropriate. Your mixing window view's panners should reflect this change.

In addition to the two main *edit* and *mix* views the sequencer has some sort of *pool* or *region list* where references to every audio clip in the session are kept. This is the place to go looking when you can't find an audio clip on the sequence view's timeline, or when you want to get detailed file information on a clip.

## The track

A track in an audio sequencer is just a sonic 'layer' or lane that can playback a mono or stereo audio file. A track can contain infinite clips in succession, but can play only one sonic event at a time. To play back more tracks at a time, add more tracks and import

The ProTools 'region list' catalogs the original and processed versions of every audio clip in the session.

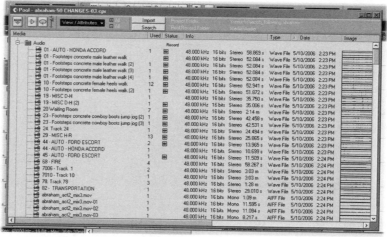

Some other sequencers keep track of the session wavefiles in an audio 'pool.'

more audio files. The vertical playback line is the tape head: when it passes over audio files on any number of tracks, it plays them back together.

The tracks' audio gets mixed/layered/ combined/summed (however you want to think about it) by the computer in real-time when the *play* button is pressed. As long as they are routed properly and not muted, all of the audio events get heard in the playback. What's great is that auditioning the audio doesn't require 'rendering' as video does in an NLE.

# THE GOOD LIFE: UNLIMITED TRACKS

Welcome to the good life. Unlike many video editing programs, most audio sequencers today allow you to easily work with an unlimited number of audio tracks. (Note that ProTools LE and M-Powered do have track count restrictions.) This means big things for organizing and processing mountains of audio clips.

Take for example a documentary that cuts between interviews of 3 different people, each using both a boom and a lavaliere mic.

Instead of keeping all of the dialogue on two tracks, we can name as many new tracks as we want and even route them to groups.

This allows us to correct Jenn's sibilance by inserting an EQ on her tracks, without affecting the others. Then we route her lav track – along with all of the other lav tracks – to the lav group, where another EQ is waiting to remove rumble on all of the lav tracks.

We have the best of both worlds: individual tracks for specialized processing, and groups that save time (and computer horsepower) by using one plug-in to affect several tracks at once. And if all of the boom tracks came out a bit too loud, one fader effectively lowers all of them. The best benefit, however, is the feeling of being organized and in control of your session.

Since audio sequencers are set up with so many tracks and routing possibilities, it's very easy to process signals through lots of effects. There are basically four ways to use effects in a DAW: *insert effects, aux sends, master effects,* and *offline processing.* Some of these routings are apparent and some work in the background out of sight.

The first three involve setting up an effect (like an equalizer) on a track and routing the audio through it. Contrarily, offline processing is kind of like applying a video filter in an NLE. (Note: ProTools refers to using offline plug-ins as AudioSuite processing.) Firstly, it is a one time, 'destructive' process (meaning it permanently changes the audio). Secondly, although the offline processing can be auditioned while being tweaked to perfection, it renders the new version while playback is stopped (not in real-time). Let's take a look at online and offline processing in depth.

## Insert effects

Each track has many possibilities for processing signals and routing them around the project. Let's follow the waveform's path through the audio sequencer (audio engineers call this *signal flow*).

The waveform first passes through the *insert* plug-in effects. *Inserts*

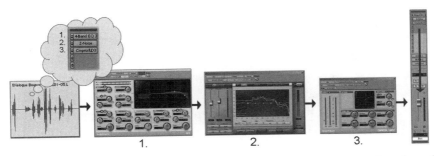

1.  2.  3.

are slots where plug-ins like equalizers or hum removers can be placed to tweak the signal in some way. Inserts are processed in the order they appear, from top to bottom on the channel strip. Each successive insert processes the output from the previous insert. Got that? They simply work in sequence one after the other. Order of operations means *everything* to complex procedures such as noise reduction, and inserts give us careful control over our signal flow.

Want to remove low end rumble before compressing the dialogue? Place an equalizer in insert slot 1 and a dynamics processor in slot 2. Reversing the plug-in order, however, would allow the low end rumble to affect the compressor, which could cause the compressor to overreact from the louder signal and over compress the speech. Want to boost the treble of a piece of music and then apply some stereo widening to it? Inserts allow you to do it, in the order you specify. You just need to mentally keep track of the order of signal flow. Look for more recommendations on using inserts throughout the book.

## Offline processing

Offline processing (called AudioSuite processing in ProTools) is a different way to use plug-ins. It's more like the way an NLE would use them. Offline is the way to go to apply a one time process that you probably won't want to

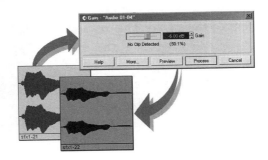

Time-out: Use an offline process instead of inserts whenever you want to make a permanent change to one or several clips.

change later. Simple effects such as *normalize* or *gain changes* are often applied this way to get volumes roughly matching between clips.

It's also a good idea to process an audio event offline instead of with a track insert when you don't want to affect other clips on the track. If just a few clips on a track have a low end (bass) rumble, it's a breeze to select just those clips, apply an offline EQ to correct the problem, and carry on with editing.

## Auxiliary channels

An auxiliary channel (or an *aux send*) is a bit different than an audio track – it doesn't hold audio clips of its own, but features all the same potential to use plug-ins. Thus, in film mixing they are used mostly for their insert effects.

Here's how they work. We tell an audio track to send out a portion of its signal to an aux channel. The sequencer automatically duplicates the signal, sends a portion that we designate through the aux channel (and its effects), and sums the aux output with the original audio. We are left with the original audio, untouched, and added to it is the result of the aux channel's processing. If there were no inserts on the aux channel, the original signal would get recombined with a copy of itself, simply making it louder.

You can insert any plug-in on an aux channel, but generally we use them for reverbs, delays, and other processes that are designed to *add* some new element to the signal. The original signal is referred to as the 'dry' portion and the aux output is referred to as the 'wet' portion.

Think of inserts as something you process audio through, in series, altering 100% of the sound. Conversely, aux sends work *in parallel* – they

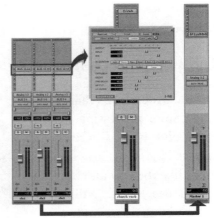

An aux channel taps off some of the audio tracks, processes it through its own inserts, and meets up with the original at the output.

split (or duplicate) the signal, process one of those splits, and re-combine the signals.

The sweet thing about this parallel setup is that any number of audio tracks can send a portion of their signal to the same aux track, which makes a great way for audio tracks to share one reverb, for example. It's a *lot* more efficient than running a reverb plug-in on every track that needs it.

## Group channels

A group (or subgroup, or bus) is a channel to which multiple audio tracks can be routed before they hit the master bus. It combines all of the audio coming into it into one super channel that outputs to the master channel (or to another group). Sonar and others call them by their generic name, 'buses.' ProTools calls them 'aux inputs' since they have similar routings. Note that they are different than 'edit groups'

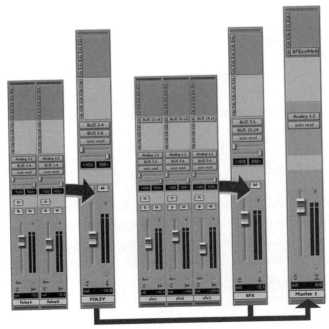

'Nest' your group tracks as deep as you like to help keep track of large sessions.

and 'mix groups' in ProTools, which do not control actual signal routing, but rather the linking or pairing of channels. There is some overlap in their organizational functionality though.

Groups are a great convenience and there are countless reasons why you'd want to send multiple tracks to a subgroup:

🎧 Groups let us control the levels of many audio tracks with one single fader. When you want to lower all of the sound effects in the picture, it's a cinch to lower that group's fader, rather than adjust every track's fader individually.

🎧 The insert effects on a group channel get applied to all of the audio coming into it. Want a simple way to take out low-end rumble on all of the dialogue? Don't use an EQ on every dialogue channel; instead, route all the dialogue tracks to a group and put the EQ on it.

🎧 Groups can be routed to other groups. You could, for example, route several dialogue tracks that need a certain kind of EQ to one subgroup, route other dialogue that doesn't need it to another subgroup, and send both groups into the main DIALOGUE group channel.

🎧 To listen to or perform a mixdown of the soundtrack, say, without the music, just mute the 'MUSIC' group track. All of the individual music tracks coming into it get muted automatically. To make a M&E mix (for international dubbing) one click mutes the DIALOGUE group, another click performs the output. Easy and organized.

## The Master Bus

The master channel behaves just like a group channel: it contains no audio clips of its own; instead, other tracks get routed to it. Except in this case *every* track is routed to it – groups, auxes, *everything*. This is where all of the audio in the session comes together; it's the last chance for affecting the entire mix before the computer either plays it back or exports it to a file.

An insert effect on the master bus affects the sum total of all tracks coming into it, and as such is a samurai sword to be handled with great care. If we wanted to make sure the loudness of the entire soundtrack never exceeded a certain level, we'd place a dynamics processor called a limiter on the master bus. If we were outputting for the web and needed to reduce the level of bass frequencies in the mix, the master bus is a convenient place to put a shelving equalizer. Choosing to affect a whole mix this way requires careful consideration and depends on what a particular soundtrack needs.

There aren't too many instances where it's necessary to affect an entire mix. It's all too easy to apply too much or the wrong kind of processing on a track, and doing this on the master bus has a huge impact on the entire soundtrack. Later, we'll learn to tame the mighty master bus to get our mixes sounding clean and punchy.

## Stereo or surround?

The two common mixing formats are 2-channel (left and right or L and R) stereo and 5.1 channel surround, which adds a mono center channel (C) between the left and right mains, a mono left surround channel (Ls), a mono right surround channel (Rs), and a mono low-frequency effects (LFE) channel. But these are not the only format choices. In fact, you might notice that Woody Allen likes his films in mono. With writing that good, who needs special effects, wide ambiences, or even stereo music for that matter! But even a dialogue-driven film can reap the benefits of surround, just with careful use of ambiences. The important thing is to decide *now* which format to mix toward – it will save a lot of time and money trying to create an alternate mix later.

A stereo mix can always be 'matrixed' up to pseudo-surround by a home theater system (more about this in the mixing chapter). But *discrete* surround means mixing and delivering six unique channels for a broadcast method or media delivery format that specifically requires or desires them.

Which format best serves your delivery medium – and your story? Consider mixing in surround when:

- 🎧 You have a properly set up and calibrated surround monitoring environment

- You are delivering the film for the HD format, where a 5.1 mix is expected

- You are producing the film for a digital-only (not optical film or broadcast TV) audience and want to make use of digital's extended headroom, wider frequency response, and greater signal-to-noise ratio. The technical advantages of digital help uphold the original sound quality of the mix.

- The film will make creative use of the extra-wide soundstage of surround, such as with creative panning or enveloping ambiences.

A fall-back stereo mix is generally included with delivery of every surround mix. Be aware of this while mixing, and use the surrounds in a disciplined way. If you're conscious of using the surrounds for ambiences, reverbs, occasional sound effects, and music, your mix should translate to stereo just fine.

## Rudiments of digital audio

Every DAW has options to establish the basic digital audio parameters of a session. These settings live in your audio sequencer and in the driver for your audio interface. Since they control the audio quality, compatibility, and 'feel' or responsiveness of your session, we'll cover them in depth so you can set them properly for your session. With a little patience, these parameters are not too difficult to 'set and forget.' (Note: Your sequencer may have several project setup and application setup screens; if you can't find the appropriate settings, consult its manual.)

| Setting | What it does |
|---|---|
| Driver | This bit of software runs in the background of your operating system and talks to your audio hardware. Like the 'Panama canal' between the sequencer and soundcard (or audio interface) it passes audio between the two and controls the soundcard's settings, like buffer size, that establish the digital-to-analog and analog-to-digital communication. Also sets and converts the sample rate and bit depth for audio entering and leaving the computer. |
| I/O setup | Your audio sequencer will have a place to set the input and outputs for your tracks. This is where you tell the program to output a channel's audio to 'soundcard XXX's output 1 and 2,' for example. This is particularly important to set properly when you are dealing with an audio interface that has multiple ins and outs. If the sequencer thinks your main outs are 'soundcard outputs 5 and 6' and your monitors are hooked up to outputs 1 and 2, you won't hear what's coming out of the sequencer. |
| Buffer size | The size of the audio packets that get passed between soundcard and sequencer. Larger buffer sizes allow more processing power but suffer longer latency (good for high track count or high plug-in count mixing sessions) while smaller buffer sizes offer less latency and faster sequencer response (useful while recording audio). |
| Latency | The time lag between passing audio between soundcard and sequencer, a direct result of the buffer size setting in the audio driver. When mixing, we use larger buffer sizes. This manifests as a lag or slight waiting period between every event you control: starting playback, tweaking an EQ, etc., and hearing that event in the speakers. When recording audio, lower latencies allow tighter sync with playback audio, helpful to the performer and reducing the need to move recorded clips around to sync them after recording. |

| Setting | What it does |
|---|---|
| Latency | Latency is measured in milliseconds. With a quality sound-card, less than 10ms is often possible with small buffer settings and is helpful when recording audio. 50ms, 75ms, 100ms or more allows use of more plug-ins without overloading the CPU and is to be used during mixing. Set and reset it according to your particular needs at the time. If you're just mixing and not recording, it should be fine to leave it at its highest setting. |
| Sample rate | Sample rate is the digital audio equivalent of film or video frame rate. Just as frame rate defines the rate of still images being recorded (and thus the resolution of the film motion) the audio sample rate sets the quality of digital audio resolution and also the limit of high end (treble) frequency response of the audio. 44.1kHz is the CD quality standard, used primarily during music based projects. 48kHz is traditionally used for film projects. The two formats exist because of legacy hardware standards and there is no real difference in sound quality between them. Regardless of an audio file's inherent sample rate, audio is auto-converted to the project sample rate upon import into the session. Upsampling (to a higher sample rate) does not increase quality but may help maintain file conformance within the session. Downsampling to lower than 44.1k a lower sample rate *does* reduce quality, noticeable primarily in the high-end treble area. |
| Bit depth, or word length | The resolution of distortion and dynamic range of a digital audio file. Upon import, the sequencer conforms all imported audio to the project bit depth for compatible processing and playback. The engineer chooses the word length of the final mixdown upon final audio export. Regardless of the bit depth of the files in a session, it is important to choose as high a *project* bit depth setting as possible for internal sequencer calculations. Choose a larger setting than the resolution of your audio files. |

| Setting | What it does |
|---|---|
| Bit depth, or word length *(continued)* | It's best to internally process audio at 24 or 32-bit while working (as a project bit depth setting) and output a 16-bit final mix later so all of the behind the scenes processing gets done at a higher resolution before finally being truncated to 16 bits. |
| Frame rate | Set the frame rate in the audio sequencer to establish a compatible time reference with the original digital video frame rate. Measured in frames per second (fps) the frame rate setting in an audio sequencer only defines the time-base for the timeline/ruler and clock/running-time display; it does not affect the audio in any way. This is important to set properly in the project setup for times when you want to visually match burned in time-code with the audio sequencer's clock, to ensure at a glance that everything is running in sync. |
| Display format | Sets the ruler and time (clock) display for the project. Most sequencers can display several rulers and clocks for ease of navigation. Choose 'timecode' or 'seconds' or whatever suits your project. |
| Pan law | In the project setup, set the 'pan law' to -6dB. This setting tells the sequencer how much it should reduce the volume of sounds panned center versus sounds panned hard right or left. Without this pan reduction, sounds panned up the middle would effectively have twice as much volume as those panned completely left or right, since centered sounds are coming out of *two* speakers at once. Some audio card drivers (such as those by RME Audio) also have their own setup screen to adjust the pan law. Set this in the driver as well, if applicable. |
| Sequencer preferences | Don't overlook the options that configure the environment for an easier workflow. Appearance settings, autosave interval, video window size, etc., are important to staying organized and comfortable during long sessions. A little time spent getting to know your sequencer's inner ways usually yields a faster, smoother workflow. |

### Creating the audio post session

Now that you're comfortable with the sequencer, let's get the project started. You'll need the extensive notes you made for the soundtrack in the *Pre Post* chapters. The ideas you came up with then are now an invaluable to do list. If you want, go back and watch the film again, perhaps with a filmmaker friend, and come up with more detailed notes. The clearer your vision for the soundtrack, the smoother the workflow will be once we start creating the elements of the soundtrack.

If you're working with QuickTime (MOV) files on a PC and haven't installed QuickTime yet, your sequencer will probably need it to play back your movie. You can download it at www.apple.com. The 'Pro' upgrade (about $30) has a host of useful features for post production, including converting video using a variety of different codecs, and easy playback of your mix into the video file for the web or other low fidelity output (such as for a promo reel).

### Setting up the session

* If you have a project template to start from, load it now. If not, we'll learn how to set up templates later in this chapter.

* Decide on a channel format. Mix in surround if you have the capabilities and a good reason to do so. If you do, set up the surround output busses in the following order:
  1. Left channel
  2. Center channel
  3. Right channel
  4. Ls (left surround)
  5. Rs (right surround)
  6. LFE (low-frequency effects)

* Create the new session for your soundtrack and open the project setup or audio options dialog box. When you create a new project the first thing to do is to check the parameters listed in the 'Rudiments' section above in both the driver and the session.

* Set the project sample rate and frame rate to whatever you used in your video session, perhaps 48kHz and 29.97fps, respectively.

- Set the project bit depth to 24 or 32 bit. For the final mix we will dither (to properly truncate a waveform's decimal precision in order to reduce file size while preserving quality) the audio down to a more compatible word length, probably 16 bit.

- Set the pan law, time display format, and any other options in the project setup.

- Set the sequencer's time display so that it reads timecode, the same timecode to which the NLE sequencer was set.

- Set your audio driver for the proper sample rate (and appropriate buffer size, while you're there). Otherwise, your audio might leave the sequencer at one sample rate, and get sped up (or slowed

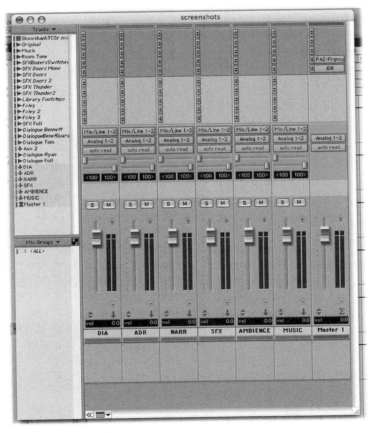

Use group channels in a way that best organizes YOUR project.

down) by the driver's different sample rate and everything will play back sounding strange.

- Create a few aux channels and keep them aside for now. Later in the mixing stage we'll use them for reverbs and other effects.

- Create some group channels for your session. You could label them DIALOGUE, ADR, NARRATION, SFX, AMBIENCE, and MUSIC.

- 'Solo safe' the group and aux channels so that they are still active when you've soloed, say a dialogue channel. See your sequencer's manual for instructions.

- Commit to easier mixing by keeping your tracks absolutely organized. Ensure that the output of every track in your sequence is routed to the appropriate group channel. As you add new tracks to the sequence later, say for ADR or for additional sound effects, get into the habit of routing their outputs to the appropriate group channels right away. The one exception to this is that reference tracks, such as rough mixes made in your video sequencer, should go directly to the master bus. These will be muted at mixdown anyway, and we don't want them mistakenly blending into the group stems.

### *Import the OMF and video*

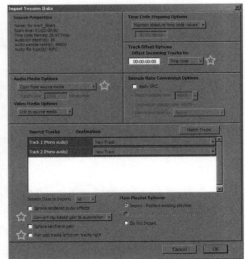

- First, be sure your new session is set up according to 'Setting up the new audio session,' above.

- Import the OMF you created in the video editing software according to the instructions for your audio sequencer (for ProTools, select 'File / Import / Session Data').

During import, choose the tracks you wish to bring in. Tailor the OMF

Upon importing an OMF into ProTools you are presented with a number of customization options. The starred options are the ones we've changed from their default values.

import according to the other options with which your sequencer presents you. Search the manual or online help for details about a particular import option.

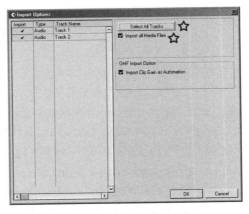

The audio sequencer sets up the tracks, brings in the media, and drops you off in the sequencer/ edit view. Quickly verify that everything is accounted

Some sequencers, such as this version of Cubase, have simpler OMF import options but offer less control.

for and in roughly the right place. Audio clips may overlap, depending on how the sequencer deals with handles and fades. Not to worry, we'll redraw fades and crossfades as we work.

🎧 If you created WAV or AIF exports from the NLE instead, import these onto separate tracks (mono or stereo as appropriate) and be sure they all line up from the same starting point.

🎧 Check the position of the 2-pops (2-beeps) that you included on every audio track. They should all be vertically in line.

🎧 It's time to import the QuickTime into the audio session. If you're on the PC platform, be sure the file has a .MOV file extension or the sequencer might not recognize it.

🎧 The video file comes into the pool or a track. Verify specifications like frame rate, video size in pixels, and running time. Then, if necessary, create a blank video track in the edit view. Drag the video file from the pool on to the video track.

🎧 If your video has burned in timecode, move the video file to the point on the track where its timecode matches the time in the audio sequencer's time display. Skip around and verify that the timecode throughout the picture matches the sequencer's time display. If not, double check that the frame rate in the audio project setup is the same frame rate you used for the video burn in.

- If you're working without burned-in timecode, the audio sequencer's timeline is a blank canvas and its time display is completely arbitrary. Just sync the video clip to the audio files. Select and move the video clip so that it starts exactly two seconds after the 2-pops on the audio tracks.

- Grab all of the audio files together and move them so that their 2-pops sync to exactly two seconds before the first frame in the picture, at the white flash frame. Zoom in close and be sure it's accurate.

- Start playbackfrom a point after the 2-pops (several 2-pops played together will be quite loud!). Check audio/video sync near the start of the project, and again toward the end. If everything plays in sync at both points, you're in good shape.

- If picture and sound start in sync and slowly drift out, the sample rate or frame rate of the audio sequence probably doesn't match that of the OMF you exported from the NLE. Go back and check these in the video sequencer. Verify them with the audio project. Find the discrepancy, re-export the OMF and .MOV at the proper rates, then repeat these import steps.

- If the video and audio are not in sync from the start, perhaps the 2-pops weren't placed accurately, or the video wasn't exported from its first frame. In this case, move the video clip around on the timeline until dialogue lines up (or use some other reference that you know) at the start of the audio. Then see if the project plays in sync, or if it drifts. If it seems ok, you have two options: tighten up the sync manually by moving the video clip a quarter frame at a time until it seems that audio is in sync, or go back into the NLE and re export, paying closer attention to picture and audio start points.

- A good troubleshooting precaution to verify A/V sync is to take the time to export a rough audio mixdown from the NLE. Using the same locators as you use for the QuickTime export, output a stereo mix of the sound as it is now, and import this file into the audio session. Line it up to the QuickTime in the audio sequencer, and visually compare its waveform and those of the OMF clips for sync.

## SAMPLE RATE LINE UP

What do you do when a line of dialogue is out of sync with an actor's lips? Somewhere, something got lost (sync is what got lost) and it looks like the scene was badly over-dubbed in a foreign language.

If it's only a few lines that have the problem, it's easy enough to manually correct them when you're working with a good quality QuickTime (or other) video in the audio sequencer. We'll cover the procedure in detail in the chapter on ADR for tightening up dialogue to actors' lips and replacing entire sections of dialogue.

If the entire dialogue track is off, first be sure your sequencer is set to the correct sample rate. If you were working in 48kHz in the NLE, check the audio app's project setup to be sure it's not set to 44.1kHz. Spot check sample rates of the audio clips in the audio pool to be sure they are all at the correct rate.

Some audio sequencers will manually move the timeline location of every audio clip if you change sample rates in the middle of working. Not a good thing – every dialogue clip in your session will go out of sync with the picture! Correcting this is sometimes harder than reverting to a backup or starting the session again (importing the OMF) from scratch. Keep track of the sample rate of both the project setting and all audio clips and you should be good to go.

## Looking ahead: Templates

Right about now it should be making sense why there were so many NLE preparations in the last chapter. With all of the routing possibilities, the large number of audio clips, the various views, etc., it's a challenge just to stay organized in an audio mix session, let alone come out of it with a successful soundtrack.

If you'll be doing more film projects in the future, now might be a good time to set up a project template. Importing an OMF into an existing template that's already set up for your personal working style makes everything easier and keeps you from having to reinvent the wheel (or the session) for every new film project. The procedures will vary from one sequencer to another but the principles are the same.

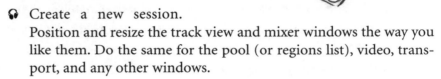

### Create a custom audio sequencer template

- ◖ Create a new session.
  Position and resize the track view and mixer windows the way you like them. Do the same for the pool (or regions list), video, transport, and any other windows.

- ◖ Set up the ruler to display timecode at the frame rate you use most (24fps, 29.97fps, etc.).

- ◖ Set the sample rate to the one in which you commonly work (probably 48kHz). While you're in the project setup dialog box set the bit depth and any other settings you want to customize.

- ◖ Create a marker track, if available in your sequencer, so you can leave a trail of breadcrumbs on the timeline for easier navigation as you work.

- ◖ If your projects normally require lots of sound effects and Foley, create several new *stereo* audio tracks. Repeat this with blank music tracks if you want to have tracks ready for importing music. Route their outputs to their respective group channels.

- ◖ Create a few *mono* audio tracks for both ADR and voiceover. Route them to their appropriate groups.

- ◖ Create 6 group tracks. Label them NARRATION, ADR, DIALOGUE, SFX, AMBIENCE, and MUSIC. Route the output of the ADR group to the DIALOGUE group. All others should be going to the same master bus.

- On the dialogue group channel, insert your favorite EQ or whatever plug-ins you might use. Do the same for the VO and ADR group channels. Disable the plug-ins, so they are ready to use but not active.

- Create four or more aux tracks. Insert your favorite reverb or other sound effect but keep them inactive or 'off' for now.

- On the master bus, insert three or four plug-ins in the following order: high-quality equalizer, mastering limiter and a spectrum analyzer if you have one. If you're working in ProTools you'll need to create a master channel first.

- Nuendo, Cubase, and some other sequencers use folder tracks to organize the sequence/edit window. Folder tracks group tracks together for easy display and navigation. Make up to eight folder tracks. Label them according to your project stems: DIALOGUE, VO, ADR, FOLEY, SFX, AMBIENCE, MUSIC, and ARCHIVE. Place all of the dialogue tracks in the DIALOGUE folder, and follow suit for the rest of the audio tracks.

  You may choose to then place the ADR group inside the DIALOGUE folder, and place FOLEY inside the SFX folder. Use the ARCHIVE folder for muted or unused tracks, or tracks with old versions of clips that you want to keep aside as backups.

  ProTools does not use folder tracks. Instead, highlight the audio tracks you want to link together and create an 'edit group' or

Some sequencers like Steinberg's Cubase allow you to nest folder tracks inside other folder tracks for serious organization of high track-count projects.

'mix group' for them in the lower left corner of the respective window. Name the group appropriately and repeat the process for all other tracks in the sequence. Use the edit/mix group selection functionality to control which tracks appear or remain hidden in the edit window.

- 🎧 Double check that *every* audio track's output assignment is going to some type of group track (or 'aux input' for ProTools), *not* the master channel (except temp mixes, which should go directly to the master bus).

- 🎧 Save the project as a new session or as a template if your sequencer supports it. Save an extra backup of this blank project, too, in case you accidentally turn your template into a project down the road.

## Looking ahead: Key commands

Often overlooked is the ability of some sequencers to let you assign commands to keystrokes. Simply hitting a keystroke to perform a common task saves the time of going to the top of the window and hunting

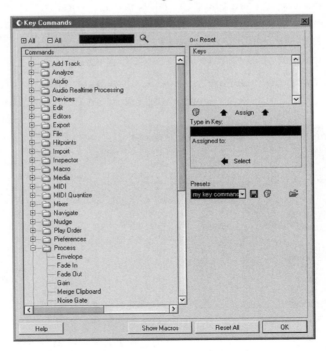

Assign enough key commands and you may never have to pull down a menu again!

for commands amongst pull down menus, or fishing through context sensitive, right click mouse menus.

Start by using the default key commands of your audio sequencer (refer to the handy key command reference guide that hopefully came with your software). Then create your own custom key mappings. It's worth taking the time now to create keyboard shortcuts that will greatly help your workflow later.

Edit faster and with less effort in your DAW by learning the key commands or manually assigning keys to commands such as:

- View settings: horizontal (timeline) zoom in and zoom out, vertical (track height) zoom in and out

- Tracks: add audio track, add aux (or FX) channel, delete current (highlighted) track, mute/unmute track, solo/de solo track

- Setup: show I/O assignments, show video window, show detailed track information, open key command assignments, open notepad, open pool

- Markers: set marker, go to next marker, go to previous marker

- Moving audio clips: file operations: import audio, import OMF, export audio (mixdown or bounce)

- Edit operations: perform crossfade, duplicate clip, mute/unmute clip, nudge forward (right), nudge backward (left)

- Transport operations: turn playback looping on/off, loop selected events, rewind, fast forward, record, return to start of last playback

- Tools: activate select (arrow) tool, split (cut) tool, mute tool, delete tool

- Snap: turn on/off snap to events or snap to cursor position (to auto align audio events with the start of other events or with the current cursor position)

- Plug-ins: it is extremely helpful to assign keys to open your favorite EQ, noise reduction, hum reduction, de crackle and de-click, normalize, gain increase/decrease, and compression plug-ins for offline processing. Highlight the audio clip you want to process, strike the key for your EQ plug-in, and you're ready to begin offline EQ auditioning and processing.

# Chapter 8

# Elements: Dialogue, Most Importantly

Dialogue is often the most important sonic layer of a film and probably the hardest to get to sound good. The tone and clarity of the characters' voices are absolutely crucial to conveying the story's message. But, since reality TV obviously does not require dialogue as clean as Robert Altman, a film's style, delivery format, time schedule, and budget determines the amount of work needed in dialogue editorial.

In this book, dialogue editing means getting organized, cleaning up noise and other issues, and making production recordings sound ready for the mixing stage. We'll consider where it's best to replace production sound with re-recorded dialogue (which gets its own chapter). We'll do the actual mixing – setting exact volume levels, applying reverb and special effects, etc. – after all elements, including sound effects and music, are edited and prepared. This is important because until all elements are in place it's difficult to determine the proper levels and effects requirements. In addition, we'll give special treatments like telephone voice, dialogue through walls, etc., their own chapter.

# Dialogue editing workflow

Dialogue editing has an order of operations that keeps the signal as pristine as possible throughout its journey to mixland. Here is an overview of what we'll be doing in this chapter:

### SET UP

- Obtain the highest fidelity versions of the production recordings, as identical to the source as possible. Create both a working copy and an additional backup from the originals.
- Set up tracks and import clips, preferably by OMF.
- Pick mics. Archive unused clips on to muted tracks.
- Delete duplicate audio clips and organize clips onto tracks by timbre, levels, or mic used. Create extra dialogue tracks as needed to keep the session organized.
- Route all tracks to the DIALOGUE group track.
- Mute or archive any production clips that won't be heard due to music or other soundtrack elements taking precedence.

### CLEAN UP

- Clean up clicks and pops, then crackle and distortion.
- Remove hums and buzzes, as well as low end rumble.
- Equalize or de-noise to remove particularly nasty low-end rumble, high end hiss, or other undesirables.
- Make specialized edits to clips where needed: fix plosives and sibilance, adjust volume of individual words or syllables, substitute other takes, and do any other finessing.

### FIX UP

- Modify start and end points of clips to follow video fades and dissolves. Apply extremely short fade-ins, fade-outs, and crossfades to avoid clicks between clips.

- Lay room tone between gaps in dialogue for continuity. Equalize and level it for consistency. Since the procedure is similar to how we work with ambiences, we'll deal with room tone in more detail in the next chapter.

- Match timbre (tone quality) within a scene through equalization and other processing.

- Even out the dialogue levels for consistency by adjusting gain of clip and track levels.

- Avoid compressing the dialogue if possible. Compression may be helpful for some broadcast outlets such as the web, but in general, use it as sparingly as possible. (Note: We're talking about dynamics compression here, not audio encoding. This is about controlling the signal's dynamic range or volume levels, not converting file formats or making MP3s.)

- Set the DIALOGUE group to the proper level. Ensure, again, that levels are even and at broadcast standards. We'll fine tune this in the mixing chapter.

### CHECK UP

- Wait some time, listen back with an ear toward consistency, and attack remaining problems.

## Setting up

There is a simple, effective way to set up and work with dialogue in a sequencer. The approach is straightforward and linear, although dialogue editing can be the most time consuming for projects with poorly recorded production tracks. Keep the session absolutely organized and troubleshooting will be a breeze.

The first thing dialogue editors do when they look at the production dialogue tracks is 'pick mics.' That is, where someone or something was recorded with more than one mic for safety (say a lavaliere and a boom) the Dialogue Editor decides to work with the better sounding one and mute/archive the other. Combining both rarely sounds natural and usually produces a thin, phasey, or unnaturally filtered sound, which you may or may not be able to hear over your audio monitors. How to choose one recording over the other will become clear after you meet the common problems that plague dialogue tracks.

The second step involves eliminating duplicate clips. Video editors double all of their mono tracks in order to have the sound come out both the left and right speakers (thus it sounds panned up the center in the middle of the speakers). Audio sequencers don't work this way, so keep only one version of each clip and delete any duplicates that came over in the OMF. Working with one clip instead of two cuts down on work and keeps the sequence less cluttered.

In the last chapter we talked about the benefits of the virtually unlimited tracks in a modern audio sequencer. This leads us to step 3. Use the sequencer architecture to your advantage and, to the extent that you feel is practical, move every dialogue clip onto a track with other clips with the same timbre or tone. If Uncle Frankie and Cousin Joey were recorded with the same mic, sound equally muddy, and are at the same volume, it's up to your own working preference if you want to keep them on separate tracks or on one track.

## THE SHOTGUN VERSUS THE LAV

Lavaliere mics, especially wireless types, are common equipment on professional film sets. However, they aren't a location sound mixer's first choice when recording narrative films. They take valuable time on set to fit onto an actor, they require multiple batteries, and their RF (radio frequency) channels can pick up interference (including mobile phone interference), often ruining a take. On top of that they sound rather bass heavy – less natural than a shotgun.

Nor are they a dialogue editor's first preference. In every case, the mic is relatively far away and out of the direct line of sight of the actor's mouth, what we call the sound source. Since all microphones sound their fullest and clearest when closest to the sound source, lav mics almost always present a muddy sound that lacks clear high frequency response (treble or presence).

Dialogue from a hidden lav is often not even usable. These mics usually get taped or pinned to an actor's body behind a layer of clothing, a man's tie, or in the hair. Almost always they pick up clothing rustle that is time consuming or impossible to remove in post. They are a good backup for narrative films but are by their nature are usually too problematic to rely upon completely on a narrative shoot.

In some cases, however, the fuller bass response that the lav provides might be just the thing – and the convenience can't be beat. Holding a boom over an interviewee's head for the duration of a long interview would be painful, not to mention a visual distraction to the interviewee. In those cases where a lav pinned on to the outside of clothes isn't a problem, it can provide a warm, full, mellow sound that lends itself well to interviews. So they are a logical choice for documentaries, industrial videos, and long-form interviews, where seeing the mic on camera is acceptable.

A shotgun microphone almost always sounds clearer, especially for narrative films. (Note: The mic is called a *shotgun* for its extremely narrow pickup area. The 'boom' is the *pole* to which the shotgun mic is attached.). There are times, however, like in an extreme long shot, that the boom might be seen in the shot. A good location sound mixer will do something creative to capture the dialogue, like hide a shotgun somewhere in the scene. Although, depending on the scene and the film, it might not be as efficient as a little ADR.

Shotguns sound better because, when used properly, they are positioned directly in the line of sight of the sound source (and have a larger and more sensitive capsule). This allows them to pick up more of the crucial treble frequencies in the 2kHz to 5kHz range that make speech intelligible.

As dialogue editor of your own picture, choose your dialogue clips *first* according to which sound the best in terms of vocal tone or performance, and *second* that have the least noise issues.

## Emergency ward: Noise

Noise is an arbitrary term for sound that we don't like or want, and that depends on your own sensitivity and standards. Cleanup is where the art of dialogue editorial begins.

To a Dialogue Editor, there are two kinds of noise: the kind he can remove and the kind he can't. And then there's that whole gray area, where the 'before' and 'after' clips sound different, but not necessarily better than the other. This is about making judgment calls that come from *experience*.

Learn to hear voice tracks in terms of signal versus noise (i.e., the sound you like and want to keep, and everything else that is in the way of that). Separate the two, even though you may not be used to tuning in to what you *don't* want to hear. You'll start to pick up on annoying vocal problems like:

- *Plosives* – bass heavy vocal popping on a close mic – when people say words with the letters *B* or *P* in them. *POP*corn!

- *Sibilance* – a whistling sound sometimes made when people speak their *S*'s – is another bane of the audio engineer but can be made less distracting.

- *Coughs, lip smacks, mouth clicks, etc.*

Then there are the equipment-related problems of:

- Clicks and pops

- ⌒ Crackle
- ⌒ Hum or buzz
- ⌒ White noise (or hiss) and low end rumble

And finally, the last kind of noise we need to consider:

- ⌒ Ambient or environment noise, including, traffic, airplanes, industry, crowds, and other jarring background events

If you've heard these issues in your own recordings, it's easy to marvel at big budget features with pristine dialogue tracks and wonder how they get their tracks so clean. We'll begin by solving these pervasive problems.

The restoration component of dialogue prep follows an order of operations for best results:

- ⌒ De-click and de-pop
- ⌒ De-crackle
- ⌒ De-hum and de-buzz
- ⌒ De-hiss

*(Courtesy of CEDAR Audio Limited, www.cedar audio.com)*

Sound restoration is actually a serious science and something of an art. In its highest form, forensic audio, engineers analyze and correct waveforms with the care that an archeologist takes to a historical site. With the proper time put into the research, excavation, and analysis, most production recordings can yield results clean enough for broadcast.

Remember to *never* equalize or compress dialogue before performing these basic cleanup functions, and *never* apply special effects or reverb until troubled dialogue has been restored. Save the effects for later.

### Removing clicks and pops

Clicks and pops are sudden spikes that come from various equipment and human error, like dropouts during recording, or digital edits that need smoothing. They are unique, isolated incidents as opposed to a constant or steady sound issue (like a hum or buzz).

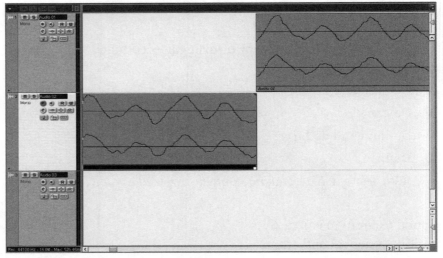

Upon playback the bottom waveform will end abruptly and the top will start with an audible click.

Zoom in close to an audio clip or two. Whenever a waveform doesn't start or end at the zero-crossing line (this is the horizontal reference line dividing the waveform into upper and lower portions), you may hear the 'click' of a sudden change in level. The remedy is to manually draw small fades over these harsh boundaries. Performed manually, this is a time consuming process. Restoration plug-ins such as the products mentioned later in this chapter can make short work of tracks plagued by clicks and pops.

**TIP:** Select several waveforms at once when you want to perform fades to all of them in one fell swoop. A half frame or one frame fade in will eliminate clicks. Keep in mind that fade-*outs* sound most natural when

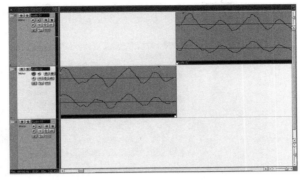

Remedy sudden starts and stops with very short crossfades.

they're longer than this, somewhere between a few frames and a half second. Avoid chopping off the actor's last syllable.

The next type of click you may hear comes from an audio dropout, where the machine decided to stop recording for a brief instant, and picked up again a moment later. The result is an abrupt change in waveform volume level, and an audible click.

You can often use a de-click plug-in to automate the cleanup if your waveform needs a lot of de-clicking (or if you're having trouble locating a click by hand).

Or you can individually redraw a click with the pen-

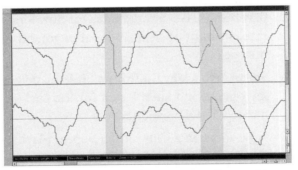

These two abrupt changes in volume were caused by recording dropouts – when otherwise clock-stable equipment (or cabling) punches out for a brief moment.

cil tool. That part is easy. Finding it, however, may take a little practice.

To find clicks, you *could* zoom in close on the waveform and scroll through minutes' worth of audio looking for the problem, but that would take quite some time. Here is a technique that can help find and zero in on a click. This type of searching also works well for pops (plosives) or any other short-lived, offensive sound that you want to isolate and remove.

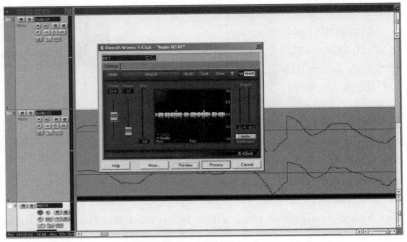

Sometimes click removal can be automated with a plug-in.

### Locate and remove clicks and pops

🎧 Play back the general area with the click. Stop as soon as you hear it.

🎧 Listen carefully for how soon the click occurs after you have hit the play button. Get a rough idea for how long – let's say there is about three seconds of clean audio after you hit Play and before you hear the click.

🎧 Start playback again from a bit later than your last starting point, say one second later. Listen for the click again: you should hear it happen a second sooner.

🎧 Now zoom in a little closer. Repeat playing it back, a bit later each time, until the click comes as soon as you hit play, until you can't distinguish it from the *natural* click that happens from simply starting playback. You have now narrowed down the click's location to within less than half a second.

🎧 When you've narrowed it down and you're zoomed in to a 1- or 2-second area of audio, begin scrolling slowly through the waveform and visually look for a jump in waveform level (for an easier time with this, see if your sequencer supports waveform scrolling using either the arrow keys, mousewheel, or a CTRL- mousewheel/ Command-mousewheel combination).

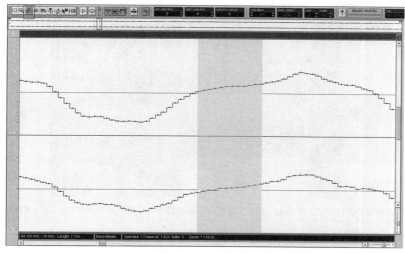

Highlighted region no longer shows any sign of clicking.

🎧 Select the pencil (draw) tool. Zoom in real close – both horizontally and vertically – and redraw as little of the waveform as
possible to smooth out the click. Play back and verify the cleaned
up audio.

🎧 Congratulate yourself on your first successful session of audio surgery.

## Removing crackle

Crackle is more of a *long-form* noise or distortion – the signal breaking up over a period of time longer than you'd want to edit by hand,
maybe a half second, half minute, or half hour! The audio sounds
crunchy because either A. it was recorded too 'hot' (the signal hit the
rails and *clipped*), B. there was an equipment or cable problem during
recording or transfer, C. battery/power level was too low in the recording equipment, or D. its non digital media has deteriorated over time.
They all result in some sort of crunchy, sputtering distortion. If they're
not too far gone, these recordings can be significantly improved.

Some de-crackling methods examine the signal waveform and
re- draw usable signal from damaged signal. Others just tame the high
treble area (5k to 10kHz) where the most offensive clipped frequencies
live. Sometimes running a de-crackling plug-in over a heavily distorted

Clipped syllables can often be improved with de-crackle plug-ins or a little EQ.

region doesn't improve things at first, but sometimes running it over a clip multiple times works better; it depends on the material. Trial, error, and undo are your best bet.

Without a specialized restoration tool like a de-crackle plug-in you can at least soften the harshness of the crackle a bit. Open an offline parametric EQ and dampen the distortion using a wide valley shaped Q and a gain of minus -3dB (Q (Quality) indicates how sharp and specific, or how smooth and broad of a frequency range we want to affect.). Increase this toward -12dB in extreme cases. Distortion bothers our ears much more at high frequencies so try 2kHz, 4kHz, or 8kHz one at a time and listen for which most effectively reduces the harshness and maintains dialogue intelligibility.

Unfortunately, EQ *cuts* such as this indiscriminately remove some of the 'good' signal, too. To minimize the loss of clarity, first scissor the offending portions into small sub-clips. Then use the equalizer on just these affected syllables or words that need it.

Now that we've applied special processing to the middle of a waveform, it's possible we caused some sudden changes in level. Listen for clicks in the restored dialogue and if necessary apply a small (half- or one frame) crossfade at any uneven seam between processed and unprocessed clips.

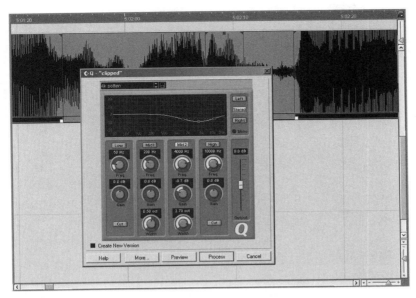

The classic way of smoothing out distortion: EQ out some high-end.

## Removing hums and buzzes

The next thing up is removing hums and buzzes, usually caused by poorly grounded equipment or recording in proximity to magnetic fields from strong power supplies or power cables. When you catch a buzz you are actually hearing a specific series of unwanted frequencies and thus it is difficult or impossible to restore completely. An ounce of prevention may be worth a pound of cure, but this is a book on post-sound cleanup so let's see what we can do to improve things.

Your best line of defense is a specialized hum removal plug-in such as the Waves Z-Noise or X-Hum, or Bias SoundSoap Pro. These tools have sharp EQ filters that are pre-set to zero in on offending frequencies.

Your alternative line of defense is to re-create by hand what these plug-ins do automatically. The hum is based on an AC-line frequency that found its way into the signal, and this frequency varies by continent. Since AC power is based on the very low bass frequency of 60Hz in the U.S. (or 50Hz in Europe and Japan), our offending frequencies will be multiples (harmonics) of 60Hz (or 50Hz). Assuming American voltage, we could theoretically cut 60Hz, 120Hz, 180Hz, 240Hz, etc.,

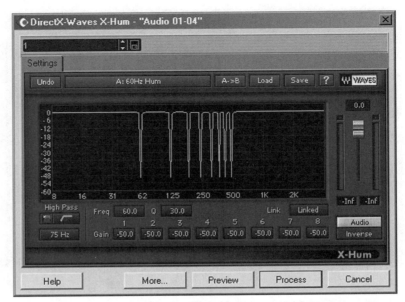

The surgical, multiband filtering capability of a plug-in specially designed to remove hum & buzz.

with several bands of EQ to reduce the frequencies of which we want to hear less. Again, this is a destructive process so we proceed carefully and apply as little EQ as needed.

### Remove hums and buzz

- First, isolate and highlight the offending clips.

- Locate the parametric equalizer with the highest available Q values (an equalizer with Qs of up to 20 or more would be helpful here). Begin an offline process with this EQ and set the frequency bands for 60Hz, 120Hz, 180Hz, 240Hz, and 300Hz (up to as many bands as you have available) for hum made in the U.S.

- Set the steepest (highest) Q values possible for all bands.

- Start with a gain reduction of minus 12dB for each frequency. Turn up the volume or listen in headphones, and increase the gain reduction to 30dB until the offending harmonics of hum are sufficiently masked by other frequencies. You may find that reducing just 120Hz and 180Hz does the trick.

If you're consistently getting hum/buzz from your recordings, first identify if it's your location sound equipment that's causing the problem, or if the hum is being introduced in the transfer into the computer. If it's the former, upgrade to a balanced audio interface/mixer and balanced audio cables, or use isolation transformers. Also check the troubleshooting tips in the Setup chapter on studio wiring in the subsection 'The power and the buzz.' This is one problem that can ruin a recording and is definitely better to solve at the source.

## Noise we like, noise we don't

The most common kind of noise is a sort of white noise made up of ambient sounds that we're not paying attention to at a given time. This includes household appliances, industrial equipment, far off traffic, hums and buzzes, insects, and low-level crowds. They're an indication

of how busy a shooting environment is. In life, a little background noise is good – it sure beats living in a sonic vacuum.

This is the **noise floor** of the world around us, and filmicly it is created from both 1. live and recorded ambiences, covered in a later chapter, and 2. *room tone*. Room tone makes up the sonic fingerprint of a particular (interior or exterior) space, absent of any obvious sound events like human motions or car horns. It is good practice for the Production Sound Mixer to record about 30 seconds of the empty, seemingly silent space of every scene, but it is not always done. It provides in-between filler to make dialogue cuts transition more naturally than going to 'black,' or complete silence.

If you don't have room tone recordings of your own, we will still be able to smooth out your dialogue and keep it from sounding choppy. You've got enough cleanup to do already, so we'll cover this in the chapter on background ambiences.

It's a common misconception that low-level dialogue clips can be simply brought up to match louder ones and *voilà* the dialogue mixing is finished. The complication comes with something called the *signal-to-noise ratio*.

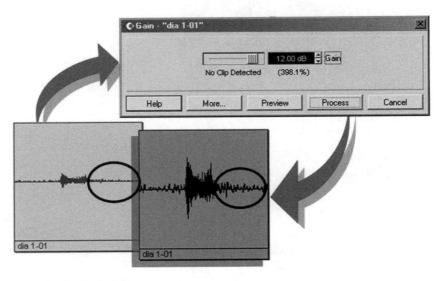

Increasing signal gain also increases noise.

Most editors find out pretty quickly that raising low-level dialogue clips also raises their background noise. After raising and lowering many individual clips of speech they are left with a nice consistent dialogue level and background noise that changes from soft to loud all over the place.

The problem requires that you start listening not to the dialogue levels but to their varying background noise levels. First, get a feel for the loudness and type of noise behind your dialogue clips. Then clean up the sound with a good de-noiser.

## Airplanes and air conditioners: removing broadband noise

Constant background noise such as hiss is usually caused by A. noisy shooting environments, B. too-low recording levels, or C. machine noise from low budget gear, such as poor microphones and mic pre-amps. It is a long-form type of problem and is best remedied with a special de- noise plug-in. It can also be partially removed with EQ which we will cover, and with noise gating, which we won't, because 'gating' is a difficult horse to tame if you've never ridden it and can easily make things sound unnatural. In addition, note that compression will lower the signal to noise ratio and should *always* be avoided with noisy tracks.

### Removal procedure with a de-noise plug-in

This type of plug-in is designed to take a 'noiseprint' of the offending background sound and then subtract that frequency fingerprint from the audio clip. They work extremely well when used with care but when applied indiscriminately will leave you with chorusy, phasey dialogue that sounds like it has been through the rinse cycle. The trick lies in how you select the noiseprint and in how much noise reduction you apply.

- First plan the work: Isolate problem clips based *not* on what the speech sounds like, but on the character of their background noise. Listen carefully to the *noise* and group clips together based on this. If all of *Robert's* dialogue in *Scene 21* has a similar constant background hiss to it, group together – on a track or in your mind – the clips that have this same hiss.

- Find the longest spot between dialogue lines (where Robert is not breathing or making even a peep) and where there is no other sound but the noise. You're looking for a pure example of just the background noise. Try and find one that is at least a second long if you can.

- If you specified handles when you exported the OMF you can also open up the leading or trailing edge of a clip of dialogue to look for a length of pure noise without dialogue.

- Temporarily divide this specimen of noise into its own audio segment. This will ensure that the de-noise plug-in knows exactly what the offending noise is.

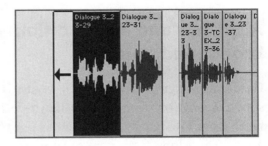

Check the handles for some good, clean background noise.

- Highlight/select the segment and open the offline (AudioSuite) processing box for your de-noise plug-in. Let the plug-in *learn* the noise. You will probably hear it loop the noise over and over. Let it go a few times and then turn off the *learn* button.

🎧 Save this as a preset in the plug-in's dialogue box. Call it anything you'll remember for the time being. Exit the plug-in box *without* applying any processing.

Let the plug-in 'learn' from an isolated portion of noise, but don't process. Then go back and apply the learned noiseprint to the whole dialogue clip.

🎧 Click Undo 2 or 3 times to re-join the noise clip to its original longer audio segment, and restore any handles you may have pulled out.

🎧 Highlight all of the segments you want to de-noise. Start the offline de-noiser again and load up the preset you just made.

🎧 This is the second critical step we mentioned above: Listening carefully, preferably on headphones, preview the process (it will loop the first selected clip). Adjust the noise reduction slider until you are comfortable with an amount of noise reduction that leaves the dialogue sounding clean without being washed out or phased out sounding.

The trade off: Your noisy dialogue tracks are cleaner, but some of the baby always gets thrown out with the bathwater. How much signal are you willing to sacrifice in order to kill off some noise? Overuse it and a de-noiser can leave tracks sounding unnatural. The trade off of an acceptable low-level background noise to washy/phasey dialogue is the dialogue editor's judgment call. Most prefer to err on the side of leaving a light din of noise, avoiding any hint of phasey side effects.

### Minimize hiss with EQ

If you don't have access to a de-noise plug-in, you'll have to try it the old fashioned way.

🎧 Minimize hiss with a low-pass filter (LPF) set somewhere between 7kHz and 12kHz.

Start with a Q of 1.0 and shape it to taste by ear. Again, we're aiming to keep as much of the signal as possible while reducing the stuff we don't want to hear. There is, again, a trade-off of signal loss versus cleanliness here.

🎧 When reducing hiss, you can restore a bit of the lost high end presence with an additional band of EQ set around 6kHz with a gain of +1 to +2dB, and a medium wide Q setting of about 1.0.

### Reduce plosives, sibilance, and other strange things people do with their mouths

These problematic human factors should be pretty easy to improve with your new surgical editing expertise.

🎧 Hone-in on the offending syllable by playing back the section over and over while gradually zooming in to the problem area, as described above in 'removing clicks and pops.'

🎧 Cut the problem syllable into its own segment. Be a little generous on either side of the exact problem area since we will need some room for crossfading later. Highlight the new clip and start an offline EQ to apply the appropriate correction.

🎧 *To remove the bass heavy POP of a plosive,* set the lowest EQ band to a high-pass filter (HPF) somewhere between 80 and 150Hz (to ear). Apply the effect.

🎧 *To tone down a harsh sibilance,* set one band of EQ for a gain of around minus 6 to minus -12dB, and a Q of 1.0. Sibilance lives anywhere between 4kHz and 10kHz. Start with 6kHz and see if it works for you, then apply the effect.

🎧 Apply short crossfades around the fixed syllable. Play back and verify that the phrases sound more natural, or undo and try again with slightly different frequencies.

## 📣 ESSENTIAL CLEAN-UP TOOLS

If you're serious about getting your production tracks broadcast-clean, you'll want to invest in some software. It's the only way to really shine up grungy tracks. Here's a rundown of some current software choices if you're ready to take your tracks to the cleaners.

🎧 The Waves Restoration Bundle (www.waves.com) includes the previously mentioned X-Noise, X-Crackle, X-Click and X-Hum plug-ins – a complete suite of problem solvers for 95% of noise issues. Waves also offers their newer Z-Noise plug-in with improved algorithms and features.

🎧 Digidesign's DINR is a popular noise-reduction staple of ProTools users (www.digidesign.com).

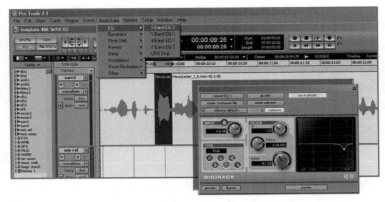

Precise sibilance control: 1. Isolate offensive syllables. 2. Apply EQ. 3. Crossfade.

- Bias' SoundSoap Pro also has a full range of tools for broadband noise reduction, click and crackle restoration, and hum and rumble removal (www.bias-inc.com).

- Voxengo makes a rather detailed and involved broadband noise reduction plug-in at a good price called Redunoise (www.voxengo.com).

- Adobe's Audition (formerly Cool Edit) is a stand alone audio editor with an excellent broadband noise reduction. This is stand alone software (not a plug-in) so you'll have to open your noisy files separately in Audition to use the noise reduction feature (www.adobe.com).

- Enhanced Audio (www.enhancedaudio.com) offers lots of advice on restoration and a 'DC' product series.

- Sony offers vinyl restoration, noise reduction, clipped peak restoration, and click and crackle removal in their Noise Reduction suite of plug-ins for Sound Forge (www.sonymediasoftware.com).

- Sony also offers a high end suite of RTAS plug-ins (DeClick, DeBuzz, and DeNoise) called the Oxford Restoration Tools that is worth checking into if you're running ProTools (www.sonyplug-ins.com).

- Finally, on a larger budget, the excellent reNOVAtor and NoiseFree! software from Algorithmix takes a newer approach to solving the problems in this chapter. Check it out at www.algorithmix.com

# Rumble: EQ to the rescue

Rumble is a warbling bass-heavy layer under your dialogue that comes from over-handling the boom during recording, machine or wind noise, or the bass-heavy emphasis of certain microphones. Since it takes a larger speaker to reproduce low (bass) frequencies, if you are working with small or budget monitors, try listening for rumble on a set of headphones, which generally will reveal the symptom more easily.

Rumble is easily remedied as a standard procedure in dialogue editing.

Rumble usually cleans up nicely with a simple high-pass filter.

### *Eliminate bass rumble under dialogue*

🎧 Apply a HPF (high pass filter) somewhere between 80 and 140Hz (by ear). You can apply the EQ plug-in as an offline process to correct individual clips, or insert it on a dialogue track to safeguard all of its clips from rumble.

You can go a step further and insert the plug-in onto the DIALOGUE group track to easily reduce this unflattering frequency area in all of your dialogue. Just be sure you aren't throwing away any good signal with the EQ.

# Level control

Now that our tracks are cleaned up it's time to fine-tune our levels. The goal is dialogue that is consistent and easily heard yet is naturally loud or soft at appropriate times. Refer to your notes of problem areas where levels are falling off.

A lot of times dialogue sounds unnatural simply because volume levels aren't consistent. For example, it is too easy to forgive or ignore one actor's speech for being louder than the other players in a scene. It doesn't register with our ears as being a problem, especially if that actor has a stronger presence in a scene. It's easy to unconsciously play favorites, to fail to be impartial to *everyone's* dialogue. Over time an editor becomes more sensitive to the finer differences between speech volume levels and gets a feel for how dynamic the range of broadcast quality dialogue should be.

What would help at this point is an objective opinion on our levels. Luckily we have that already, in the form of our sequencer's built-in level meters. We'll use them later to ensure even, overall dialogue levels. For now we're concerned with making small edits to improve the worst problem areas. Just use your ears to listen for clues.

Here are some things to listen for:

🎧 Some people naturally trail off their speech at the end of a sentence. For a polished sounding (as opposed to natural style) mix, the ends of these phrases need to be manually brought up to the common dialogue level. You can often see waveforms getting smaller at the end of people's phrases while your ears have a bit more trouble making out exactly what is being said.

🎧 The mic goes *off-axis* because the actor turned away from the shotgun for part of a sentence. Although this affects the EQ and overall timbre of the speech, by raising the level of these segments by about 2 to 4dB we can easily Band-Aid the situation.

🎧 A syllable, word, or phrase seems unnaturally loud for any reason.

🎧 A phrase is rushed and unintelligible.

🎧 An actor intentionally whispered in a scene and the result is too low in volume for the scene or intended broadcast medium.

🎧 One actor is louder than another throughout the scene. Try listening without picture for a minute to see if this is the case.

If you want to really be able to tell where your dialogue levels are going south, find a way to play the film through tiny speakers, such as a small TV, a boom box, or the famous Auratone studio monitors. You'll be more sensitive to varying dialogue levels on a small, midrangey speaker.

Here are a few cures for common volume related ailments:

🎧 Improving syllables or even phrases that are for some reason just too loud or too soft is as easy as making cuts around the loud section and adjusting the gain up or down a few dB for the new clip. But always apply tiny crossfades around the newly cut segment so it transitions smoothly back in to the rest of the dialogue. This procedure is preferable to relying on a compressor to tame levels.

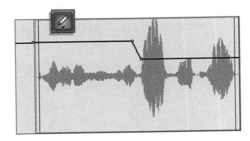

🎧 Where dialogue trails off at the end of a sentence (or a similar situation) make a cut where the dialogue begins to go soft. Make another cut at the end of the phrase, where the speech is

Sometimes it's fastest to zoom in and draw simple automation by hand.

softest. We've just isolated the softer section. Raise the gain on this segment by 3-4dB. Lengthen the first (louder) segment by pulling it far out to the right so that it greatly overlaps the softer segment and crossfade the two segments. The volume will gradually be brought up by the end of the phrase, compensating for the trailing off.

🎧 Where levels are particularly dynamic and impractical to even out by hand, or when you want a quick fix, you can run to a compressor. Compressors can be used as either an offline process or a track insert. Suggested settings: ratio at about 3:1, threshold set so that the compressor's gain reduction meter takes a 2 to 6dB hit only

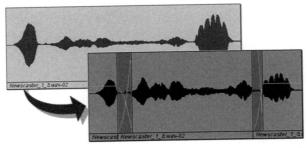

Some sequencers allow you to make smooth level changes by cutting segments where they change volume, apply a gain change to one segment, then overlapping them with crossfades. (example from Cubase)

during peak levels (audition the track while watching the meter), attack and release set to about 2ms and 150ms, respectively. These are rough guidelines that will vary depending on your program material, plug-in quality, and intended distribution medium.

Keep in mind that compression is a common pitfall of many new sound editors. It's too easy to overdo it and end up with lifeless, squashed speech that can't be fixed later. Better to not compress if you don't know exactly what you're doing and why.

## Chapter 9

# Elements: Replacement Dialogue (ADR) and Narration

While we're on the subject of dialogue, let's finish the dialogue editorial with the magic of ADR. With automatic dialogue replacement you can fill in missing lines, add off-camera dialogue, replace noisy or problem parts, or re-record entire scenes. While the process isn't entirely 'automatic,' it's not as hard as you may think.

Whether this is your first foray into recording actors in the studio or if it's old hat, the approach in this chapter will offer some insight. Since the process of capturing good ADR shares many similarities with recording narration, we'll hit on them both in this chapter. If you only need to record narration then you can skim over the next few sections. But for now, let's approach replacement dialogue recording as if for the first time.

## ADR: Do I have to?

You've read a lot up to this point about re-recording dialogue. If you're new to the idea perhaps you feel it's beyond your time schedule or studio expertise. When you are working with talent capable of giving both emotional and accurate repeat performances in the studio, dialogue re-recording can allow you to build the scenes of your dreams with low noise and a high production value. Crafting a scene from scratch is both a luxury and a challenge. But when should you clean up the recordings you've got, and when is it best to scrap it all and start fresh?

ADR is a good alternative to production dialogue when:

- The production sound is so dirty that restoration will leave undesirable artifacts.
- You want to build a scene completely from stock or re-recorded elements.
- The delivery of the dialogue isn't exceptionally emotional or wasn't performed under hard-to-duplicate circumstances.
- You want to lay in music, drones, or ambiences that won't mix well with the production ambience.

Re-recording the dialogue has its disadvantages, too, and there are things that make it difficult:

- Actors' inability or unwillingness to come in for ADR sessions.
- Actors' inability to re-perform satisfactorily in the studio.
- Production sound that has a unique emotional delivery, desirable ambiences, or other extraordinary qualities.

It's satisfying to create your own soundtrack completely from scratch in post. It starts, as most scenes do, with the dialogue. Of course, scenes with no dialogue or narration do not need this chapter. That said, let's get on with the "how-to" of recording your actors.

## Recording techniques for ADR

Let's illustrate two different cases of dialogue re-recording. One occurs when only certain lines in a scene need to be replaced, either due to the actor's delivery, nature/traffic/airplanes/etc., bleed in the recording, or mechanical failure. Regardless of how (good or bad, clean or dirty) the production dialogue sounds, the studio ADR needs to match the original in terms of timbre, frequency response, and amount of background noise or room tone. It follows that the production dialogue first needs to be de-noised, EQ'd or otherwise prepared for mixing in order to have a tonal target for the ADR.

The second approach to ADR occurs when the Director wants to replace *all* of the dialogue in a scene. In this case there is no need to match any existing production dialogue. However, it is still important to match the ADR'd scenes to the others in order to preserve the flow of the film. We don't want the tone or volume of the ADR'd scenes to stand out from the others.

## CAN YOU HEAR IT?

Dialogue recorded in a studio has a certain sterility or dryness to it that doesn't blend perfectly with production dialogue. Re-recording Mixers try to minimize this and make a scene sound like one consistent performance. Sometimes they have to go against the grain, using their skills to *reduce* the quality of the ADR clips so that they match the dialogue from the shotgun.

While most audio engineering involves making things sound as good as they can, in this case the challenge is more about getting two different bits of dialogue to sound similar to each other. This sometimes means processing the ADR to make it sound worse – less hi-fi – than it is. A high quality studio condenser microphone for ADR will likely make recordings that are much fuller and clearer than they need to be. In that case you'll need to do a bit of processing to bring out the midrangey quality of a shotgun. (EQ'ing a bit out of the high and low frequencies with shelving filters would be a good start.) Likewise, a cheap $30 high-impedance dynamic mic will be muddier and lack the high frequency sensitivity of a shotgun. It requires even more reduction (EQ shelving or a high-pass filter) of the lows (200-400Hz) as well as some pushing of the 4 to 8kHz region to even begin to match the fidelity of a shotgun.

Another effect is at work on ADR versus production recordings. Studio dialogue is drier than on set recordings. This lack of ambience or reverb is another clue to picking out ADR in a film. It can be terribly apparent in older films when microphone and recording technology was less advanced. Matching the volume levels between ADR and production dialogue was also more difficult then. If you listen closely, re-recorded dialogue might start to pop out at you, even in modern films.

It stands to reason that if we want punched-in dialogue to sound as close as possible to the production dialogue, we use the same type of microphone that was used during shooting. Furthermore, we place it in the same position as it was during production. We also need to place the mic at approximately the same distance from the actor's mouth, and at about the same angle. When in doubt, asking the Boom Op about the technique he or she used for the scene is not unreasonable.

Ideally, ADR sounds as natural as production sound and this includes the sound of the location in which it is recorded. Even a sound-treated vocal booth has a unique sound to it and therefore a large impact on the tone of the scene. In a pinch, choose a muffled, dead sounding location similar to that of a large walk in clothes closet. With a touch of reverb and the right underlying ambience, crystal-clean, natural-sounding dialogue isn't far away.

Most ADR is done with a shotgun mic held on a high boom stand a few feet from the actor's head, pointed down toward their mouth. When matching existing lines in a scene, this implies that the same was done on location. In any case, always match the original recording equipment and method used on set. Use whatever lavaliere, camera mic, or stealth microphone that you originally used on set. Otherwise, use a shotgun mic for most pictures, or a studio condenser if you feel the need for a more pristine sound quality. A high pass filter (HPF) at 80Hz or higher (some mics have a switchable rolloff built into them) will help tame low-end rumble.

If you don't know how your source dialogue was recorded and you're not sure what to do in the studio to mimic it, try various mics and listen to the differences in sonic quality. Listen for bass boominess, high frequency sizzle, harshness versus smoothness in the midrange, and overall presence. You may also want to ask an experienced (either music or film) sound engineer to listen to your tracks and give you an idea of what miking techniques might match your original source material.

Are you ready to record? Equipment check: computer, soundcard, microphone preamp, headphones for both yourself and the talent (and possibly the director or producer), and the appropriate microphone on a sturdy stand. If you originally recorded dialogue into a camera, then you should use that. Studio check: quiet surroundings and an acoustically-neutral sounding room with very little reverb or machine noise.

### Recording replacement dialogue in the studio

🎧 It may help to prepare the lines to be re-recorded, creating in effect a list of cues for the talent to follow. Be sure to derive these cues word for word from the film's actual performance – not the script – before beginning the session since the scene may differ slightly from the script.

On the other hand, since the actor will be hearing the original line before re-performing it, it is possible to just 'wing it' without a written cue list.

🎧 If you have only one headphone output, split the headphone out of your soundcard using a Y-cable that has one male and two or three female ends (obtainable at any Radio Shack or pro-music retailer) and send a feed to yourself and the artist. You may need a headphone extension cable for long cable runs. Turn off the studio monitors, quiet the surroundings, and check for anything that could interrupt a good take: squeaky chairs, household appliances, etc. Silence the phone, the dog, and the kids if necessary!

🎧 There is no substitute for a good vocal booth, but not all of us have this luxury. However, when you're forced to record in a room with a particularly strong source of noise, say a computer, minimize picking up the noise by facing the mic in the opposite direction of the noise source. Then set up your actor around this mic placement. Also place a baffle – such as a thick blanket on a second mic stand – between the mic and the noise source. Of course, be careful to make no body movement or computer noises during the recording.

🎧 Where you're punching just a few lines that have to match the tone of the production dialogue in a scene, your goal is to make the new lines sound as close as possible to the old. Use the same microphone used during production of these scenes, distance it from the talent's mouth as it was on set, and angle it in similar way as it was angled. Do a test: listen to some of the original dialogue, then have the actor speak a line or two through the mic. What's different? Which one is bassier, too trebly, etc.? Some things can be fixed later but it will save time if you can get as close as possible now to the sound you're after.

- Make some new mono tracks in your sequencer and get a level check from the artist by having them read through a couple of lines at the volume at which they expect to be speaking (or shouting or whispering). Adjust your microphone preamp for a good level that won't overload.

  Aim for the input meter to show about 60%–70% on the loudest words when getting a level check from the artist. With digital recording, it's better to come in a little low than to risk clipping.

- An easy way to work productively with ADR is to play one line or paragraph at a time for the talent and have the actor simply re-speak the line into the mic right after they hear it. Most talent will be able to mimic lines like this by ear without even needing to see picture. This makes for a fast and easy ADR session without even needing to set up a video monitor.

- With long paragraphs or where several lines are close together, you need to keep the actor from hearing the ensuing lines while they are re-speaking one, or they will be very confused. In other words, there needs to be silence following the line to be re-recorded so he can repeat it without hearing the dialogue that follows it. There are at least two ways to achieve this.

  1. Prepare the lines you'll be re-recording by cutting them into phrases ahead of time. Keep lines relatively short since the actor has to remember them word for word upon hearing them once. Then, just before recording a phrase, mute the clips that follow the phrase you're recording. This provides silence for the actor to speak over after hearing the line. Unmute the next phrase and proceed in the same way to record it.

Aim for the input meter to show about 60%-70% on the loudest words when getting a level check from the artist. With digital recording, it's better to come in a little low than to risk clipping.

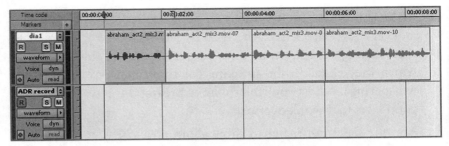

1. Cut the reference track into bite-size phrases 2. Mute the phrases following the current take so the actor doesn't speak over existing dialogue while speaking their lines. 3. Have the actor repeat the line after she hears it.

2.   Or, while recording, play back the phrase for the actor and, as soon as the phrase finishes playing, mute the track on the fly right after he hears his line, allowing him to speak the line over silence.

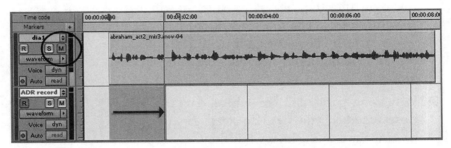

Alternatively, during recording, be ready to mute the reference track to create silence over which the talent can re-perform the line.

- 🎧 Cut up the recorded take and move it backward to line it up with the actor's lips in the picture. Use the original production dialogue waveform as a visual reference.

- 🎧 Get several takes of a line if you're not sure about the delivery or tightness of the performance. As you go, compile the best takes on to one track for each actor. Label each track something like 'ADR Harry' and send its output to the ADR group channel. Be sure to save the session often while working.

- 🎧 Archive the unused takes, as you may need an alternate at a later date. Place these outtakes on muted tracks – hide them, disable them, or place them in a folder track labeled 'ADR outtakes.'

# Syncing dialogue

Once you're satisfied with your new replacement dialogue there are three ways to line it up in your sequence: by ear, by eye, and by lips. Consider it a three-step process, or, in some instances, you may be able to get good sync in just one or two steps.

### By ear

Rough place the new clip by ear by playing back both old and new phrases at the same time and adjusting the timing of the new one to be in time with the old. Set the playback transport to loop the phrase for easier editing.

### By eye

Here's a tip that may save some time. The waveforms of different takes of the same dialogue line, especially when spoken by the same actor, usually end up looking very similar. Visually compare the waveform of the new clip to the existing waveform. Vertically lining up the before and after clips on adjacent tracks allows you to easily see where words line up and where they may need some timing adjustment.

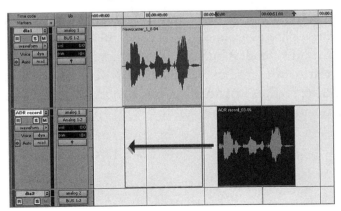

Slide the new ADR waveform underneath the old dialogue. If it looks like the syllables line up, it will probably sync fine to picture.

---

### *By lips*

Regardless of how you line up the dialogue, it's always important to listen to it against the picture and carefully check for sync with the actor's lips. You need a fairly hi-res version of the picture to see where the new dialogue lines up to the actor's lips, and where it goes off.

It's likely that your first ADR session will teach you a lot. One quickly learns to be organized and prepared with mic setup, dialogue cue sheets, pre-cutting playback dialogue into phrases, and a comfortable working environment in order to have a successful session. ADR not as hard as many first-timers think, in fact it saves time in trying to restore production dialogue – and typically gives better results.

## Mic choice and recording techniques for narration

Narration or voiceover (VO) recording calls for a slightly different approach than engineering ADR. We usually want voiceover to sound fuller and warmer than the more natural sounding dialogue of the production tracks and ADR. And we always want it to be drier; that is, without room ambience or reverb. We achieve this by recording in a proper vocal booth (or at least a warm sounding small room) and with a good quality studio microphone. A shotgun mic or on camera mic will sound too colored, lacking the vital clarity and warmth of a studio condenser.

Luckily, the pro-audio market has been deluged with studio condenser microphones in the last ten years, mostly with hobby musicians in mind. With prices as low as around $150, a condenser mic is not out of reach of even the most modest budgets. If there were a way to 'fake' the warmth and clarity of a close mic'd condenser, I would describe it here. In this case there really is just no substitute: a good condenser mic is a worthy investment for any project studio.

## ARE YOU SURE YOU NEED IT?

Narration can enhance the sense of storytelling and create a direct connection with the audience. Sometimes it's also used for creative effect, like voices in dream sequences or when a character is talking to himself.

However, sometimes a voiceover track is written in as a crutch for a story that might not be telling itself clearly enough through the action, dialogue, and music. Sometimes it's not as necessary as the writer or director may think at first. If you're among the many directors who aren't sure how clear the story is coming through without voiceover, get the opinion of test audiences (friends, colleagues, spouse, kids) before investing time into VO recording. See how much they're getting without the VO, then you can always record the narration, have a re-watch, and see whether it adds to or distracts from the story.

At this point, you've chosen your VO artist, prepared their lines, and are ready to record. How do you get big, warm, professional sounding narration? Let's go through the process step by step, but remember that 'less is more' when it comes to narration. A close-miked, full-sounding, clean, noise-free recording is what we're after.

### Getting great narration recordings

Follow the basic recording setup for ADR. This time, use your nice studio condenser and a vocal booth or similar small, warm area for recording. You might want to have the actor sit, to help get a more relaxed performance.

- Position the mic about 6 to 8" from the talent's mouth. Set it to a cardioid pattern.
- Use a pop filter, available at pro-music stores, and even department stores, to help avoid plosives. You can use a double-layer of pantyhose stretched around a bent coat hanger as a makeshift pop filter.

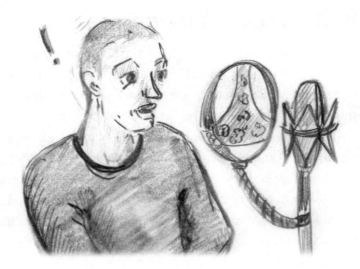

🎧 Do a mic check and get a good level from the talent. Narration usually stays remarkably consistent in level and tone. The talent probably won't be raising their voice much so get a good strong level on your microphone preamp, leaving a little headroom for the loudest syllables.

🎧 Listen carefully as you record and be proactive about correcting any problems you hear. Get an alternate take whenever you're not sure of a performance or technical issue. It takes only a few seconds to play back and ensure you've got a good take. It takes a lot longer to schedule the actor to come back in to re-do the lines.

🎧 Be critical during recording. Listen for good diction and be sure every word is clearly pronounced. It's a common mistake among actors and singers to trail off at the end of phrases. Inform the artist of any volume drops and have them take the phrase again where necessary.

🎧 Listen to make sure that the first word of every phrase is coming through. If the audience doesn't catch the very first word, they can get hung up for the rest of the sentence wondering what the narrator was starting to say. The last word of every phrase is also crucial. Likewise, no one wants to be left wondering what the narrator just said!

- Adjust the mic by turning it 5 to 10 degrees or so off-axis to reduce plosives, if necessary. Inform the talent of which words they are hitting too hard, of when their S's are sibilant, or of when you are hearing any undesirable mouth noises. Retake.

- Check out the techniques in the section below, 'Getting the best take.' They apply as much to narration recording as they do to re-recording dialogue.

- Listen for a calm sense of interest or passion behind the talent's voice. Most anyone can read something and sound like they are reading, but your talent should sound natural, like she is speaking to you without a script, and probably enthusiastic about it (depending on the material).  Make it a goal to get consistency in volume and tone across the whole film's narration.

## Narration editing

Prepare the narration in much the same way as the dialogue itself. Keep in mind that voiceover is usually clean and warm, adding a high-fidelity vocal element to your soundtrack. This is why we take care to record it in a good, quiet studio with a quality mic. If your VO tracks do happen to need restoration or cleanup due to a challenging recording location, follow the procedures in the Dialogue chapter, and then come back here to complete your narration editing.

Once you are happy with the performances and the recording quality of the narration it's time to do a little editing.

# Edit and clean up the narration

- Start with clean, noise-free tracks with a good, solid level. Make the narration clips uniformly louder if necessary by applying an offline Gain or Normalization process equally to all clips.

- Cut the performance into the desired segments, placing them reasonably in time with the movie, if desired. Cut fairly tightly around the VO speech, muting or deleting all silence between segments.

- Eliminate the first breath (and any mouth clicking noises) of every passage (not of every sentence, but rather of every segment of narration).

- Perform a short (half-second or one-second) fade-in and fade-out of every clip so that very low-level background noise isn't abrupt when played back on loud systems. Again, a quick way of applying fades to multiple clips in most sequencers is to select them all first, and then draw in the fade. Check on headphones to ensure that you don't hear the narration clips start and end abruptly.

- EQ the narration if you like, to make up for microphone deficiencies or to bring out certain aspects of the voice. If needed you can enhance bass and a sense of authority by adding a little 150Hz (male) or 225Hz (female). Try a Q of about 1.5.

If you feel the need to get the narration sounding warmer, try a high shelving filter to cut out some high end. Start with a shelf of around 9kHz with a gain of minus -1, and lower the frequency or the gain to taste. Err on the conservative side to avoid creating muddy and unintelligible narration. It should probably sound a bit warmer than the dialogue, though.

If you feel you need to improve clarity, set your parametric to boost somewhere between 3kHz and 6kHz by perhaps 1 or 2dB. Use a wide Q between 0.2-1.0.

If the narration is still not cutting, you may be trying to use narration in too busy a mix, or need to use a different mic, or need to boost the 1-3kHz range by a couple of dB (again with a wide Q).

For now, set a rough level for the narration track. Later, in the mixing chapter, you can adjust it to how strong you want it in relation to other tracks. Three to 6dB louder than the dialogue's average level is common, but depends on the desired effect.

## Getting the best take

Here are several additional tips to make your ADR and narration sessions go smoothly:

🎧 Consider the talent's comfort level. You'll get the best performances if you help everyone feel relaxed, interested, and excited about helping to finish the film. Sometimes overlooked, creature comforts such as beverages, soft lighting, and a comfortable place to sit, mean a lot.

🎧 Be professional when coaching actors. Be polite but firm in your expectations of their performances. Give them clear, honest, short feedback that encourages them to do better on the next take. Follow their energy level – are they getting tired, is it time for a break? Or perhaps the takes are getting better and better, but it's not quite there yet. Inspire them: tell them the last take was almost perfect and let's do one more a little slower, faster, softer, clearer, or stronger this time.

🎧 One approach to re-recording scenes involving two actors is to schedule both actors for the session, prepare each a dialogue cue sheet, and have them re-perform the scene in front of the microphone. Record both at once, on to one track, with the same technique of playing a line or two and having them repeat it while you mute the playback track. Sometimes two people can re-perform many lines at once this way. It works especially well when their dialogue doesn't overlap or interrupt each other. Even when it does, it can add naturalness to the scene when the actors time it exactly like their original performances. Sometimes recording both actors together helps the performance as they feed off each other's energy and work out scene details together. Be prepared to cut each person's lines to put them on separate tracks, if need be.

🎧 A good ADR take is one that combines a good performance with good timing and recording technique. When you get a good take, check it right away against the original dialogue or against the picture for timing. Visually line up waveforms and/or watch the actors' flapping lips as you move the clips around to get them in sync. Then you'll know if you need to do another take or if it lines up. Encourage the talent to be patient with you while you check the take for sync.

🎧 Also listen for tone quality. Does the mic sound like it's further from or nearer to the actor than it was in the original? Adjust accordingly before doing another take.

🎧 Many performers, trained actors, and voiceover artists included, have a tendency to fall off in volume at the end of phrases. Listen for consistent volume and clear diction throughout their performances and decide whether it's best to try problem lines again, or keep the take and adjust levels later. Usually it's easiest to just have the actor re take problem lines. Tell them clearly and politely that they're trailing off at the end of the phrase and that you want to re-take the line.

🎧 Make as many edits as possible as you record, including lining up takes to lips as close as possible, performing short fades and cross-fades as necessary, adjusting levels to match the other clips in the scene, etc., but above all keep the session moving. Don't leave your actors waiting around for you to do technical editing that can be done later. Get them while they're hot.

🎧 You'll usually know when you've got a good take. The performance and the recording quality are both solid, the tone quality matches the rest of the dialogue in the scene, and the new phrase is in time with the actor's lips on screen. Feel free to cut up ADR to match the picture timing, as long as the phrases still sound natural. Whenever you're not sure, it doesn't hurt to put down another take. It's not uncommon to record 5 or 10 takes of an important line, even with experienced actors.

## Chapter 10

# Elements: Sound Effects and Foley

Second only to dialogue in modern films are the sound effects. They carry not only the excitement of many a picture but also the believability of character actions. When an actor sits down on a hotel room bed, is the mattress soft and comfy or do the springs squeak? What does this tell you about the hotel? It's easy to take the meaning of a scene up a notch with carefully-chosen Foley and sound effects.

Location Sound Mixers are concerned with getting as much clean dialogue as possible. Unfortunately, time constraints and shooting environments often don't allow them to do even this. They certainly can't be bothered with trying to get clean recordings of every footstep, car start, and dog bark that sound editorial is going to want in post. Sets are often too busy – and acoustically biased – to get clean recordings of these essential elements. Furthermore, tight shooting schedules and budgets on indie pictures require that much of the soundtrack need be built in post.

On professional projects, the post-production Foley and sound effects teams re-record much of the extra sound *custom* for each picture. Those of us on a budget, however, can turn to pre-recorded sounds from stock libraries to bring our props and actions to life. One reason that SFX added in post sound is bigger and cleaner is because they were recorded better than most of us have the time to do ourselves. In this chapter we'll talk about both stock sound effects and recording custom effects for your picture.

If you prepared a list of the Foley and sound effects that your film needs back in the 'Pre Post' chapters, you're a step ahead of the game. Indeed, you will probably think of more SFX you want to include as you continue shaping your sonic masterpiece. Don't depend on memory to retain these ideas; keep track of them in your notes. Later, we'll find the ones you need and lay them in while they're on your mind.

## SFX INSPIRATION

Most every action in a cartoon or animation piece needs an associated sound, either recorded manually or added from a stock library of some sort. Without a doubt, quality animation soundtracks require serious effort to build – one sound effect at a time – and need to contain interesting sounds that make sense of the action. Animations are a Sound Designer's dream – or nightmare.

Interesting sound effects (and distinctive music) brought the old Hanna Barbera and Warner Brothers cartoons to life. Modern animation features from Pixar/Disney and DreamWorks do the same. Modern TV animations have to sacrifice this level of detail due to tight syndication deadlines, though still create a believable soundtrack out of thin air. And just as with narrative films, animation starts with the dialogue (voiceover) and then fills in the sound effects, ambiences and music to magnify the action: to make it real, make it huge, make it funny, make it *something*.

Watching a good animation for its soundtrack can be overwhelming, but inspiring nonetheless. The number of actions that require sound effects in a single episode can be staggering. Listen to how they use classic Foley and sound effects. Notice where  they sound natural and where they are distorted, processed, or layered for creative effect. What action or feeling are they bringing to life? Are they all literal or diegetic? Do all sound effects have to illustrate an on screen action, or are they used to mark transitions and provide flourish, too? Turn off the tube and just listen to the soundtrack – you'll really start to get a feel for the number of sound effects that animation needs to bring it to life.

# Where to find Foley and SFX libraries

What is a stock sound effects library? It's an organized collection of pre-recorded sound effects with the ability to search by keyword. It affords the sound editor the ability to quickly find, audition and import the sound of a household appliance or a car starting. Some libraries are general and contain common sounds used in all types of pictures and some libraries are sound specific, like those just for, say, boating sounds, footsteps, or drones. Sometimes making a certain type of picture, say a horror picture, calls for investing in a library created for that genre. It's a lot easier to save up the money for an off-the-shelf library than to try and record all the strange SFX you'll need for a horror movie. Then again, it might be fun to try, if you have the time and inclination.

## SOUND IDEAS

Brian Nimens is the president of Sound Ideas (www.sound-ideas.com), the world's largest publisher of professional sound effects. He has a few creative tips on improving realism and adding interest.

*Why is it important to keep SFX and Foley separate from the dialogue?*
There are a couple of good reasons to keep the sound effects and Foley tracks separated from dialogue tracks. When you keep everything on separate tracks, you have control over the spectrum of your mix. You may choose to pan a sound effect or a Foley action to the left or right (or rear channels during surround sound mixing) but it's important to keep your dialogue front and center. For this reason you will want to keep it on a separate track from the Foley and sound effects.

Also, when it comes time to make a M&E mix ('music and effects') you want to make sure that you can still keep the original sound effects and Foley in your film when you replace the dialogue. If they are recorded on the same track as the dialogue, you will have to start all over to put the sound effects and Foley back in with the new dialogue. This could be a real pain, especially if you have several different foreign language versions to make.

*How can I improve the realism of re-recorded dialogue?*

Dialogue recorded in the studio is pretty bare! Placed back into the picture, you really notice a total lack of movement in the characters' actions. Clothing rustle and chair movement, particularly, become very important. Take notes on where these actions are missing. Foley them or fill them in with sounds from a library. When replacing dialogue tracks, as is done in most professional filmmaking, it's also important to add room tone from the actual set to give it dimension. If you didn't capture room tone, get it from a stock library or layer the scene with a light ambience track, which always masks the room tone anyway.

*How do I design ambience tracks that add to my film's character and believability?*

When looking for the right ambience from a stock library, really listen to each track as you audition it. Go slowly and play out each one for 20 or 30 seconds. If you're looking for midtown Manhattan, don't just trust what the filename says: does it sound like the New York you're looking for? Perhaps it's not a busy enough day, or the weather (wind, rain, etc.) is not appropriate for the picture. Also, listen for authentic animal sounds for your scenes. Do the birds, crickets, etc., in the file sound native to the area shown in your scene? One last thing you can do is to not be shy about layering as many ambient events as possible – to a point, of course. Layers of off-camera events create interest in and involve the viewer more in the location or space.

*Do you have any advice for fight scenes?*

It depends on the character of the punches, gunshots, etc., that you are going for. Combining multiple body hits and other sounds to add extra punch can sound great or it can be too over-the-top. Layering is quite common though. Perhaps you have a cannon going off. Feel free to dial in a bass heavy version to the original sound effect if you feel you want to bring the subwoofer more into play. The important thing is to listen at the proper level so you can hear everything in the right proportions. Your ears will tell you when a sound needs replacing or layering.

*What about levels of Foley and SFX?*

Imagine a woman walking on cobblestone in high heels. This should be very audible. Then she stops and sees a car blow up: that sound effect should be huge and hit the viewer right in the chest. You want to be sure some of that explosion is coming out of the LFE (subwoofer) channel as well. We have a library called 'Just Boom Tracks' – it's all subwoofer material. When they need more 'ooomf' our customers use it to layer some in to taste.

*What can be done in production to help things go more smoothly in post?*

When you're on the shoot, look around: what props, animals, vehicles, etc., are being used? Record the heck out of them. Record them doing any action you can think of that they might do. Later, you might need a pass-by of a specific vehicle and this will save a lot of time in post.

Not quite ready to invest in your own effects libraries? Enter the internet. You can often find common sound effects online by searching the web or asking folks on filmmaking and editing forums. Be warned that a lot of these sounds are old, 'crunchy' sounding (lo-fidelity) and probably overused. For the stuff you can't find for free, sites like sounddogs.com let you audition and shop for sounds so you can buy just the ones you need. Otherwise, get out your camera and mic and start building your own library for free. We'll learn how later in this chapter.

# Getting organized

A sound effects library is useless unless it's fast and easy to find the sounds you need, when you need them. A feature might require individually placing hundreds of sound effects in post, so there's no time to waste. This means putting time into logically organizing your library of sounds, and being able to search it by keyword.

### Make an efficient SFX collection

🎧 Hard drive space for desktop computers is cheap these days. Consider compiling all of your sound effects on to a dedicated hard drive for fast, easy searching. Dedicating a drive to them also makes for effortless one-step backups of the whole collection once every few weeks or months.

🎧 As your commercial SFX library grows, copy newly-purchased collections to your dedicated SFX hard drive and organize them by library name. Each unique library, for example 'Hollywood Edge Foley,' becomes a folder on your SFX hard drive. Then store the original CDs, if applicable, where they won't get damaged.

☊ Keep a separate folder for miscellaneous SFX like individual downloads and personal recordings. Further organize this inventory by creating categorical subfolders under the MISCELLANEOUS heading.

Each commercial library will come with a listing of its contents, in the form of a database application or as a searchable document (often in Adobe PDF format). Copy or install these listings to the root of your SFX hard drive (or folder on the hard drive) for easy access. When it comes time to search for a sound effect, you can either open the database or the appropriate document and search by keyword.

When building a large sound effects or music collection you can really get organized and work faster by investing in a good asset management system like the ubiquitous Soundminer software. This type of program helps you organize, edit, copy, convert, audition, and import sound effects and music into your sequencer for a faster workflow.

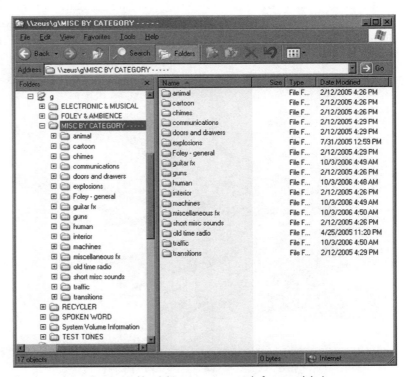

Be prepared: A well-organized hard drive sets you up to do fast sound design.

Most sound effect and stock music producers include keyword meta-data in their files that these programs use to build a searchable database.

## Foley: The pits, the props, and the pain

Foley, the term we use for the natural sounds of the on screen action, requires a sensitive ear and a patience for details. To perform the live recordings that Foley artists create while watching a picture requires some resources that most people don't have in their studios. Six or eight Foley "pits" with various floor and ground surfaces allow the Foley artist to re walk the actors' footsteps on any surface used in the film. They also get to shake, shoot, and smash a myriad of household props, industrial tools, food, and half broken *stuff* in order to make the sounds the picture needs. It's easy to hurt yourself doing this all day but you'd be hard-pressed to find a Foley artist that doesn't have an intense passion for their work.

### MAKE JACK PROUD

The humorist/stuntman/sound effects pioneer Jack Foley had some unconventional ways of making prop sounds for movies in the mid-20th century. His creativity in coming up with missing sound effects saved the studios the high costs of re shooting scenes just to capture clean sound effects.

Since Jack's heyday, it became standard practice to re-record sound effects in the studio. The sources of these sounds make great conversation pieces. Fortunately, we do not have to keep bunches of celery and carrots on hand for bone breaking horror scenes, crinkle cellophane to make fire, or run out to the hardware store for sandpaper to simulate a man shaving. Today, thanks to Mr. Foley, we can buy these sounds in stock libraries.

In the end, Foley is like housecleaning: it's a lot of work for something that the viewer usually takes for granted. But when it's not there, the film drags from lack of sonic interest, and the audience senses that something is missing. And when it's done carelessly or incompletely the film feels 'fake' like a bad kung fu movie and is condemned to the annals of the B grade. Every bit of credibility counts in an art like film which is built on an illusion of reality.

Foley is, in part, a necessary evil. However, when the Foley is working well, it may still go almost unnoticed but it adds a subtle level of personality to the action. Carefully-chosen or well-recorded Foley lends personality and emotion to a scene. The action and locations get infused with new meaning that goes beyond the original performances and writing.

## Footsteps first

You're waist deep in post audio editing on your movie. The dialogue is clean, the music is in, but the film sounds empty in places and lacks sonic detail. You sense that it's going to need a healthy injection of additional sound to take it higher. Start at the bottom: footsteps.

The audience takes them for granted – and it's only natural. At the minimum, footsteps have to sound believable enough to give a subtle impression of authenticity while not being inappropriate or distractingly loud. In order for the audience to properly *ignore* them you really do need to consider the type of footwear, the person doing the walking, the walking surface, and the environment.

Beyond this, professional Foley artists also interpret *how* actors walk (hurriedly, languidly, drunkenly, etc.), how hard or soft they step, how much they slide or shuffle, and other natural movements. Going the extra mile here enhances the emotion of the scene on a subconscious level. How someone walks is especially important in slower moving, sensitive scenes because it fills in quiet spaces and keeps the viewer engaged in the downtime between lines of dialogue.

## Footsteps: A superfluity of permutations

| Character | Action | Footwear | Surface |
|---|---|---|---|
| man | run | barefoot | carpet |
| woman | walk | sneakers | wood |
| child | jog | leather shoes | metal |
| animal | jump | high heels | grass |
| | skip | boots | concrete |
| | single hard step | | snow |
| | shuffle | | |
| | slide | | |
| | climb stairs | | |
| | descend stairs | | |

### *Fit footsteps to the footage*

🎧 Determine the best footstep sounds for your scenes. Mix and match each scene's footstep needs – for each primary actor – using one element from each column in the table.

What's that? Your film doesn't feature a *child* wearing *high heels* in the *snow*? Even still, many combinations are possible. Go through every scene in your picture and determine the needed footsteps. Simply jot down which combinations you'll need for each scene.

🎧 Import all of the appropriate footstep files at once. Trim out the parts you know you will not need, place the clips in their approximate locations, but do not do any detailed editing. Continue placing the rest of the footsteps.

🎧 Then focus on detailed placement and editing of each set of steps. Take special care when placing shuffles, slides, stair steps, and other unusual types. Be critical, work one step at a time (literally) and ask yourself, does the type of step I'm placing here fit, or is there something 'off' about it? Perhaps the action calls for a slightly harder, softer, longer, or shorter type of step.

Working in stages like this, instead of selecting, importing, and editing each file one at a time, is a sort of specialized "assembly line" approach. It keeps you focused on one task at a time, developing your ability at that task so you can work faster. It also helps keep the picture sounding consistent from beginning to end.

Getting the most out of the actors' performances and scene locations requires tireless sound effects placement. Here are a few tips that might help.

- ☊ Invest in at least one general purpose, high-quality commercial sound library or start building your own library from sounds you find online. The FilmSound community maintains a comprehensive list of places to find sound effects online at www.filmsound.org/sound-effects/libraries.htm.

  Quality libraries include the aforementioned Hollywood Edge (www.hollywoodedge.com) and Sound Ideas (www.sound-ideas.com) as well as PowerFX (www.powerfx.com) and DeWolfe Music (www.dewolfemusic.com). Popular retailers of sound effects include www.prosoundeffects.com and www.sounddogs.com.

- ☊ Use the library's search engine, its PDF, or Soundminer to locate appropriate footsteps and audition everything appropriate to the actor's particular footstep needs. Don't be shy about importing several tracks and pitting them against the video one at a time to get an idea of which might be most appropriate. Delete any unnecessary clips and portions of the chosen clip that you won't need.

- ☊ Your imported footsteps will most likely be walked in a different rhythmic step as your actor's. Start by lining up one footstep and then make a cut between each subsequent footstep. Zoom in close and line up each step, one at a time, as you watch the actor's feet in your video preview window. This is sonically preferable to time stretching the entire string of footsteps.

- 🎧 Placing footsteps can be slow going at first. Save time by just roughly importing clips where they need to be, for all actors and all scenes at once, then go back later to do your editing.

- 🎧 Take extra care when placing off camera footsteps. Focus on the midsection of the torso and judge where feet hit the ground based on the height of the actor's hips.

# Beyond footsteps

By now you have developed an increased sensitivity of reading into your scenes, looking for detailed actions to highlight with sound. Most every film has plenty of opportunities to add clothing rustle, car and vehicle sounds, body hits and falls, furniture movement and squeaks, door openings and closings, and a plethora of household sounds. Jog your imagination with the following list, refer to your scene notes, and re-examine your scenes for opportunities to add ear candy.

### FOLEY and SFX

- 🎧 Vehicles – consider the model of car, truck, or motorcycle when placing doors, engine starts and stops, windows, wipers, exhaust, pass bys, engine revs, screeches and skids. Perspective: from inside or from outside the vehicle near or far?

- 🎧 Misc household: appliances, clocks, kitchen and dining sounds, windchimes, etc.

- 🎧 Clothing rustle, bed squeaks, fabric and pillow motion

- 🎧 Machinery and industrial sounds

- 🎧 Guns, fight sounds, bodyfalls, military sounds, explosions

- 🎧 Dogs and birds such as crow calls can add a level of either comfort or anxiety

- 🎧 Whooshes, sweeps, falls, and other more 'musical' sound effects for scene transitions, fast camera movements or moments of drama

- 🎧 Bass drones: constant bass heavy tones or pads as a quick and dirty substitute for music. Great for enhancing suspense.

- Noise drones: constant, slightly evolving tone layers that unnerve or distance the viewer. Great for sci-fi films, dramatic and industrial scenes.

The manual process of placing sound effects is like that for placing footsteps. Proceed scene by scene, looking for opportunities to add subtle or not so subtle sonic enhancements to the scene. For each needed sound:

### Find and lay in sound effects

- Think of a keyword or two that might identify the sound you need, e.g., 'clothing' or 'fabric.' Keyword-search your commercial sound libraries databases, document (PDF) listings. If you are using Soundminer or a similar program, your process will be a little different that described here.

  Leave the audio sequencer open and open the database in the background. You may need to keep several document listings open at once and search each one separately if you own multiple libraries.

- Highlight a stereo sound effect track in the sequencer and place the cursor approximately where you want the effect to start. Open the import audio-dialogue box.

- Browse to the appropriate folder and audition the relevant sound(s) from within the import audio dialogue box. Audition similar sounds as necessary to find what you like.

- Choose one or more files and import. They get placed on the sequencer timeline.

- Decide on one and move it around to be in approximate sync with the picture. Trim it to just the portion you need and delete the unused portions.

- Set a rough level for the chosen sound effect by adjusting its individual clip volume. Create fades as needed but don't get hung up on perfection just yet. Better to keep moving and get everything you need placed in the timeline.

- Repeat, ad infinitum.

🎧 Later, go back through the picture and 'detail' all sound effects to the picture. Set better levels, tighter trims, and closer sync to picture.

If you're working without a database program, there's no way around the tedious work of finding and placing sound effects. But you can get pretty fast at it by following the above steps like a mantra. It looks like a long process in print, but with some practice – and a well-organized library – you'll be placing sound effects in a matter of seconds instead of minutes.

These tips might speed up your work:

🎧 Try importing several sound effects into a scene before you start editing them for exact placement. Roughly line them up to the video to be sure you like them, and then move on. Leave the detailed editing for the next session. You'll work faster this way.

🎧 While you're doing your detailed editing, only roughly set each clip's volume. Again, leave perfection for the mix process. Better to keep moving.

🎧 Eliminate silence around the sound by cutting in fairly close to the start and end of the sound. Be careful not to cut off the tail of the sound (zoom in vertically to check for this). Be liberal about customizing

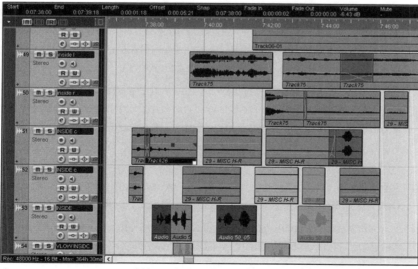

In some sequencers you can quickly set the overall level for a sound clip. Notice the different levels of thin horizontal lines in each of these clips from a Cubase session.

Line up the starting point of a clip's waveform to just before the associated action.

start and end points according to the action. For example, cut up, copy, paste, and crossfade windchimes to shorten or lengthen them as appropriate for the shot.

- Apply time stretching as needed (see your sequencer's manual for how to do this) where a sound is a bit too short or too long for the on screen action. Be aware that time stretching always degrades a sound, and some sounds inherently hide the distortion better than others.

- Apply offline processing such as equalization if you know the clip absolutely needs it, but don't go crazy since all sonic layers may not be finished yet. We can always fix it in the mix later.

- When it is time to go back and line up Foley clips more accurately, a common technique is to visually line up the start of the wave-form to a point just slightly before the visual cue. Experiment to see what works best for the particular sound effect.

- After placing effects for much or all of the picture, create a rough sound mix if you know how, sync it to the picture, and watch it on a different, larger screen. Take notes of where any sound effects seem to come too early or too late. Then go back and make the needed changes.

- For help on extending and looping drones using crossfades, check out the chapter on ambience editing. Both work in the same way.

- If you're consistently not finding the sound effects you need, it may be time to invest in another library, perhaps one specific to the sounds you need for your current project, e.g., 'Human Impacts' or 'Water and Boating.'

# THINKING IN LAYERS

How big do you want your sound effects? It's an individual decision for each sound, and for each film genre. It can help to think in terms of frequencies: do you want more bass from the sound in question, is it lacking the high fidelity of clear high end treble, or perhaps it's having trouble cutting through the music from a lack of midrange clarity. Sometimes EQ or other processing helps, and sometime layering similar sounds on top of each other is the answer.

It might work to layer several bodyfalls, punches, explosions, fireworks, gunshots, and other sounds you want to be 'huge' in the mix, but be careful not to sacrifice authenticity when making a big noise. Layering can result in smearing, the naturalness of the sound disappears. Of course, this might be a magic element for your scene. Some films have a fresh sound to them because the designers layered common sounds in a tasteful way that recalls the individual sounds, but makes for new and exciting textures. Let the picture decide the tone quality of the sound design it needs: is it real/natural, futuristic, corny, or perhaps vintage sounding? Select and process your sound effects to style.

So go ahead and lay four gunshots over each other if it gives you the sound of that massive gun from the future that you're imagining – but keep their combined volume under control. Mix just enough of each layer so that each contributes to the overall sound you're trying to create. If the result is to your liking but comes out too soft or too loud, select all of the clips and raise or lower them by the same number of decibels. In the mixing stage we'll do the final tweaks.

## Off-camera sound effects: interpreting emotion, creating tension

We touched on this idea in the last chapter on ambiences. Sometimes there are interesting breaks in the dialogue, where there is no music, no Foley, nothing really happening except perhaps an actor sitting in a lull for a moment. These are sometimes great places to add low-level, off-camera sounds to enhance the location or create tension. The philosophy of it lies somewhere between adding sound effects and building background ambiences.

Take two actors having a conversation where a woman is trying to get a man to do something he doesn't want to do. She tells him what she wants and this makes him uncomfortable. He pauses and looks off in the distance instead of responding right away. For the audience this could be a long and awkward moment as we await his response. Consider the meaning that an off camera sound effect would add to the silence. A disturbance of birds, a far away siren, subtle helicopter, or an industrial sound might be just the thing to build tension. Now the man seems legitimately distracted for a moment by something we can't see and we're pulled into his point of view, no longer alienated by the silence. We identify with his tension for a moment and look forward to his next line.

When trying to come up with appropriate sounds for fill in moments such as these, consider what is happening in the *diegetic* world of the film. Ask *where are they?* If the players are in a monastery, a church tower might toll the bell for them more suitably than, say sirens. Or perhaps thunder? If it's appropriate, it will no doubt add to the scene.

If our cast members were in a tender moment instead of a tense one, perhaps if they were discussing the prospect of marriage, we might hear children playing, or an ice cream truck going by, off camera. Or the weather might settle down a bit to create more space for their next lines. Sound has the possibility to reach far outside the boundaries of the camera. Great films use this technique to their advantage.

Also watch the actions of the cast extra carefully. Consider adding off camera sounds for any actions that the audience might not see them do, but that we assume they will do, like opening a door, setting the car's emergency brake, or hanging up the phone.

Watch carefully how actors are performing. If an actor is stumbling home in the dark there might be opportunities to add fill-in Foley of objects getting knocked over. If an actor is supposed to be sick, there might be places where you can insert sniffles or coughing in places where we don't see her face. Tell the story with sound wherever you can, and you create a richer world that reels in your audience on a non-verbal level.

## Can't find it? Make it: Recording SFX and Foley

There are at least two types of sounds that will from time to time be difficult to find: sounds that are hard to describe by keyword, and sounds that are performed in a very specific way in a scene. An example of the latter is the sounds of writing or typing. As usual, if the pencil or typewriter wasn't miked, you'll either need stock Foley or a short recording session. These kinds of complex and unique motions are better off being re-recorded, whereby you perform the pencil-writing along with the actor by watching his movements on screen. Trying to line up stock sounds is often much more difficult.

At some point you may need a certain sound that you can't find in your library. You decide to try to custom record that unique sound for the scene, though you're not sure what materials to use to make the right sound. You know what object makes that sound in real life, but what does it *sound* like? Close your eyes. Think like a Foley Artist. Narrow it down by the character of the sound – does it have a sharp attack, does it rattle, does it thud, is it rubbery, watery, indistinct, strong and punchy, does it need to be a machine or synthetic sound, a human body sound, or something that might be in a science fiction library, something heavy, something old, something new…Try talking it out with a friend: sometimes when trying to describe the sound in words you'll hit on some possible materials.

The recipe for cooking up your own Foley and SFX is similar to that for ambiences. Some can be captured in the controlled environment of the studio and some must be done in the field. Some of the things you'll need for getting good SFX recordings:

🎧 The props (the car, boat, footwear, guns, swords, etc.) that you need recordings of in the scene. Of course, it doesn't have to be the same exact prop used for the shoot, it just has to make the *sound* you want. Test it: close your eyes to listen if your props sound like you want them to, even before you mic them.

- Repeatable performances, for getting a variety of choices at different recording levels, angles, mic distances, etc.

- Acoustic baffles or blankets are helpful to deaden reflections from hard surrounding surfaces.

- Microphone – a mono shotgun mic or camera mic will do on a budget, but consider a studio quality condenser for indoor – or outdoor for that matter – recording. Invest in a stereo mic for capturing passing cars, ambiences, and other wide-field sounds.

If you're in the market for a studio mic, don't be shy about auditioning different ones in music stores. Speak through different ones. Get a feel for their sensitivity, harshness or smoothness in the treble frequencies, and fullness and body. A clean, neutral mic is what's needed for effects recording. Aim for a neutral, even frequency response that doesn't exaggerate the highs, mids, or low end.

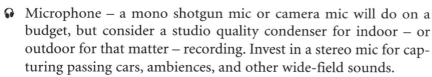

- Of course you'll need a camera, minidisk, DAT, digital multitrack, laptop, or other audio recording device, and media for it. There are all kinds of low-cost digital recorders on the market that allow for easy USB and firewire transfers to computer and that use reliable media cards or internal hard drives. Any pro-audio retailer should carry several types.

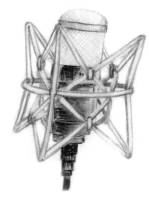

- An assistant to either do the recording or perform the Foley (or be a human mic stand). If you need a stationary mount for the mic, invest in a boom-style mic stand from any pro-audio retailer.

- Patience, and a willingness to break stuff (the law maybe?) to get the really good recordings.

Experiment: make a recording, listen back, and identify what's right or wrong about it compared to what you want to hear for the on-screen prop. Is it too bright for the scene – could it be that the room you're recording in is too bright, or is it something about the props you're using that have a different timbre? Are you getting too much reverb or 'air' in the recording – try moving the mic closer to the source, or use an assistant to help. Mentally subtract the tone quality of sound you envision with the sound you are getting on tape. Describe that difference in words, out loud to someone; identify what you need to change on order to get closer to the sound you need. With all of this creative experimentation, you may find yourself enjoying your new side career as a Foley Artist.

### Remember:

- Record in a small, warm sounding location wherever possible. Use blankets as acoustical baffles, much in the same way a DP uses lighting diffusers around the subject. The room is always part of your sound; try and minimize its effect as much as possible.

🎧 For indoor recordings, use the best studio-quality condenser mic you can. For exterior props and effects sounds, try the same condenser, weather permitting. If phantom power is not available on your equipment, you may not have the option of using condenser mics. A shotgun, handheld dynamic, portable stereo mic, or some other type might be more appropriate. Always keep the mic close to the sound source. Reverb and echo can be added, but not removed.

## Bodyfalls and fireballs: Creative SFX

Once all of the essentials are in place, try taking your SFX to the next level.

### Fight scenes

Fight scenes require careful sound design. While timing (placement of sound to picture) is obviously very important, so is the sounds you choose. How much bass did you want in that punch?

Punches and bodyfalls can sound anything from naturally 'thin'-sounding to over-the-top like many fast-action Hollywood movies. Most general-purpose libraries have quality fight sounds that work great for most dramas. However, you may want to go beyond these into the more stylized sounds of dedicated impact effects libraries. Sound designers will often layer two or more sounds to create stronger body-blows, and having a variety of sonic options is always a good thing.

### Custom FX

There is a moment toward the beginning of the movie *Constantine* where we see a car door close from an extreme long shot. The sound is not that of a car door, however; the designers used a gunshot echo with heavy reverb to add to the tension and estrangement of the scene. While 'less is more' when it comes to applying reverb to a sound, the occasional exaggerated, washed-out sound effect can create an eye opening moment of power. In the Home Stretch chapters we'll talk more about using reverb.

### Transitions

You can get a fun, comic effect by adding sounds to camera zooms, swish pans, and scene transitions. The concept is similar to that used in dance music where production effects like sweeps, swells, hits, falls, and explosions are used as transitions between musical sections. Check out playful dramas like Guy Ritchie's *Snatch* for creative uses of sonic swishes and swells. Animations also use plenty of production effects to add energy and keep things moving. You can also listen to house or trance music, or the sound libraries used in creating urban dance music, for inspiration for using these sounds. The same idea can be adapted to thrillers. Use ominous production effects to add drama and tension to scene transitions in a similar way.

### Creative stuff

The sounds of a stock library are yours to mold as you see fit. Shape them by cutting off their attack or long decays, reversing them, pitch shifting, or time stretching them. All of these processes should be available as stock offline (or AudioSuite) processes in your sequencer. At some point any of this processing will distort the sound into something unnatural or unrecognizable. It is up to you to decide what makes the sound fit best with the picture.

Animal sounds are great fodder for sound design. Fun things happen when you start reversing or pitch shifting lion and elephant roars. They can add a fresh dimension to an action, horror, animation, or even a quirky comedy. Layering them under real sounds can keep the soundtrack sounding authentic while hinting at something sinister.

Experimental and art house cinema defines itself with unconventional uses of sound. One of these is non-sync sound. It is a bold move to first see say, an airplane, without sound and hear it later, perhaps in the next shot. Used outright, it calls attention to the artifice of the film medium. Used tastefully, it can do many things like transition shots in new ways or engage the viewer's memory of characters or events between shots. Building a soundtrack from scratch allows you to imagine any kind of bizarre effect and make it believable.

## Chapter 11

# Elements: Ambience and Room Tone

Background ambiences in narrative films aren't always heard but they are always felt. Quality ambiences make a huge difference in the naturalness and believability of a scene. A film without them is like a wall with out wallpaper. They aren't just a textural backdrop – they are also a secret weapon for keeping the viewer's interest between lines of dialogue, as a custom music score does.

In this chapter, we'll solve the problem many novice production recordings face: too much background bleed, where the dialogue is fighting to be heard over the location noise. We'll discover the importance of room tone and how to lay it in seamlessly. We'll build the layers of ambience you wanted for your scenes when you were dreaming up your ideal soundtrack back in the *Pre-post* chapters. We'll discover that we can even steer a viewer's emotional response with carefully-chosen background ambiences.

## What's in an ambience?

Let's talk about what ambience really means, and why it's treated as a separate layer of the soundtrack. Generally recorded with the dialogue in budget pictures, ambience is made up of environmental sound events both constant and singular in nature. Some unique events might be dog barks or car and airplane fly-bys. Constant ambiences and what is called room tone include the noise inherent to your recording equipment (hums, buzzes and hiss) and the recorded atmospheres of machinery, traffic, nature and the like. The quality of these background tracks either lend credibility to the actor's performances and make the world of the film more interesting or, without proper care, they can make a scene sound empty or inconsistent.

Some soundtracks make use of natural, uncontrolled sound environments quite well. Documentary, reality genre, Italian realism, and deliberately 'lo fi' or low-budget indie films come to mind. Where production ambience is deliberately left in, the ambience track work in

audio post consists mostly of cleaning up the distracting events between dialogue phrases. Additional unique ambient events can be inserted around the dialogue and one can even layer in additional constant ambiences to build more complex environments. But often these types of pictures live with their production sound relatively unchanged.

## LISTENING TO THE NOISE

What exactly is signal, and what is noise? Signal is anything we want to hear and noise is basically anything we want to ignore. But as a new Sound Designer it's important to get intimate with both. After all, both are part of your final mix.

How often do you listen to the noise while watching a picture? Have you noticed that certain genres, like documentary and reality pictures, tolerate more background noise than others? Narrative films incorporate natural and stock ambiences and scenes with none at all. What is the noise made up of – is it the hiss of old tape recorders used in production, the natural sound of a field, the racket of the city?

Can you hear where ambiences or room tone were captured in production, and where they were added in post? Does the dialogue give it away? ADR always demands a new layer of ambience or RT for realism. Does the camera give it away? Is it an extreme long shot, where the actors are too far away to be captured with a boom mic? Wireless lavalieres on those actors wouldn't provide adequate ambience, so if you hear it, it must have been added later. What about those B-roll sunset shots between scenes? Are they layered with non sync sound – ambiences from stock libraries or wild soundtracks?

The name of the game in building a more polished and refined soundtrack is control: creative control of each sonic layer in order to design whatever world you would ideally like to have for your scenes. If you have relatively clean dialogue tracks (or will after re-recording them in the studio) you can take delight in building a custom environment of your choice under them. This allows you to shape the scene to your liking. You can sometimes find ambience tracks on the web, record them yourself, or buy them in sound effects libraries, such as the ambient series of libraries from www.sound-ideas.com or www.hollywood edge.com.

## Pouring the foundation

Earlier the *Pre Post* section introduced the typical structure an ambience track built from scratch. Any of three discrete layers can be sandwiched to create an environment that adds a unique character to scenes with clean or no dialogue. These ambient layers are:

- Room tone or ambience of the immediate room or vicinity
- Low-level, far away ambience
- Specific ambient events including unique animal sounds, vehicle pass-bys, airplanes, etc.

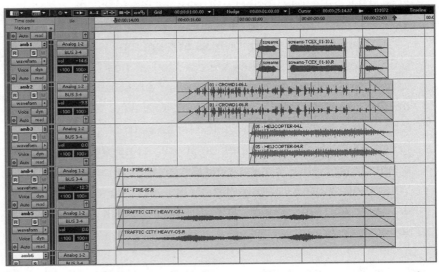

This full-bodied ambience track starts off with a layered background and gets more interesting halfway through the scene.

Here are some of the most common ambiences you're likely to hear in a soundtrack. Some of these might conjure up ideas for specific, one time ambient events, say for filling in spaces between dialogue, and some are designed to be used as constant, long-form background layers.

## Ambiences

| Interior | Exterior |
|---|---|
| • Appliance hums, refrigerators, A/Cs, vacuum cleaners | • Weather (wind, rain, thunder, ocean) |
| • Stores, malls, markets, bars, restaurants, cafes | • Animals (crickets, birds chirping, etc.) |
| • Offices, conference rooms, hospitals, libraries, banks | • Traffic (city, suburban, or rural? Distant highway? Close cars or motorcycles?) |
| • Airports, bus and train stations, subways/trams | • Construction sites |
| • Manufacturing and industry | • Crowds (adults? children? close or distant? loud and busy or quiet?) |
| • Live sports games, concerts, casinos, and other crowds | • Airplanes and helicopters (close or distant?) |
| • Television (sports game, news report, sitcom, etc.) | • Parks, forests, rural country atmospheres |
| • Talk radio, TV commercials, etc. | • Playgrounds, schools |
| | • Fire and emergency: accidents, police sirens, helicopters, flames, fire trucks, explosions |

In addition to these, layers of machine noise and drones customary to horror, thriller, and science fiction films can be used in films of all genres. Used much in the same way as ambiences or music tracks, drones build drama and tension, usually at low-volume levels under the dialogue. Find them at the same stock library houses, on the web, or create them yourself from synthesizers.

# ENOUGH ALREADY ABOUT AMBIENCES, OR, HOW I LEARNED TO STOP WORRYING AND THROW OUT PERFECTLY CLEAN PRODUCTION TRACKS

It might sound like a bold move to *mute* the Sound Mixer's hard work but sometimes it might be the best thing for the scene. Here are some reasons why you might do such a rude and inconsiderate thing.

### CREATIVITY

Choosing instead to build a soundtrack from scratch, even when you have a usable production track, gives you the creative option of designing a very different soundtrack for a scene. This is even easier for scenes with little to no dialogue and no particularly unique location sounds. Be prepared to build the scene with stock library sounds and re-record the dialogue. This option affords you much more creative control than dealing with dialogue that's married to its location ambience.

### EASE

Sometimes it's faster and easier to build a convincing background environment from scratch than to bother dealing with the production sound just to save a few lines of dialogue. Consider how little effort will go into re-recording a few lines and laying in some ambience versus futzing with noise reduction, matching noise levels between shots, etc. If you've got a good stock sound effects library, let *it* do some of the work.

### CLEAN UP

Noisy dialogue? Uneven noise levels behind shots? Wind-blown production backgrounds? Restoration/noise-reduction is an option, but perhaps you're still not convinced that you can re-record dialogue in post. If you're concerned that your replacement dialogue will come out unusable or take too long to engineer, you may be surprised at how easy it can be to ADR a scene. Build your dream soundtrack free of the noise pollution of the production track.

## MUSIC

Consider how much presence music will have in your scenes, and save yourself a lot of work building ambiences and sound effects tracks. Music alone – with no production sound, ambiences, or dialogue – can be all you need to reinforce the emotion of a scene that already explains itself through its action.

When music is in the foreground, you often don't need extra ambience at all. However, where music seeps in at low volumes, you may choose to keep the action anchored in a real space by layering it with an ambience track. It's the Re-recording Mixer's judgment call. Generally speaking, to put the scene in a natural (or unnatural for that matter) environment, add ambience. To let it float in space like a music video or silent movie, mute the production and ambience tracks and let the music carry the action.

Unsure? Play the scene with the production sound, play it with the music, and play it with both. See which brings out the meaning of the scene. Watch other movies with similar music to yours and listen to where they mute production sound and where they don't. Get opinions from others. Then you can lay in your ambience and/or music beds out of creativity, not necessity.

If you haven't brainstormed about the backgrounds you'd like to hear in your scenes, now is a good time. Take into account what you own for stock libraries, but don't compromise what you imagine to be ideal environments since they can always be purchased or recorded in post. Consider whether you want each scene driven by music, natural ambience, drones, room tone, layers of sound effects, or a combination of these.

# More ideas for ambience and tone

🎧 When considering traffic, decide: Close or distant? Suburban, urban, rural? Local or highway? Few cars or many? Dry weather or wet?

🎧 For unique vehicle pass-bys consider the weight of the vehicle. You can't make a Honda sound like a big truck. Also be aware of the direction it passes, left to right or right to left.

🎧 Appliances, machinery, and industrial sounds, real (in the scene) or just as low-level ambience. If you're not sure, try adding one in. Does it help the scene or create clutter?

🎧 Bass drones: constant bass heavy tones or pads can be a great substitute for music. Enhances suspense in thrillers.

🎧 Noise drones: steady white noise types of layers useful for unnerving, distracting, or distancing the viewer. Great for sci-fi films, industrial scenes, or any thriller.

🎧 Record your own radio, TV, or PA announcements for scenes at train stations, airports, supermarkets, etc.

Ask yourself for each scene: What was recorded on the production tracks behind the dialogue? Is the nature of the dialogue in any of your scenes such that it can be re-recorded, or is this not an option? Were your environments chosen and carefully considered or were they left to chance? Do they sound relevant to the atmosphere you want to create in the scene? Are they too loud, overpowering the dialogue, perhaps interrupting the actors with distractions like car horns and airplanes? If you had it to do again, would you have taken more care in customizing or choosing your locations?

## Room tone: Good noise

The natural assumption of dialogue tracks is that they should be as clean as possible. While this is true, dialogue tracks often have some kind of audible noise floor, as either a side effect of audio recording equipment or from the unique din of random noise that defines a location. Perhaps you are not used to listening to low-level noise under the dialogue (it's more apparent the older the film is). When it's not treated with care, the audience hears a distracting jump in background noise levels. With today's digital recording and increased use of dialogue re-recording, dialogue sounds cleaner than ever. With good recording technique, a consistent noise floor is sometimes a moot point.

*Room tone (RT)* is traditionally made up of the slight hum, buzz, or hiss created by the location recording equipment and a low-level ambience of machinery, traffic, or nature, or a combination of these. Since independent pictures often rely so heavily on the production dialogue (versus ADR) maintaining a consistent background noise floor is important, especially between cuts within a scene. Volume jumps and gaps in the noise floor are the mark of unprofessional work. A consistent noise floor – or ambience – is an almost inaudible/imperceptible threshold of hearing in a film and gives a sense of character and contrast to the much louder dialogue.

Modern films recorded on digital equipment aim for pristine tracks and show it off in whisper clean speech so intimate it seems to come out of nowhere. Since it's not anchored in a bed of noise, ambience, or even reverb, this clean and dry dialogue sounds close up and larger than life. The intro narration of the 2006 film *The Fountain* comes to mind. The intense intimacy created by a lack of any noise whatsoever behind the high-fidelity voiceover is engaging in such a way that the viewer feels someone is speaking directly to him. On the other hand, the lack of ambience under an entire film of re-recorded dialogue such as in Godard's classic *Le Petit Soldat* can leave the viewer tense and unnerved. It's up to the director.

The most important use of room tone, then, is for patching up and creating a consistent dialogue track. In the course of dialogue editing you may want to cut out offensive and stray elements such as microphone bumps, crew coughs, stray footsteps, and other short problem sounds. If you have room tone to fill in the gaps made by these cuts, you'll be able to take out any oddities that might have been captured by the Sound Mixer's mic. A problem sound can easily be cut out in post and replaced with a segment of room tone – so long as it doesn't occur during a line of dialogue.

There is another use for room tone. Dialogue that has been through extensive noise reduction or that was re-recorded in the studio can end up sounding too clean, sometimes having slight artifacts from the noise reduction. Take an indoor scene that doesn't have the benefit of the din of traffic or a bed of nature sounds. If recorded in the studio, the lines can end up sounding sterile and bare. Layering RT under the dialogue is one option for gluing a scene together or providing a sense of light, neutral ambience as a foundation for the scene. RT is smooth and consistent – with no breaks or unique elements that jump out. It's mixed almost unnoticeably low in level, and it's not particularly audible until the viewer purposely listens for it. We'll talk more about levels for ambiences and RT in the chapter on mixing. Let's get right into finding and laying in RT and ambiences.

# Where to find room tone

There are at least four ways to get hold of a sample of room tone. Let's talk about each, starting with the easiest method.

### 🎧 Use the room tone recordings done by the Sound Mixer

If you are fortunate enough to have separate room tone recordings for each scene, you are in luck. Solo the track and listen on headphones for the cleanest 2-, 5-, or 10-second portion of tone you can find for each scene that needs it. Keep these clips handy and reuse them when you need tone within that scene.

### 🎧 Lift short pieces of tone from between phrases of dialogue

Dialogue Editors commonly lift bits of tone from quiet moments between the dialogue or from the start of a scene. Listen carefully for moments where neither cast nor crew is breathing, moving, rustling clothing, etc., and you might find a second or two of tone to use during scene surgery. Usually the best tone is found in the 'handles' (before or after the start of a clip). With some copying, pasting, and crossfades, you can extend this one second of tone into as long a phrase as needed. The danger here is that tone bites that are too short will start to sound noticeably looped. We'll see exactly how to do this properly construct them in the next section.

### 🎧 Obtain room tone from stock 'ambient' sample libraries

Choosing the right RT from a stock library is an obscure art. It's not immediately obvious whether a light drone, a type of white noise, machine noise, or hum is the best underlay for a scene. When in doubt, a light bed of hiss or white noise gives a 'colder' tone to the scene while a soft machine type hum makes a warmer bed. Consider how natural or synthetic the noise sounds, and match it to the feel of your scene. These are subtle points and difficult to describe without actually listening to them. David Lynch pictures are a great education on what can be done with drones and artificial room tones.

### 🎧 Go back to the location and re-record the ambience

If the original locations are still accessible, consider going back to them with a DAT, minidisk, video cam, or other recorder to grab additional ambience. You may find that the background sound of these locations stayed consistent enough to provide you with tone similar to your existing production tracks. Use the same mic you used for the dialogue to get the best matching RT you can.

# How to lay in ambiences and RT

If you are building a scene's sound from scratch in post you have the luxury of laying stock ambiences or those you've recorded yourself into the picture, with no competition from noisy production tracks. Choose your ambiences from your libraries, or record what you need (in stereo), and proceed to edit them into smooth backgrounds.

### Import long-form ambience tracks

- Create several new stereo audio tracks to be your palette for imported ambiences. Be sure they are routed to the AMBIENCE group.
- Stock ambiences are provided louder than necessary for most scenes. It might help to bring down the level of the AMBIENCE group channel to about -15dB, since most ambiences sit pretty low in the mix anyway. Or you can just lower the individual track levels as needed.
- Search for and import the ambience tracks you desire. Roughly adjust their clip levels as you like for the scene.

Adding stock ambience or room tone to your soundtrack implies that there is sonic 'room' for it. If your production tracks already have loud backgrounds, then you already have a bed for your dialogue and there may be no need to add any more drones or room tone. However, you may be able to enhance the scene with specific ambient events.

### Enhance the ambience with layers and specific events

- Listen for opportunities to layer additional ambient events over each other for more complex textures. For example, far away traffic mixed in to the din of closer, louder crowd conversation.

Distant church bells over a nature scene. Make it a point to deliberately create interesting sonic wallpaper that adds texture and meaning to every scene.

🎧 For scenes that seem to be moving a little too slow, a more interesting soundtrack can help keep things moving. Listen for lulls in the dialogue where an off-screen bird chirp, dog bark, church bell, siren, plane flyby, or other specific ambient sound event might keep things moving on a subliminal level. Search for, audition, import, and edit these as you wish. Set their volumes appropriately.

🎧 Likewise between dialogue lines there may be distracting sounds that can be cut out. Do this and patch the holes according to the next set of procedures. Let your ears decide if the result is working and sounds natural.

Creating seamless ambiences for each scene requires plenty of cutting and patching with smooth dissolves. The audio equivalent of the dissolve, and your secret weapon in editing RT and ambience tracks, is the crossfade. The ease and flexibility that most sequencers give you in crossfading makes light work of creating flawless backgrounds.

Often you'll need to cut out a syllable, thump, or other undesirable from your production track, leaving a hole of dead air. Use the procedures below to patch these up.

### Patch up holes in the production track with room tone

🎧 Patch holes in the production track with room tone and listen for clean passages of "silence" (room tone) between dialogue phrases. Be sure there is no breathing or other noises and try to find the longest segment you can, at least one second long.

Sometimes the best room tone occurs before or after the actors' lines. This is why we specified 60-frame or longer 'handles' in the OMF export. Open up (stretch out) the beginning and ending of a production dialogue clip to check for usable tone.

🎧 Copy and paste this small bit of clean, consistent room tone to extend it into as long a segment as you need. As you paste, nudge the clips back a few frames so that they overlap enough to make a tiny crossfade between them.

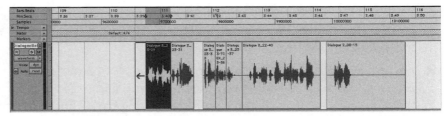

Extend the beginning and end of dialogue clips into the 'handles' region to find good, usable room tone.

🎧 Solo the new multi segment and ensure that it sounds smooth and natural. Remedy choppy or loopy sounding results with longer crossfades, or go back and look for a longer, more usable segment of room tone.

Often you'll import an ambience track, lay it under your dialogue and find that particular undesirable events are sticking out of the track, drawing too much attention. Edit those out to make a smooth, unobtrusive background track.

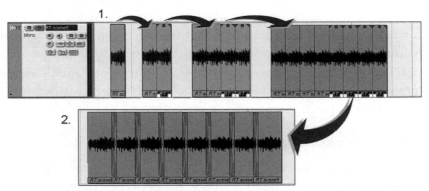

Doing the above: copy one, paste 2. copy two, paste 4 etc. Quickly generate long segments of repetitive clips by copying & pasting one clip, then two clips, then four, then eight, etc.

### Remove undesirable events in the ambience tracks

🎧 Solo the ambience track that needs editing.

🎧 Listen for the offending element. Sometimes car horns, harsh animal sounds, or strange tones in added ambience tracks will obscure the dialogue.

🎧 Cut out jarring or undesirable events in your ambience tracks.

🎧 If you haven't performed any fade ins or fade outs and aren't married to the exact position of the ambience track in the timeline, simply move one of the clips so that it overlaps the other, and mend them with a crossfade of one second or so in length. Solo the ambience track and check that it flows naturally through the crossfade.

🎧 If you need to keep the ambience track exactly where it is, then you'll need to find a patch of similar ambience that you can graft in to the hole you just created. Once you've done this, create two generous 1-second or longer crossfades at the beginning and end of the new, inserted clip.

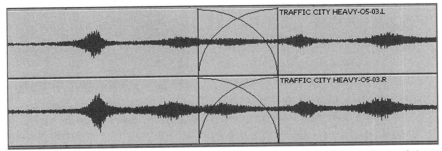

Often you can just cut out offending sounds in the ambience tracks, close up the gap, and crossfade with no audible artifacts.

You may want an ambience to start off strong in a scene and then reduce down in volume once the dialogue comes in. This is sometimes used to 'duck' the ambience track under the dialogue.

### Create volume changes in the ambience track

There are several ways to automate level changes – for any clip, not just ambiences.

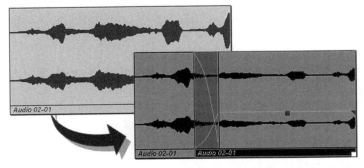

One way to make volume changes: Cut a clip into two segments, adjust the volume of one clip, overlap the two segments, and apply a crossfade.

1. If your sequencer allows you to set volume levels for audio events (clips), try this method. Cut the ambience clip at the point you want it to fade down and perform a long crossfade by overlapping the resulting two segments. Lower the volume of the second segment and then upon playback you'll hear a gradual reduction of volume during the crossfade. You can time this fade to be as sharp or as gradual as you like – a few frames, 1 second, 5 seconds – to cause sharp or very gradual volume changes.

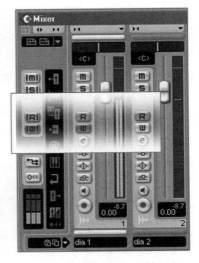

Using automation is easy: 1. enable write mode, 2. play back the track and move the faders, panners, and other controls, 3. enable read mode.

2. Draw volume automation by hand. You can pencil-in just a couple of points on the volume line and the application interprets the slope for you.

3. Turn on the automation 'write' mode and move the track fader in real-time. Even if it doesn't come out perfectly, you can later edit the automation line by hand. Check your manual for details on automation recording and editing.

Unmute the dialogue to audition it with the new level change. Tweak the clip levels or edit the volume automation until it's working well with the picture.

## ANATOMY OF A CROSSFADE

Perhaps you've noticed how many ways there are to crossfade two segments of audio. Is the type of fade really important? When do we use each type, and how audible are the differences between them?

A crossfade is simply the sound of one audio clip fading down while another clip fades in. In visual terms, it's a high-maintenance dissolve, with many ways to control the timing and volume levels of the two coincident events.

There are two basic choices to make when shaping a crossfade. One influences how abruptly versus smoothly the first sound ends and the second begins, and the other determines how constant the volume remains at the midpoint of the fade between clips.

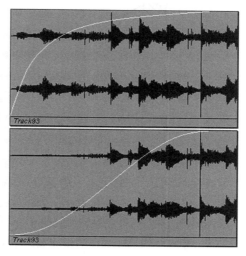

Long fades – whether fade-ins, fade-outs, or crossfades – have very audible differences. It pays to audition a few different curves and see what works best against the picture.

### Spline versus linear fades

When you crossfade, you are in effect making two fades, each with a shape that determines how quickly or how smoothly the sounds make their transition. The longer the crossfade is, the more obvious the sound difference between fades. The shape of fades less than a second or so in length is usually of little consequence. Longer than that, however, and the listener can hear how strongly or how naturally the first sound dies and the second one comes in.

Generally, a linear curve (or modified linear curve, see the following illustration) is fine for short crossfades. There are times when different shapes sound better, though there are too many unique instances to try to describe here. Best to solo the track and audition different types of fades on the material. Listen for levels staying consistent – the fade should sound 'invisible.'

## Equal-gain versus equal-power

Dialogue transitions and short crossfades in general often sound fine with equal-gain crossfades, where the computer maintains constant attenuation during the fade-out and constant amplification during the fade-in. That doesn't necessarily mean it sounds like a smooth, natural transition. That depends on the program material.

Constant sounds like drones, RT, music, and also longer crossfades in general usually sound best with equal-power fades, where the energy of the sound stays consistent for the length of the fade-in and fade-out. When you've crossfaded two segments and find that they aren't maintaining a loud enough volume in the middle of the x-fade, switch from equal-gain to equal-power to bring up that midpoint area to a constant level. Do the reverse for the opposite problem, where the midpoint gets too loud.

Try it: Cut a drone or other constant sound into two pieces. Crossfade them across two or three seconds: first with an equal-gain, then with an equal-power x-fade. Notice the difference in volume around the midpoint of the fade. Which one sounds more consistent, more transparent? Which one hides the edit better? The answer may depend on the particular audio material.

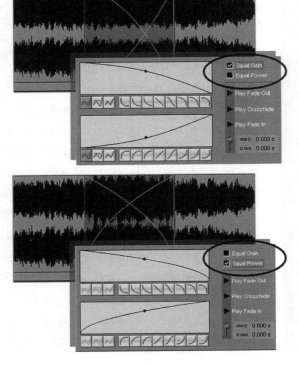

Take the extra time to make smooth fades and crossfades; it adds a professional polish to your work and reduces jarring 'jump cuts' in the audio.

## Excess ambience

Budget production recordings often bleed too much background into the dialogue tracks. There are at least two remedies for this, depending on the type of background noise. Let's recap:

🎧 As we mentioned earlier in this chapter, you can re-record the dialogue in the studio and build the ambience and sound effects tracks to your liking. Starting from scratch for a troubled scene allows for a clean, controlled, custom soundtrack, but sacrifices the original emotion of the acting. Sometimes this is fine – sometimes performances can even be improved in the studio. Although it may not be appropriate for documentaries, reality genres, and any scene that would be difficult to re perform, done with care, studio re-recording usually results in a cleaner, slicker, more big budget type of sound – if that's what you're after.

When you decide to mute your noisy production tracks (or where you have no production sound) follow the procedures for laying in ambience and room tone. First, re-record the dialogue as described in the 'ADR and Narration' chapter, add your sound effects and Foley, and finally add music as desired.

🎧 Sometimes a production track has noise problems but the dialogue performance is too important to throw away. Cleaning up your production sound is the other option. Perhaps it's just a low-level din of noise that you want removed, or the scene contains special performances that you don't want to lose, or you're making a documentary for which re-recording the dialogue is not an option. You can use noise reduction to partially remove constant, unchanging background noise such as air conditioners, heaters, blowers, tape hiss, and the like (see the sound restoration section of the 'Dialogue' chapter) without losing much signal quality.

In these cases, revisit the procedures for noise reduction that we outlined in the 'Dialogue' chapter. You'll want to arm yourself with a quality noise reduction plug-in and a good parametric EQ. As you reduce the noise in your production tracks, be careful not to go too far. A little remaining noise is more easily accepted by the audience than the alternative – phasey, warbly sounding dialogue.

There is a variation on the clean-up theme, especially useful when the offending background noise is different from shot to shot. It's a kind of Zen approach: to clean up scenes where noise levels vary in tone from shot to shot, *add* a noise bed under the scene. This technique works best when the quality of the background differs from shot to shot, but not their levels. Also, the noise needs to be low in level compared to the dialogue (i.e., the signal-to-noise ratio should be fairly high). These scenes can sometimes be made to sound more consistent by simply stacking on additional ambience, drones, or room tone under noise-reduced dialogue.

For shot-reverse-shot (crosscut) dialogue, there are several ways to keep background noise levels consistent between shots (or takes). The method you use depends on what works best for the scene. If one character dominates the dialogue, consider using only the dominant character's production track under both characters' shots, and ADR the less vocal actor. Or you can do what's described above: restore both characters' tracks as clean as possible and layer a new ambience track under the whole scene to help it gel.

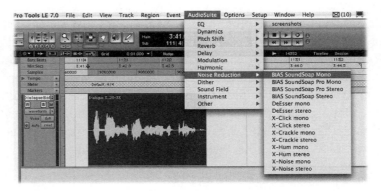

Noise reduction, revisited. Check out the Dialogue chapter for full cleanup procedures.

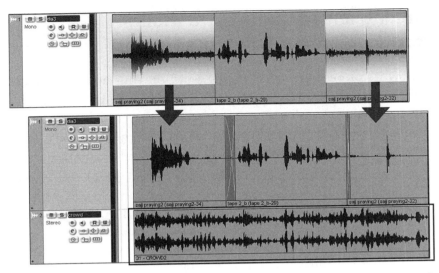

Noise levels vary from clip to clip. 2. Noise levels cleaned up. 3. New ambience bed added under to gel it together.

### *Clean up noisy backgrounds*

🎧 Use EQ and noise reduction to get rid of as much noise as possible without sacrificing the tone quality of the dialogue. Scrub the clips as clean as you can. (Work efficiently: process similar sounding clips together by selecting several of them first before opening the offline plug-in.)

🎧 Equalize the dialogue as necessary to get it sounding consistent, like it was recorded with the same microphone, in the same place, at the same time. Add a little low-end EQ to thin lines, brighten up dull spots, etc.

🎧 When you're satisfied that the tone of the dialogue is reasonably consistent, lay in your ambience or room-tone track. Don't be shy about adding in machinery, appliances, nature sounds, traffic, or just plain low-level room noise to fill in the clarity you just created in the dialogue. Roughly set the level of this noise bed; we'll tweak it later in the 'Mixing' chapter, when your ears are fresh.

## Looking ahead: some extra thought in production saves headaches in post

By now if you've done some editing work on your ambience tracks you've realized how important it is to keep backgrounds separate from dialogue. It's a lot easier to maintain consistency of levels and tone when you have independent control of each layer. With every post-audio mix you learn things that might be prevented next time.

🎧 On your next shoot, encourage your Sound Mixer and Boom Operator to focus on getting the cleanest dialogue possible. Ironically, elimination of all background sound from the production track is the key to a clean, consistent ambience track. Close windows and doors, use sound absorbing blankets, and maintain an absolutely quiet set while recording.

🎧 Be sure to leave time to record 30 seconds of pure uninterrupted room tone for dialogue-critical scenes. Do it at the end of shooting the scene, when the production assistants and camera crew has left the room. Assure the sound crew that they have your support in quieting the set so that absolutely no other sound is made while recording this critical, low-level ambience. Use the same mono, shotgun mic at the same time of day with the same recording setup as for the dialogue to capture room tone that will later blend perfectly with the dialogue track.

🎧 You may also want to record ambiences in addition to room tone, especially if you don't own your own stock libraries. This includes ambiences such as traffic outside the window of a scene, children in the playground next door, the rustle of people walking, restaurant ambiences, etc. You can do it on-set or not during production – anytime, really. Invest in a good stereo microphone and portable digital recorder and you can quickly build up your own custom library of ambiences – and have fun doing it.

# Chapter 12

# Elements: Music

Nothing can bring out a scene's emotion like music. Carefully chosen music tracks can do wonders for a scene's mood, pacing, and interpretation. A good custom score heightens the perceived quality of the picture. At this point you may have placed some temporary or even final music tracks in your session. However, it's easy to shy away from adding music to a picture considering the complications of acquisition, negotiations, and licensing.

In this chapter we're going to tackle where to find music, how to properly license it, how to edit and fit music to picture, and how to skillfully use it to round out your soundtrack.

# Temp tracks

Even if you haven't found your dream music tracks yet, decide as soon as possible where music will be laid in to a scene. It's especially important to determine those places where you want it to carry the action as the only sound for a scene (or portion of a scene). This will keep you from unnecessary work. There is no sense in cleaning up the production sound in scenes where it will be muted. Likewise, we don't want to waste time adding Foley or ambiences to sections where music will drown them out.

As soon as possible, lay in temporary tracks of artists' or composers' works that get across the emotion you are trying to bring out. Keep in mind that rhythm and timing may change once you find your final music, so don't bother tightly timing your picture cuts to the music, unless you are certain of its licensing status and your decision to keep it in the scene.

Also spend some time mapping out where music will be 1. a low background presence under other the sound elements in a scene, 2. playing at a significant level along with sound effects, ambience and/or dialogue, or 3. carrying the scene all on its own with no other tracks playing. Knowing your sonic goal for every scene saves time and better prepares you for mixing.

## NOT-SO-SILENT FILMS

Music can lay low underneath the dialogue or it can capture the audience by taking over the soundtrack. Check out how many times music takes center stage in your favorite films, trumping the dialogue, sound effects, and ambiences. It's probably more often than you realize. The right music can sometimes express everything you want to say in a scene.

Audiences of all ages actually love silent films, whether they realize it or not. That's not to say that there isn't any sound at all. 'Silent' pictures are those that rely on the music to interpret their

emotions. Animations, music videos, action movies, romantic films, even documentaries and reality shows have scenes that ride exclusively on music. It's a timeless, effective device for filmmakers of all genres to engage audiences.

There is a classic scene in Stanley Kubrick's *2001: A Space Odyssey* where the man-ape first uses a bone as a hammer and a memorable, triumphant fanfare is all we hear as he smashes the tool on all the rocks around him. No Foley, no backgrounds, no production sound. At this point *2001* is essentially a silent film – like its predecessors made before 1927 – and expresses itself *exclusively* through the powerful score.

The impact of music over picture is timeless and can offer a welcome 'breath' between dialogue heavy scenes. Indeed, some on screen action is self evident and better described through a score or a song than through dialogue. Characters falling in love, chase scenes, scenes of suspense, fascination, or discovery are easily told through the action and music alone. 'Silencing' a scene with music a powerful device – unique to action-based arts such as film, theater, and dance – and crosses language barriers to reach a universal audience.

Sometimes you want to cut picture in time with the rhythm of the music. Here is a trap that many editors fall into; it's a chicken or egg type of problem: do you cut the picture to the music, or the music to the picture? Where you've made your final choices of music, you're able to edit video to the rhythm and phrasing of the music. Doing so creates that dynamic punch of sound and picture hitting the viewer simultaneously.

The dilemma comes from needing a final cut of the picture before sound work begins, yet being unable to finish editing until you have found final music. The disadvantage of watching a rough cut picture is outweighed by the benefit of attaining that all important, dynamic sync-lock between music and picture later. Since swapping out the music will mean changes in rhythm and phrasing, the timing of video cuts will be off, and the impact gets lost. There are two ways to remedy this.

🎧 Rough-cut your scenes to temp tracks and leave extra footage around each shot for further fine tuning later. In other words, don't perfect your edits without final, cleared music. Import a small extra margin of footage before and after the log and capture points for each shot (as you probably would anyway). This leaves you with video handles that you may need to alter the timing of each shot in order to sync it to music of a different rhythm later. This method works best when edits don't have to closely match on action or where there is no dialogue to sync to.

You will, however, need to commit to an exact running time for these scenes, regardless of music choice. Since the video and audio need to be exported for audio mixing, it is vital that overall sync be maintained; the audio and video need to be back in sync following this loosely-edited section. However, edits within the scene do not have to be final. You can later re-edit the video during the scene to match future music. However, its end point needs to be decided upfront since you need to know exactly on which frame the picture will return to sync. This is particularly effective for scenes that fade to black without synched music hits at the end.

🎧 Or, take care of licensing and procurement upfront – or at least get estimates of availability, cost, and delivery time of the music – and decide on final music choices as soon as possible, before making your final cut. Use low-quality versions of your final music choices if necessary while editing, as long as they are rhythmically accurate. Note that the musical timing of tracks ripped from CD or obtained on the internet, especially MP3s and other compressed formats, can vary greatly. Skips and dropouts from flawed encoding or inaccurate CD readers are common, so always strive to obtain high-quality masters where possible, even when using a track temporarily.

## Licensing pre-existing music

If you have a budget for music or if you intend for your picture to play to large audiences, you'll want to get familiar with music licensing. Some budget independents forget to consider the seriousness of proper licensing due to financial restrictions and the lack of time for post production. Acquiring permission to sync music to picture requires significant research and can become a tiring process, especially for a full length feature. For indies with any kind of budget, it's best to hire a good Music Supervisor to control those precious funds (and future payouts). However, if you're going it solo you'll first want to understand basic music licensing concepts and then how to go about procuring permission from music publishers, production houses, and record labels.

Music licensing involves some understanding of copyright law. (Note: Keep in mind that this section offers general information only. Please don't let this be a substitute for a detailed discussion of copyright law, contracts, or music licensing. Music licensing is serious business and it's always a good idea to consult an attorney or other expert.)

Recorded music breaks down to two legal components: the written composition or work, and the recording, or manifestation, of that work – which cost some record label (or independent artist) time and money to produce and manu-facture. Composers, performers, and producers need to eat too, and performing rights organizations like ASCAP, BMI, and SESAC collect royalty fees based on airplay or public performance for the parties of ownership of a musical work. In addition to royalties, musicians earn their living through upfront flat rate 'sync fees' paid by the licensor for use of their work. Sync fees can get expensive, from a few dollars a track (for the smallest audiences) into six figures for advertising purposes and large scale viewings.

You need to license pre-existing music when your film will play to a group of people beyond a circle of your family and friends. (This constitutes a public performance.) In fact, you need to obtain two licenses: the right to marry the composition to picture (a 'sync license') and access to the recorded work, a 'master use.' The sync right is granted at the discretion of the music publisher (the copyright owner or their publishing agent) while the master fees go to the record label or whomever controls the actual recording.

There are a couple of exceptions where it's not necessary to obtain two licenses. One is when music being played in the background of a shot is innocently and unintentionally picked up by your production microphone, such as on a documentary or news broadcast shoot. The other is if you plan to re-record the track yourself, you will then own your own master recording, and thus will not need to obtain a master license, just a publishing (sync) license from the copyright owner.

### License pre-existing musical recordings in two steps:

### 1.  Sync license

The first priority is to clear the publishing, or sync, rights from the party who controls the composition. While there are sometimes several master recordings of a composition to consider for licensing, there is only one publishing entity to grant you permission to use the composition at all – in *any* recorded version. Plan ahead: allow one week to six months, depending on the parties involved to clear licenses.

In order to request and negotiate a sync license from the music publisher, you'll need a way to contact them. Sometimes the publisher is simply the artist themselves, and sometimes it's tricky to track them down.

🎧 Search the Harry Fox Agency (HFA) (http://www.harryfox.com/) to find most music publishers. If the party of ownership is not listed at Harry Fox, probe the performing rights associations in order of popularity: ASCAP (http://www.ascap.com/ace/), BMI (http://repertoire.bmi.com/startpage.asp) and SESAC (http://www.sesac.com/repertory/sRepertorySQL.asp) (Note: These four agencies can only tell you about rights held within the United States.)

CD liner notes also contain publishing credits for each track, but contact info may not be so visible. You can try asking the record label to refer you to the publisher.

### 2.  Master license

When wanting to clear the master you can use the standard procedure of contacting the record label or other entity who owns the recording. You can also try to appeal to the artist themselves, if you can find their contact information. You may be able to get them to lobby their publishing agent and/or record company on your behalf. When an artist feels there are benefits to featuring their music in your film, they may be able to expedite negotiations with both parties.

🎧 If you're not going through a music licensing agent or production house, the standard procedure is to contact the label and request a master-use license. Find the record company's contact info on the back cover of the CD, at the artist's website, or at the album's product page at a retailer site such as amazon.com.

Later, if you plan to sell a soundtrack (online or through a record label or other distribution network) you'll need to get a mechanical license (and a new, associated master-use license). At that stage you will need additional permission from the artist or composer. Since it's customary to outline separate types of uses in separate legal agreements, new-use permissions get negotiated separately, at a later date, from the original sync and master use licenses you procured. Artists and composers receive mechanical royalties (based on physical and online product sales and rentals) from a soundtrack in addition to the writing and publishing royalties they receive for performance, airplay, and distribution.

## Budgeting and fees

Although every type of film approaches its music budget differently, let's consider what an independent feature would budget for pre existing music in a picture. A general rule of thumb is that 10% of the overall film budget gets earmarked for music. This may sound unrealistically high for a lot of indie filmmakers, however, who might budget 5% or less. It is the filmmaker's decision as to how recognizable or high-quality the music needs to be in order to enhance the film's message and enjoyment.

Although it's important to know as soon as possible in order to get the licensing ball rolling, costs of using pre existing music from production houses, licensing agents, and labels vary widely, making discussion difficult. For film festival or industrial/internal corporate use, common outlay might range from $200 to $500 for the master and the same for the sync (publishing) right. Again, it's hard to say but the cost for using under 30 seconds of a music composition showing on up to 250 screens might increase to $1000 per side. This is in itself on the lower side of indie film broadcast rates and can increase to $3000 or more per side depending on territories, length of term, type of picture, and other factors. If your film gets picked up by a network or studio, they may end up paying the performance royalties or they may try to negotiate a buyout.

## STEP DEALS

Using pre-existing, published music can easily seem like a cost prohibitive effort. But there are alternatives to paying high upfront sync fees with music publishers, labels, *and* composers. We've mentioned that the film's potential success creates a bargaining position for future compensation based on broadcast, distribution, downloads, webcasts, and perhaps also product sales. And thus film music deals can be creatively structured based on stages of the film's potential success.

If your picture is currently running in the festival circuit and has a real possibility of being sold, distributed, or syndicated you may have that extra bargaining power. Go directly to the label, artist, or production music house and tell them outright that this picture has a good chance of being picked up and aired widely. They can help push for rights clearance and negotiate better sync fees. Or negotiate a step deal: 'I can pay you this much now, and if it gets picked up, I will pay you this much more at that point.'

Step deals may sound like a no-brainer to help save a film-maker's ever-diminishing funds but experienced producers know to be very careful when negotiating these types of deals. Consider the prospect of selling or licensing the picture: the studio or network that picks up the film will have to buy out these prior negotiated contracts in order to gain a clear 'title' to the picture. If these future obligations lead to high costs, it could influence the studio's decision to pick up the picture. In extreme cases, heavy prior contract obligations could kill the picture deal because the business is no longer worth it to the studio.

Take the case of one rather successful and beautifully-done indie picture, made recently for a modest $3 million. The producers made step deals for various services – mostly music. These deals totaled about $18 million in additional payouts based on the level of box office success the film achieved (around $20 million).

Hopefully, the royalties from DVD sales made up the difference!

Only you can gauge how much you should leverage your picture's future. Certainly ask friends and read online forums, but start by visualizing your film's success as a realistic possibility. Put yourself in that future place where you are negotiating with a major studio. What kind of step deals will you wish you had – and hadn't – made?

Cost of license fees go down if you only need use permissions in small territories. Only showing the picture at a year-end corporate party? Reduce the scope of the request and negotiate for lower fees. Conversely, music for a film's opening titles will demand heftier fees. Everything is negotiable, or at least negotiated. A filmmaker with big plans for a picture should always start negotiations with a territory of 'the universe' and a term of 'perpetuity.' However, if this film won't ever need to play on all 2500 to 3000 movie screens coast to coast, then money can be saved by scaling negotiations accordingly.

Wedding videographers and small productions with no plans for distribution can license professional tracks for very small audiences at extremely low rates through a personal use music agent. It's sort of like group health insurance. And remember that royalty free stock music is always available, even via the internet, and at last minute.

If you are making a not for profit picture – one which will never receive any type of compensation – you may be able to procure 'Creative Commons' and/or public domain licensing of composed works at low or no cost. In the next section we'll look into these and every other possible way to procure music.

## Finding music for your film

We've seen that the costs involved in using pre existing music in a film range from virtually nothing to utterly exorbitant. Even more daunting is that the research, negotiation, and administration involved can add upwards of six months to your post production schedule and can be so involved as to require a specialist's skill. Make no mistake – artists and record companies have a complex system in place that helps them get the rewards they deserve for their work. The good news is that today's independent filmmaker has a virtually endless body of work from which to choose and a number of ways to legally acquire rights to this music. Let's sketch a quick profile of the most common resources for pre existing music: (Note: This section assumes United States copyright and licensing laws. For detailed information and for other countries, please check with a legal professional.)

| Resource | Pros | Cons | Licensing issues | Cost |
|---|---|---|---|---|
| **Music in Creative Commons or the public domain** | Free sync license for compositions and arrangements in the public domain. | Limited availability of modern works; still must pay a master use or re-record the music. Variety of CC licensing agreements to navigate/interpret. Often limited to non-commercial use. | Sync license of CC arrangements are free; license of an existing master still needs to be cleared in the usual manner. Must give proper credit. | Free sync license; cost for using a particular existing master recording varies and could fall into any of the categories below. |
| **Stock music libraries** (e.g., Sound Ideas or The Hollywood Edge) | Able to purchase individual tracks or entire libraries of music quickly and easily; available via internet. | Generic ('MIDI') or dated sounding tracks at worst, good quality at best; some gems can be found; particularly useful for backgrounds. | Usually none, you can use the music for any sync or non-sync purpose. | Flat rate; royalty-free; As low as $1/track, $200+ for a collection of themed tracks. |
| **Production music libraries** (e.g., DeWolfe Music, Killer Tracks) | Creates source music in house specifically for TV, film, events, etc. More unique than straight stock music. | Music is still somewhat generic since is produced for commercial vs. artistic purposes. | Very straight-forward; license is negotiated for and restricted to an intended use. | $200-500 for festival use; negotiable; can often be as reasonable as stock libraries |

| Resource | Pros | Cons | Licensing issues | Cost |
|---|---|---|---|---|
| **Music licensing agents** (e.g., The Orchard) | Large selection of independent music since they aggregate a wide variety of artists worldwide. | High quality music but relatively unknown artists. More instrumental availability than vocal music. | Handles licensing; license is negotiated for and restricted to an intended use. | $200–500 for festival use; $10k-15k for nationwide theatrical release. Scaled based on the piece, sync purpose and intended audience. |
| **Personal use music licensing agencies** (e.g., Zoom License) | Access to major and minor label artists; does the legwork for you when dealing with labels and publishers; expedites negotiations with labels; possible option for web broadcasts. | Restricted use. | License is for personal use only: non-broadcast, non-distribution up to 25 copies of a project. Appropriate for videographers and multimedia presentations. | $3-10 total per track. Upcharge of ~$300 for web streaming license. |
| **Independent musicians, unsigned artists** (e.g., via MySpace) | Fresh talent; wide variety of genres; ability to negotiate directly without administrative overhead; ability to avoid obtaining master license and re-create covers ('soundalikes') of well known songs at low cost. | Production quality varies widely with artist's experience; artist may be inexperienced with contracts, deadlines and negotiations. | Need sync license from music publisher; master is usually owned by the producer. | $100-$5000+ per track; negotiable private contract between filmmaker and artist (or artist's manager). |

| Resource | Pros | Cons | Licensing issues | Cost |
|---|---|---|---|---|
| **Artists on independent labels** | Large selection of high quality, often recogniz-able (popular) original music. | Cost could be a major factor depending on the artist; use restrictions. | Depends on the label. Probably a more expedi-tious licensing process than the majors. | $500 to $50,000+ depending on sync require-ments, artist popularity, desire for exposure, etc. |
| **Artists on major labels** | Catalogs the most well-known artists of all time. | Length of time to license; possible refusal of license; cost; use restric-tions. | From 1-2 months min. to 4-6 months max; least flexi-ble terms. | $500 to $50,000+ depending on sync require-ments, artist popularity, desire for exposure, etc. |

(**NOTE:** Unless specified, estimated fees shown are costs are per track, **per side.** Double this figure for both sync and master licenses.)

🎧 Public domain (any work published before 1923, and many recent works at the discretion of the writer) or music copyrighted under one of the several Creative Commons partial copyright licenses allows a user certain usage rights without paying sync fees. Costs to license an existing master recording of the work would still be determined by the owner of the master. If, for example, you con-tracted a pianist and recording engineer – both on a work for hire basis – to create a recording of Erik Satie's *Gymnopédie No. 1*, since you paid for the session and performance you own the master and can use it as you wish, royalty-free. (www.pdinfo.com/list.htm has some great info and search tools for public domain works pub-lished post 1923.) Creative Commons (www.creativecommons. org) is a non-profit agency that allows copyright owners to give up some rights to a work, placing it somewhere between public domain and fully copyrighted. Their various licensing agreements allow some types of sync-free and royalty-free use. Use restrictions vary depending on the rights the creator chose to relinquish, but most commonly include a not-for-commercial-use requirement.

🎧 Royalty free (stock) music spans a wide range of quality from generic sounding, widely available MIDI files and ringtones to unique vocal and instrumental productions that begin to sound like real music. These tracks can make for some particularly cost effective background music, especially with their sometimes convincing classical reproductions. They're the easiest to obtain: just point, click, and buy – one track at a time or as a library. And the contract is usually liberal; the music can usually be used for just about anything you want (except sampling and commercial reproduction of course). Royalty free music is available for quick purchase one track at a time online but is often sold as a library and delivered on CD or portable hard drive. A quick keyword search of "royalty free music" returns thousands of hits – well, perhaps not hits – let's call them music choices.

🎧 Production libraries usually have composers on staff, writing music for TV and also film, specializing in seasonal music, music

for specific events and purposes, and the hot styles of the moment. Quality ranges from stock music quality to rather high-quality commercial productions. Rates are pre determined and scaled, probably based on subjective track quality or demand of the piece. Networks pay the performance royalties or film studios will negotiate a buyout for production music. Some vendors of this type of production music include: Majong Music, One Media Productions (for covers and karaoke versions of songs), Nightengale Music, and DeWolfe Music.

🎧 Music producers and artists have seen the distribution options for their music blow wide open in the last 10 to 15 years. No longer confined to major or minor labels, producers and artists can license their music non-exclusively with them, meaning artists can offer their music through several of these services and use their music for other non exclusive purposes as they like. This is good news to filmmakers on the hunt for new music.

Independent music licensing agencies such as Orchard Music Services (TheOrchard.com), Pump Audio (PumpAudio.com), Ioda (www.iodalliance.com), and InGrooves (www.InGrooves. com) offer one-stop music shopping and rights clearance. They are aggregators of most any musical style in the world. The Orchard's style is to take your sync requests and present you with suggestions from their library of over a million songs for consideration, or let you browse them online. Pump Audio lets you browse their catalog on a hard drive called a Pump Box, allowing you discover what you like at your leisure. Quality ranges fairly widely but can be among the most professional sounding music you'll have access to without dealing with the big labels.

Prices for these aggregated music houses cover a wide range and can be very reasonable for filmmakers. It depends largely on the size of your audience and the integration of the song into the picture. Using a track as background music versus foreground or title music will generally impart very different rates. Feature films and advertising clients make up the high range of their client base.

Some of these agents connect their artists to iTunes, eMusic. com, PureVolume.com, and similar sites, bringing worldwide distribution into the hands of relatively unknown artists, and online shopping to consumers. These sites are another great resource for filmmakers to get acquainted with new music. Some allow reverse lookup searches to find the artist or even music publisher of a particular track.

- Personal use music licensing agents such as Zoom licensing (www.ZoomLicense.com) are a niche market option for very small productions. They use their relationships with major labels to pre-clear tracks for use in wedding videos, corporate meetings, and other very limited audiences. They've pre-negotiated rates with the record companies and publishers and the costs to a filmmaker are almost negligible. A web-streaming license is usually available at additional cost. They're another resource for obtaining cover versions of hit tunes for set fees, much like a production house. The drawback is that these inexpensive music licenses cannot be reassigned for broadcast or distribution use.

- Artists and bands want exposure. Some songwriters and bands will go to great lengths to gain exposure for their music. Online portfolio sites like MySpace have created a revolution in the availability of independent music for listening, research, artist exposure, connecting artists with their audience and peers, and bringing the music to the people. Here are just a few places where you might find these artists:

www.myspace.com
www.mandy.com
www.versusmedia.com
www.productionhub.com
www.fanfilmsforum.com
www.harmony central.com
www.craigslist.org
www.musicyellowpages.com
www.theindustrydirectory.com/
    pages/Film_TV_Music/index.html

If you're a student or new to filmmaking, another great way to find musicians is by posting flyers around colleges, universities, and technical schools – or placing ads at school websites. Google for sites where musicians buy and sell gear: you might find a gigs oriented classifieds forum where you can put the feelers out for musicians who want to be part of a soundtrack.

Negotiating with independent artists, producers, and managers is an open playing field and it's best to do some research first. If you have licensed music through a label or a production house prior to dealing with an independent producer, you'll have at least some background in contracts. There are many potential bargaining points. For example, less experienced, independent musical artists are often willing to give up upfront fees for the prospect of generating royalties or simply gaining exposure. In every case, however, it's always best to put all expectations of schedules, terms, and compensation in writing. The table in the next section of this chapter compares the bargaining scenario of filmmaker versus composer and offers some information relevant to dealing with any type of independent artist.

🎧 Both independent and major labels offer the prospect of obtaining recognizable songs for your film – for a sometimes hefty fee. This is the most expensive way to license music. It's worth pursuing, however, even if you're on a budget because labels will sometimes be sympathetic to your cause.

Be prepared when contacting record companies and music publishers for use permissions. They will probably ask for details about how you will use the music, whether it will be sync, background, or opening/closing music, the names of actors in the film, whether intended distribution is DVD only, theatrical only, or all media, and other pertinent questions – anything that will give them an idea of how their music will be represented in your film.

Plan ahead: give yourself plenty of leeway – up to six months for some sync requests, less for a label to come back to you with a quote for using the master recording. Granting of sync licenses are at the discretion of whoever owns the publishing. It's up to them if they want their music heard in the context that you want it played. And as mentioned earlier, appealing to the artist directly may help expedite the process.

Sometimes it costs larger records companies and publishers too much to carry out the licensing administration and they will refuse to grant permission. In this case, a particular track that you have your heart set on may not be within your budget. If you have been granted a sync license, your options now are to seek out another existing master or pay for re-recording the tune yourself.

🎧 Lastly, let's also mention that there are informational resources all over the net that can be of great help in both pre-production research and in post. Sites such as www.AllMusic.com offer 30-second clips, album reviews, and the opportunity to learn about artists' backgrounds. Say you need a Brooklyn hip-hop artist with music from 1995, a site like this catalogs that kind of information about artists. www.OceanParkMusic.com is a commercial music licensor but also offers a comprehensive link library of indie music labels. Where there is a need, there is help.

## Custom scores and working with composers

A quality custom music score can shape the texture of your scenes and bring out subtle emotions as only you the filmmaker can imagine. It also puts a stamp of professionalism on a film and is, in the end, well worth the time and expense of finding and working with a composer.

### Enlist a composer's services

🎧 Search for, interview, and decide on a composer. Audition work samples online or solicit reels and resumes through ads. Meet with your best candidates and show them the film in its current state. Check the sidebar on artists wanting exposure for some sites where you're likely to find composers.

🎧 Once you've decided on a composer, discuss rates and terms. Everything is negotiable, but indie film composer rates vary based on budget and relationship. Usually they are paid per minute of music or as an overall flat fee for a certain deliverable. Front-end money depends also on back-end negotiations (deferred payments due to future film sales or a distribution deal). Remember, contracts are your friend and it pays to hire a lawyer if needed.

🎧 Negotiate a contract and give them a copy of the picture in QuickTime (or other requested) format. A script may be helpful as well. Map out each scene. How present should music be in each scene? Where are you sure of what you want to hear and where are you open to interpretation? Direct him as to what you want the audience to feel in each scene. Exaggerate your sentiments, amplifying your passion for the film so he really begins to understand the emotional heights each scene could reach.

Discuss instrumentation choices (Orchestral? Electronica? Rock?), sparseness or busy-ness of the pieces, tempo, and any other specific musical direction that may help the two of you get on the same page. Talk about the films or directors that inspired the making of this picture, in terms of style or emotion.

## A CONFLICT OF INTEREST?

While the director and composer have the same goal of making the best picture the best they can, the business relationship between them is riddled with apparent contradictions.

## Clash of the filmmaker and composer

| | Director/ Producer | Composer (copyright owner) |
|---|---|---|
| **Negotiations** | Tries to leverage exposure, film credit, contacts and their reputation in lieu of payment. | Wants to secure front-end payment, back-end royalties, and ownership rights at every stage of creation and distribution. Sometimes willing to sacrifice future rights for exposure or credit. |
| **Front-end compensation** | Wants to pay as little upfront as possible. | Wants as much money upfront as possible, paid at predictable time intervals. |
| **Back-end compensation** | Wants composers to work on a work for hire basis with no responsibility of back end compensation. | Wants broadcast and distribution publishing royalties for every media: screen/TV/ web/DVD. |

The composer retains any rights to her music not expressly given away in the contract. But composers need to distinguish between work for hire and other types of agreements. If not considered work for hire, a contract may specify that their work is subject to a 'belts and suspenders' condition. This may translate to the composer involuntarily assigning their copyright over to the film production company. As always, consult a legal representative for the proper language and meaning.

Terms can be negotiable. A production company may acquire the right to use the compositions for a film's five year release schedule. The possibility of extending this can be written into the original contract. During any period, however, a composer should normally retain the right to promote their own work via normal advertising outlets.

A composer registers their work with their performing rights organizations, which collects, tracks, and dispenses publishing royalties as her work is broadcast or performed. Broadcast compensation

|  | Director/ Producer | Composer (copyright owner) |
|---|---|---|
| **Territories and terms** | Wants exclusive rights to all music, cleared for all media (cinema, DVD, CD/soundtrack, etc.), in all territories of the world. Wants to be able to universally exploit the composer's material. | Wants their music cleared in as few territories for as limited a term as possible. Wants the ability to negotiate additional usage rights every step of the way as the film garners more exposure. Wants to retain rights to promote their compositions physically and online. |

is tracked primarily through network video editors' cue sheets, that list every musical piece used in all on-air programming.

Once you've got the ball rolling, get the business stuff out of the way first: set up payment, terms, dates and expectations before you start working. The composer needs to know the future potential of the film in order to give the director a good upfront rate. The director can leverage back end royalties when she knows the picture will get heavy distribution. Step-deals offer many more options for both sides. When both parties are aware of the various forms of compensation and are sensitive to the other's position, it shouldn't be difficult to structure a deal where everyone wins.

🎧 Some novice and student composers may be willing to work for experience and credit only. It's particularly important for these budding talents that they get a copy of the film for their reels and that they feel like an important part of the project, getting positive feedback and experience in the process.

🎧 Set realistic goals and stick to them. Be proactive: don't go too long without hearing from your composer and reviewing their progress.

🎧 If you engage a composer before achieving final cut, ask for rhythmically-accurate rough mixes in order have something to which you can edit picture. The composer can always complete the orchestrations at a later time.

# Music editing

Once you've obtained music, licensed music, and placed the final tracks into the audio sequence you'll want to cut them tightly to picture. The usual challenges with music editing include editing glitches and pops, controlling levels, and equalization.

A preventative approach to avoid clicks and pops is to cut an audio clip only at points where the waveform meets the horizontal zero-crossing line. At these points the waveform has no amplitude and thus no volume spike results. This can be difficult with stereo files, however, since their two unique right and left channels don't often meet the zero-crossing line at the same moment. In addition, music has to start and end at specific times in order to line up with events in the picture. Enter fades and crossfades.

## MUSIC SERVES THE STORY

Cutting music in time to picture may seem almost routine, but it is a delicate art. Music editors are very sensitive to the emotional difference that a couple of frames, or decibels, make. When editing a picture it's easy to become 'too close to it' and lose sight of the nuances of emotional timing. It's important to take breaks, get other opinions, and keep perspective.

The director – and the film – is telling a story and music should always serve the interest of that story, even when it takes center stage (as discussed earlier in 'music takes over'). When music comes in loud on a hard scene transition, the emotional impact should be for good reason and at a carefully-considered volume, otherwise the audience may get desensitized by the film's unruly dynamic range. When music creeps up under two lovers in an embrace, exactly what is the right moment for it to hit full volume and have the melody line come in? The difference between turning the audience on and turning them off can even come down to a type of crossfade!

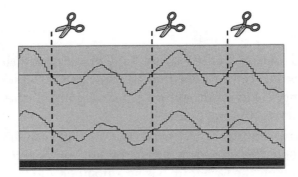

For glitch-free cuts without having to make short crossfades, cut where waveforms meet the zero-crossing line.

When cutting music to picture, don't let music lead the emotional shift; let it come out of the emotion being created. Time it so that it expresses what is *already* being said through the dialogue, character actions, or whatever is driving the meaning of the scene. Let it support the story, not try and create it.

## Music-editing basics

- It's mentioned several times in this book, but remember to always work with the best quality WAV or AIF file you can get a hold of. There is no making up for lack of fidelity at the source.

- When cutting music clips, get in the habit of adding short fade-ins and fade-outs to eliminate glitches. Use inaudible one-frame or half-frame fades so the music seems to start (or end) instantaneously.

- While equal-power crossfades generally keep volumes consistent in the middle of a crossfade, equal-gain crossfades sometimes sound better. It really depends on the source audio and in and out volumes of the two clips. Just try them and listen to the difference. Also review the sidebar on crossfades in the 'Ambiences' chapter for a full discussion on types of crossfades.

- With music processing, remember that less is more. Keep all music tracks as dynamic and pristine as possible: don't compress, EQ, or apply other effects unless absolutely necessary. To a finished mix, every plug-in means another generation loss. Also, every digital-to-analog and analog-to-digital conversion is another loss, and will eventually enhance the 'grain' or pixilation of the waveform. It's all too easy to tarnish a polished master with repeated processing.

# Looping and extending musical passages

Sometimes you want a musical passage to play longer than the music clip's running time. Video editors often need to fill out a scene by repeating instrumental sections of a musical piece. When music doesn't last long enough to cover the video that you want it to, you have two choices: look for longer music or customize the fit. Luckily it's not hard to extend and loop sections of music. Find the section you want to loop, copy and paste keeping the rhythm in time, and smooth out the cuts. Rhythmic music like pop music is easy to work with since the drums are visually obvious in the clip's waveform. Music without strong downbeats is more challenging.

If you are musically inclined and can count bars and beats when you hear a piece of music, you've got an advantage. Knowing where beats one, two, three, and four are will help you line up measures in a more pleasing musical way. Let's first create a musical extension:

### Lengthening a music clip

🎧 If you haven't already, import and place your chosen music on to a track in the DAW. Route the track to the MUSIC subgroup.

🎧 Set the in point of the music as you like it. Perform any initial fade in as you normally would.

🎧 Duplicate the track below the current one. You now have two music clips, directly above and below each other.

🎧 Working with the new version, roughly cut out around the passage you want to loop and discard the rest of that version. Slide it over to the right to the approximate location of where it will pick up where the first version ends.

🎧 Solo this second track and listen for an obvious reference point, like a strong downbeat on beat one of a musical bar. It doesn't have to be the starting point of the extension or loop but it should be visually obvious.

🎧 Locate a similar downbeat toward the end of the original clip that is also on beat one of a bar. Line up the strong beat in the beginning of the new version to the strong beat you just found toward

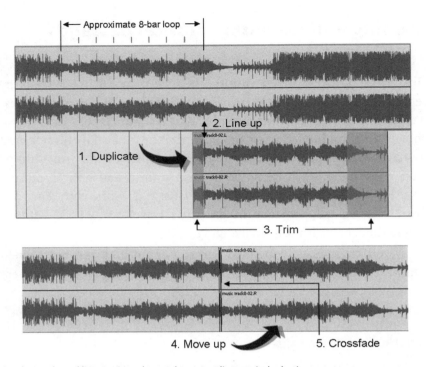

Overlap tracks and line up strong beats when extending musical selections.

the end of the original clip. Also pay attention to phrasing. Most music sounds best when cut into passages of 4, 8, or 16 bars so time your edit points to these natural musical phrases. You should be able to pull off completely invisible (inaudible) edits this way.

- Zoom in and visually line up the two beats by nudging the new clip around until it vertically lines up with the beats in the original clip.

- Cut the original clip just before the reference beat. Delete the remainder of the clip.

- Cut the new clip an extra beat or so before the first cut and move the new clip up to the original clip's track. It should overlap by a beat or so.

- Crossfade the clips. Move your crossfade to just *before* the reference beat (where it is least audible) and minimize its length. Generally, a crossfade length of around 5 or 10 frames will work; in some cases you might want a longer transition if it helps a drum fill or key change sound better.

🎧 Zoom out, play back, and adjust the crossfade length as necessary. When you're satisfied with your new musical extension, feel free to delete the second 'work track' you created (or hold on to it for next time).

You can create a musical *loop* – something you can copy and paste indefinitely to extend a selection – by applying the same principles of cutting a complete musical phrase out of a music clip. Here's an example of how to make a 16 bar loop starting on, say, bar 64 of a musical piece.

### Loop a musical section

🎧 Again, copy your music clip onto a new track to create an edit version. Solo the new track for easy listening.

🎧 In the new clip, find bar 64, the first beat of the first bar you want to loop (bar 64, beat 1 for example) and make a rough cut just before this beat.

🎧 Play the music, count 16 bars, and visually locate beat 1 of the next (17th) bar. In this example, you'd be looking for beat 1 of bar 81. Roughly cut the clip just after this beat and discard what's before and after it. This new loop is about 16 bars long, with an extra beat or so before both the start and end points.

🎧 Cut the old track at beat 81. Discard the portion on the right.

🎧 Vertically line up the new clip's bar 64, beat 1 exactly below the old clip's bar 81, beat 1. Zoom in close and get them in perfect sync.

🎧 Move the new clip up to the old track. It will overlap the old clip by about a beat. Crossfade them. Audition and select the crossfade type that sounds the best.

🎧 Adjust the crossfade length shorter or longer, whatever sounds most musical.

🎧 Copy and paste the new loop again as needed, using the blank track for editing as you did before.

# More ideas for using music

## *Transitions*

🎧 Once you've imported a music track, it is time to cut it up and place it. (However, you must, of course, abide to the terms of any agreements that specify where and how music tracks must be used.) Consider which parts of the song best present the emotion you want to portray. You can start at the second verse, use only an instrumental section, or the chorus, etc., according to what part of the music works best with the picture. Remember when making cuts to use short crossfades to prevent clicks and pops.

🎧 Consider sneaking the music in gradually under the previous scene – it creates a foreshadowing sense that gets the viewer excited about the upcoming scene. The music can start 2 seconds, 5 seconds, or more before the scene change. Keep it low in the mix, fade it in slowly during the prior scene, and go to full volume on the cut.

🎧 Starting a scene with the strong downbeat of a pop or rock tune brings power to a scene transition. Furthermore, hitting a scene change with a strong vocal melody punctuates the narrative with song lyrics, waking the audience up even more.

🎧 Doubling up hard music starts with musical sound effects like sweeps and falls or with gunshots or other types of hits can add character and make a transition even more powerful.

## *Drones*

🎧 Using drones instead of music is not only cost effective but can also add an ominous, floating presence to a scene. Thrillers and sci-fi films create many of their moods with drones alone. There are stock libraries of drones available from most major library manufacturers, or you can make your own.

🎧 If you have access to a synthesizer, check out the 'pad' patches. Mixing an original keyboard drone into a scene is easy and is a great start to creating a painlessly unique musical soundtrack. Slow moving, one note synthesizer melodies can easily add originality to your movie. Select a sound (keyboard patch) that works with the scene and keep your melody simple with long sustaining notes.

## Chapter 13

# Home Stretch: Special Effects

The little things really matter when you're absorbed in a movie. Special effects are the silver stars that make one picture stand out from the rest: brief audio and visual moments of technical genius that took hours upon hours to create. The viewer will never know how much time went into developing that CGI effect, or how hard it was to work in a hard-to-shoot-in location, or what it took to design a special sound effect from scratch. But these effects make a memorable impression. At these moment audiences become engaged – the filmmaker has won her audience over and her film gets burned on their brain. The long hours of attention to detail finally pay off. There are a number of common special effects that sound editors and re-recording mixers use for added realism – or surrealism.

## Tiny speakers: put it through a telephone

To make dialogue or music sound like it's coming through a telephone (or radio, etc.) first, think like a telephone. The effect of a small speaker is to limit the frequency spectrum while compressing the signal's dynamic range. These signals are also riddled with distortion. No problem, since these are three effects – equalization, compression, and distortion – that we can apply quite easily with plug-ins in any DAW. Used where appropriate, the effect can add a unique flavor to both dialogue and music.

- The frequency range of a land-line telephone is about 300Hz-3.5kHz. Set up your EQ for a pretty sharp high-pass filter (HPF) at 300Hz and a low-pass filter (LPF) at 3.5k. This alone may give you the effect you're going for.

- If you want to take it up a notch try a little compression: a ratio of about 3:1, threshold so that the compressor is working most of the time (i.e., the gain reduction meter is sweeping from -3 to -9dB. Attack and release settings should be set for dialogue, around 1ms and 200ms, respectively. Note that heavy compression will lower your overall signal level and you'll need to apply a few dB of make-up gain to get it back.

- Most DAWs have an overdrive or distortion plug-in, generally used with guitar sounds. Try putting your new frequency-limited sound through it. Play with the settings, season to taste, and stay on the conservative side until you've had a chance to live with it a little while.

For telephone dialogue, these techniques are usually enough for imitating either a land line *or* a mobile phone, although mobiles have smaller speakers and micro-phones. For replicating the sound of a radio with a very small speaker, try taking out even more lows, perhaps a HPF at 400 or 600Hz. For walkie-talkies, get a little more extreme – maybe compress a bit harder (increase the ratio and lower the threshold) and definitely add more distortion.

### Principle

A small speaker of any type will only be good at producing mid-range and high (treble) frequencies; it won't be able to recreate lows. It takes a larger driver (speaker cone) to pump out any kind of bass. If you're trying to recreate the effect of a speaker the size of the one that's in your cell phone, simple physics tells us to limit the frequency spectrum to a range appropriate to the size of the speaker.

## Massive ambience: put it in a huge room

We saw in the mixing chapter that in order to sound natural and realistic, every sound needs a sense of the space in which it occurs. Sound effects from stock libraries, ADR dialogue, or music made in a studio often sound *dry*; that is, without the natural reverberation of the room or space around the sound. It may be punchy and clear, but if every sound was that dry it would lead to a boring, lifeless, and unnatural mix.

🎧 To put sounds in a large space such as a church, club, or large music venue, add just enough hall reverb until you hear the sound start to smear. Best to do this on headphones, since headphones often exaggerate reverbs and delays. That way you won't add too much effect. Used occasionally, an extra-large reverb can add another dimension to a scene, where appropriate.

### *Principle*

Large untreated spaces combined with loud volume levels have a smearing effect on the sound. Its echoes ricochet off every hard surface and their levels build up in uneven phase responses (timing). The louder the sound, the harder the surfaces, the longer distance for the waves to travel, and the more of an effect the room will have on the sound. The larger the room, the louder the reverb, and the sound gets more washed-out and indistinct.

## The muffle: put it in the room next door

Say you've recorded some ADR that is supposed to sound like it's coming through a wall, from under a jacket, through a pillow, etc. This kind of speech is harder to hear since it is both lower in volume and has a skewed frequency response. That is, the high frequencies that help us understand consonants (approximately the 1 kHz-5 kHz range) get severely attenuated.

No problem. You don't have to re-record the ADR with the mic in the next room or anything like that. Just pull out your favorite equalizer, reach for the knobs of the highest frequency band, and set a high-shelf filter to cut the treble down to about 1kHz with a gradual slope. From there you'll need to adjust the frequency

or slope up or down to ear, according to your specific scene. Dense walls are going to attenuate the frequency spectrum more and require a steeper rolloff than a character speaking through the lapel of a coat. Some EQs allow you to adjust this slope, or Q factor. Mother Nature generally uses a smooth, not sharp, rolloff so start with the gradual curve of a low Q value and adjust from there.

You may want to apply a bit of reverb to convey how close or far the sound is. Use a room reverb for rooms, hall reverb for larger spaces, etc. If you're going for an intimate, close-sounding effect, skip the reverb. If the person should sound like they're talking from an adjacent hallway, a touch of a short hall reverb may add a realistic smearing effect.

### Principle

To understand what happens to sound that makes its way through walls, pillows, or other absorbent material calls for a little background in acoustics. Again, there are inherent differences in the frequency spectrum. High frequencies, with their shorter wavelengths, aren't robust enough to make it through dense materials. The lower the frequency, the longer the wavelength, and the greater chance of it making it out the other side.

In addition, the more porous the obstruction (like fabric curtains or a couch) the more energy gets inside it and bounces around in there, causing some attenuation. But it is *density* that is the real culprit. The denser the material, the more energy the wave loses as it tries to pass through it. That's why sheetrock, brick, and thick concrete walls make great soundproofing. They're heavy, and that's the point when it comes to sound *proofing* (as opposed to sound *treating*) a room. Both of these factors attenuate the signal – especially its higher frequencies where short, little waveforms get trapped in the material.

## Dream weaving

A dream sequence is an example of a place where you can get really creative. Almost anything goes for these points in a film. Classic techniques use delays and reverb to add tunnel like repetition and blurring of the sound. Try other plug-ins, like the *modulation* effects in your DAW. Effects such as chorus, phaser, and flanging can add plenty of psychedelic dreaminess.

Try routing a portion of the sound – via an FX channel – into an interesting reverb patch. Try a phaser or chorus inline after the reverb. Also play with EQ – maybe filter out some of the low-end (with a high-pass filter) to thin out the sound. Generally, heavy effects work better on short passages. The longer the dream, the clearer (less effected) the sound should be, just for practical purposes. Again, experiment for fun and check your work on headphones for clarity.

### Principle

There really aren't any hard and fast rules here since we are trying to create a deliberately unrealistic environment. Still, there are conventions that audiences are used to. Light reverb and delay make good starting points. Play with these as well as modulation effects, either as inserts or by routing a portion to an FX send bus with these plug-ins inserted on to the FX channels. Check your work with a friend to see if clarity and your intention are coming through.

## An approach to narration

Narration is normally left natural and dry in a mix, and effects are only used as necessary to maintain consistency among phrases. Re-recording mixers generally avoid time domain and modulation effects like reverb and chorus to keep narration clear and neutral. For certain actors (and certain film genres or broadcast intentions) some light compression may help keep levels consistent, though generally it is not needed.

In order to achieve a clear, full sound for your narration and voiceovers, you'll need a good studio condenser mic and some type of sound absorption. See the chapter on ADR and narration for a complete explanation. Leave the tracks dry. Remember to aim for consistent speech with no sibilance, plosives, odd mouth noises or words lost to low volume levels. Adjust loud syllables or words with cuts and crossfades as necessary.

### Principle

Narration, when well recorded and carefully edited for consistency, is best left untouched in mixing. The fullness and clarity of a studio condenser

mic, as opposed to the strong colorings of shotgun and lavaliere mics, automatically convey a warm and pleasing contrast to the dialogue. Conventional narration should be dry, present, warm, and 'natural' since it doesn't come from a particular diegetic place in the film.

## Creative panning

With dialogue centered, music in stereo, and sound effects coming from all over, the soundstage of a film mix can be large and dynamic, yet strongly focused if carefully arranged. This tip picks up on what we will revisit in the mixing chapter: 'the soundstage.'

There may be times when you want to deliberately disrupt the sense of focus. Dream sequences are a perfect example. Characters hearing voices in their head is another. These are good times to break convention, even with something normally predictable like panning. Try panning dreamy, effected dialogue partially left or right for effect.

Another example might be a drunk or drugged character where the world is moving strangely around him. One way to put the audience in his shoes and capture his sonic point of view is by panning the music or ambience slightly left, then leisurely to the right, then back to the left, etc. A strange effect, and strong, since it feels like the entire soundstage – and theater – is moving left to right like an amusement park ride. This is just one example of some bold, creative panning.

### Principle

Reverb helps us determine how close or far a sound is based on how clear or washed out it is. Multiformat (4, 6, 8, or 10-channel surround sound) options allow even greater control of two dimensional placement. Likewise, stereo panning locates a sound at a specific place along the horizontal left right axis. Normally, it is important for dialogue to be panned up the middle. Doing this creates a sort of sonic anchor for the film's entire soundtrack. It is precisely because the dialogue (or music, perhaps) stays centered that the audience feels a sense of place and focus throughout the duration of the soundtrack. But as with any convention, there are times for exceptions. Be conscious of when you are breaking that sonic 'third wall,' panning specific elements across the left and right spectrum for special effect.

## Doubling

So far we haven't touched on much beyond the basic plug-ins that come stock with most sequencers. Let's say you want to make something sound larger than life or perhaps confusingly busy. There are several ways to do this and one of them is by adding delay.

A short delay of 50-200ms will add a slightly time delayed doubling of the original sound. Set up on its own aux channel, a delay plug-in is a flexible tool that creates sound that can be further processed by subsequent channel inserts. Try following the delay with an EQ to filter out the low and/or high end frequencies, or a chorus for a washy, dreamy effect. And just a touch of reverb can send the delay back in the mix for an echo effect.

Crowd ambiences can benefit from this technique, making your walla (crowd ambiences) instantly bigger. The trick is to hide the delay by using very short feedback times, processing it through plug-ins, or keeping the delayed signal low in the mix to avoid creating an obviously audible doubling of the sound. When you've got it right, it can thicken the sound, creating a busy, spiraling cacophonous effect.

*Principle*

The delay effect duplicates the original sound at a time delay of your choice. It's used in music quite a bit but can be too obvious or contrived in film mixing. Used sparingly to create extra 'busyness,' it can be quite effective for short durations.

## More sound design, please

Sometimes we want to create an unnatural, unusual environment. Dream scenes, narratives set in the future or the past, or creative animations are just a few great candidates for some fresh, original sound design. Here are some popular processes for creating unusual sounds from SFX, drones, music, or even dialogue:

- 🎧 **Reverse:** reversing creates a strange, recognizable sweeping sound that establishes a time warp or disorienting kind of feeling. Try it on transitions and moments of drama, both for dialogue and sound effects. It's very recognizable, so be careful of losing your audience with overly long reversed segments or overuse.

- 🎧 **Pitch shift:** Remember the '80s film *Legend*, which pitch shifted all of the dialogue of the devil character? Pitch shifting a drone a half step or more can help it sound in key with the music. Too much of a shift and the sound will start to break up and get pretty useless (the threshold is different for every sound, you just have to try it).

- 🎧 **Time stretch:** Today's sequencers can easily stretch out a sound over time without changing its musical pitch (or frequency). Slowing something down – or speeding it up – is a quick way to get Foley footsteps in time with the action. Be careful, the sound will break up and get 'pixilated' if pushed too hard.

- 🎧 **Reverb:** Intentionally heavy reverb on a word of dialogue or a sound effect, at a moment you want to emphasize as important or other worldly, can add an unexpected dream like effect. Try a cathedral or church reverb, with a high pass filter (at 400Hz, maybe) after it to keep it from muddying up the low end (and maintain clarity, especially if there is music in the scene). Keep in mind that even a short burst of heavy 'verb on dialogue might obscure it to the point of unintelligibility, but can add interest to a special sound effect like a door slam or a word of dialogue transitioning into the next scene.

🎧 **Musical samples:** You may have worked with film sound effects libraries, but have you considered musical libraries, especially those for dance music? The production effects in a dance library offer a plethora of useful sweeps, swells, falls, keyboard drones, textures, drum hits, and computer sounds that can bring thrillers, animations, comedies, and any exciting film to life.

🎧 **Layers:** Again, let's mention that a drone under a sound effect, or a noise texture under the music, or some other layered combination, creates a relationship and depth that is greater than the two sounds themselves. Don't muddy it up, but when you want to venture outside the sonic box, a gunshot layered with a very light scream in the background, for example, is something you can get away with if you keep it subtle.

## Working methods for special processing

🎧 There are a few ways to go about working with clips that require special processing. If you find that you are re-using a particular effect (such as a certain reverb) many times, it's easiest to set up an aux send with that effect on it, and route a portion of the signal to the aux. Be sure to set the wet/dry slider in the plug-in dialog box to 100% wet when using it as an aux send. Put clips you want to have this effect on one audio track and route a portion of the track to the new aux send channel. Of course you can send multiple tracks to this bus, too, in varying amounts by adjusting their send levels.

🎧 Alternatively you could insert an effect on to the audio track, when only that track will need to use the effect. Some plug-ins have a wet/dry slider that allows you to adjust the portion of the signal you want to affect. This comes in handy when using the effect as an insert and you only want to slightly affect the signal.

🎧 Another way of applying effects to audio clips is with offline processing. This is a more decisive and relatively permanent way to affect the audio. It's good for saving CPU resources since you don't have to keep an insert or aux send effect active for the whole session. Great for applying a quick EQ or gain change that you're reasonably certain you won't need to change down the road. See the previous chapter on mixing for more ideas on working with plug-ins.

Always keep a backup handy of any clip on which you want to try some special processing. You might want to duplicate the clip first, before you process, and move this copy to a muted audio track labeled 'FX Backup.' Some sequencers like Nuendo and Cubase keep track of your offline processing and allow you to remove one or more offline jobs you've done to any audio event. Whatever working method you choose, having a fail-safe backup plan is worth the little extra time upfront to save yourself the trouble of rummaging through the audio pool, region list, or hard drive for the original.

It's also a good idea to listen back on several playback systems (especially headphones) when experimenting with effects like reverb and equalization. Be sure the effect you are going for is coming through on all systems. It's natural to overdo it, no matter what you're doing, when trying effects for the first time. Listen for intelligibility of speech and dialogue that gets overly harsh/distorted, or reverbs that wash out the sound so much that you can't easily understand it.

## Chapter 14

# Home Stretch:
# The Mix

Mixing is a glorified term for the stage where we bring in all remaining audio, tweak levels, finish up detail work, create special effects, and make sure the result will sound good on – and be compatible with – a variety of playback systems. Make no mistake, this is a fair amount of work, and this last stretch may make the difference between a muddled and ineffective soundtrack and a balanced, enjoyable one.

Much of what we're going to discuss here can be done in the comfort of your own studio. Most of us wish we had access to our own private theater in order to hear exactly what our *oeuvre* will sound like on a big screen. Alas, we only have the tools at our disposal so first we'll learn to maximize them. Then we'll get on with preparing the mix for any form of broadcast or distribution.

## Ready to mix

Here is a general workflow for mixing. There are all kinds of films, and some of these may apply and some may not be relevant to your process. Several of these points are reminders to finish up every editorial stage before clearing your palette for mixing. Refer back to previous chapters where any additional editing needs to be done.

- Calibrate the monitoring environment. If your room is off, your mixes will be off, guaranteed. (Headphones aren't a cure-all to the monitoring mess, either, since they are speakers with their own coloring, they exaggerate the stereo spread, and they don't allow for calibrated listening levels.) If you want your mix to hit anywhere in the ballpark, carefully follow all of the procedures in Chapter 5 in the section 'Calibrating the monitoring environment' before proceeding.

- Add any last minute audio as needed, such as new music versions, missing sound effects, end credits music, etc.

- Perform all of the editing necessary to clean up your production tracks. From this point forward you shouldn't need to make very many individual edits, fades, crossfades, etc.

- Spot check every track in your session; be sure each is routed to the appropriate group channel. The only tracks that should be going directly to the master bus are reference tracks (such as pre-mixes made in the NLE) that won't be included in the final mix. Be sure any of these reference tracks are muted.

- Ensure consistency of timbre and levels amongst the dialogue and replacement dialogue (ADR) throughout the film. Finish equalizing the ADR to match the tone of the dialogue.

- Finish editing narration as needed. Ensure consistency of level and tone throughout the narration track.
- Perform any additional music editing not already done. Check that short crossfades are used to eliminate clicks and pops.
- Create a dynamic mix by controlling the dialogue level and working other elements around it. Use both your ears and your eyes, being aware of both peak and average meter levels.
- Create an effective soundstage with conscious use of the center channel, surrounds, and subs in multichannel mixes.
- Apply reverb, EQ, etc., as necessary to add realism to ADR, Foley, and other sounds recorded in the studio.
- Use plug-ins to create special effects as desired (see the previous chapter, 'Special Effects').
- Output a temp mix and check it on other system(s). Make changes to the mix if desired, re-output.
- Output final mix and lay it back into the video. Check for sync on both small screens and in larger rooms, if possible.
- Archive the session and clean up the audio drive.

## Loudness, dynamics, and compression

Dynamic range refers to the spread of soft versus loud levels of a mix and how effectively they are used. Just as cameras have a limited contrast range of lights to darks that they can effectively capture and display, recorded sound has a dynamic range to keep under control in order to avoid washouts (clipping) and to preserve detail (low-level sounds). We want to be able to clearly hear whispers and breaths as well as endure shouting without overloading the equipment or adding too much noise. We want sound effects to overpower the dialogue in the right amount, so the viewer doesn't cringe in pain or run for the remote control at every loud event in the picture. We sculpt the dynamic range of a mix in two ways: by programming clip and track levels (volume automation) and sometimes by using compressors to restrict the dynamic range.

A *compressor* is a samurai sword: without proper training, new sound editors usually end up shredding their mixes and hurting themselves in the process. Compressors track audio levels and automatically reduce them when they approach the threshold of volume that you set. This pretty much allows the engineer to put a ceiling on how loud a track will get. Contrary to popular opinion, however, in film mixing, they are rarely used. Mostly because 1. where possible, it's always better to keep the signal path as pure as can be by avoiding unnecessary plug-ins, and 2. compressors take the control away from the engineer and, left unattended, can raise noise levels or squash your signal. If you feel the need to compress, remember several principles:

🎧 Less is more. How much you're compressing the signal is determined by the 'threshold' and the 'ratio' settings. The compressor's 'gain reduction' meter should light up only rarely, reducing the signal by say, 2-3dB when it kicks in. Except for deliverables that require a  very restricted dynamic range (say, website audio or webcast) any more than this points to out-of-control levels that need further volume automation.

A bit of reigning in the levels never hurt anyone, but do it consciously. If you're concerned about the wide volume range of your dialogue, compare it to that of a similar feature film. Dialogue is supposed to be dynamic, especially for feature films. Perhaps yours is right on. Or you may need to manually adjust the levels of a few loud bits that are just over the top. Choosing to manually adjust only the offending clips keeps the entire track from traveling through another unnecessary plug-in.

🎧 Compression has its disadvantages. Noise is one of them. Not that your particular plug-in is necessarily noisy, rather, it's a general characteristic of all compressors. Taming volume peaks as a compressor does implies bringing up the overall volume to compensate for the loss. This make-up gain also brings up any noise in the track. If noise is a concern, avoid compression at all costs.

🎧 The attack and release settings of a compressor shape the sound in ways that sensitive listeners can hear. Since we're trying to tame initial dialogue peaks (transients), fast attack times of less than 2ms work best. In addition, long release times (>100ms) hide the compression better than short ones. This is about as much detail we will go into here since compression techniques for a variety of signal types are widely discussed online, in product manuals, and in music-magazines.

A *limiter* is a compressor with less user adjustments. It is more of a safety valve that keeps signals absolutely under a certain level. It can be useful as a brick-wall defense against overload. The trade offs again are sound quality and control. Putting your signals through plug-ins always takes away some bit of clarity. Remember that less is always more.

When using a limiter, keep an eye on it to see when it's compressing the sound. Although it sometimes takes years to become sensitive to, compression does change the timbre of a sound, and we want to avoid this. Let's say that if your limiter is showing gain reduction of more than 3dB at any point, there's something wrong with the track or clip levels. Better to go back to the drawing board and make manual adjustments than blindly rely on a plug-in.

High quality limiter plug-ins are offered by numerous developers including Waves, Voxengo, Focusrite, Universal Audio, Bomb Factory, and Roger Nichols Digital to name a few. Multichannel (mastering) limiters take the concept a step further and, for example, compress only the low end when the bass is about to overload, leaving the dialogue midrange intact. They call for a samurai/engineer who can wield *two* swords.

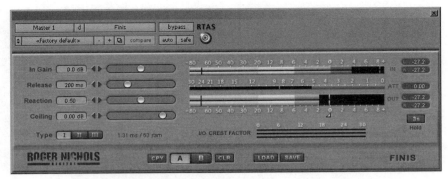

Limiters can help prevent overloads, but it's better to keep a careful eye on your levels.

### Using a limiter

🎧 If you want, you can place a high quality limiter on a group channel or the master bus to prevent clipping. Know that this is a quick fix, perhaps more appropriate for lo-fi material destined for the web or amateur videos. Avoid running stems or an entire film mix through any unnecessary plug-in. In a pinch a limiter *will* pin down any stray waveforms that try to overload your meters, though.

🎧 By default the limiter will have a cutoff of 0dBFS. It will curb waveforms that attempt to cause any digital 'overs' (overloading) by softening their dynamic peaks as they approach digital zero. You can change this to say, -6dBFS to keep your mix from going over -6. If you find the limiter performing a lot of gain reduction, manually reduce the level of the audio events causing the hits instead.

## Crash course in equalization

Any kind of waveform – including final mixes – break down into two important and controllable sonic components: its dynamic range and its frequency spectrum. Equalizers are audio filters that help us shape this range of frequencies like how a sculptor adds and subtracts clay from their work.

Frequency is another word for pitch and spectrum and refers to the range of bass, midrange, and treble of a waveform, or of a mix. When all are represented in proper proportion, music, speech, and other elements sound natural. Sometimes we deliberately alter the frequency spectrum of a portion of audio, like boosting the bass in a radio DJ's voice, or filtering out the treble in an ambience to simulate it coming from the next room. But we want most things to sound natural, which in itself may require some sculpting to achieve.

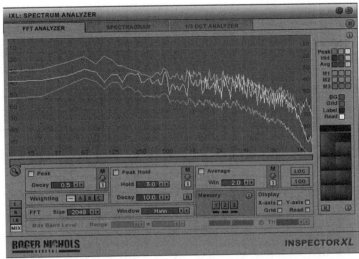

Frequency spectrum analyzers allow you to see what's going on in every frequency range of your mix.

## EQUALIZERS: ANYTHING BUT EQUAL

A parametric equalizer is the engineer's hammer: an absolute staple of every toolbox. All EQ plug-ins are not created equal, however. If you've ever tried to use the equalizers in some of the popular NLEs you've experienced their confusing interfaces and unnatural sound. Luckily, there are dozens of after-market choices in this arena. But why would anyone need more than one?

Well, there are framing hammers, finish hammers, ball pein hammers, rubber mallets, etc., and every equalizer sounds and behaves differently. The longer you use one the more sensitive you become to the nuances of user interface and timbre of an EQ. When you turn a knob, you want a specific result. You want the frequency and gain knobs to behave linearly so they affect the signal predictably over their full rotation. You want a choice of Q values so you can control how much of your precious signal is being affected.

Parametric EQs are the most common type of EQ we'll refer to in this book. Parametrics allow both tight surgical adjustments for notching out specific offensive frequencies and wider, more 'musical' slopes for making less noticeable changes. The former uses high Q values of, say, 3 or more (to affect as few frequencies as possible) and the latter uses wide Q values of 3.0 or less for a smoother response over a broad frequency range. Most parametrics have a range of Q adjustments wide enough to allow all kinds of frequency shaping.

*High-pass filters* (HPFs) and *low-pass filters* (LPF) sound confusing at first, but they do just what they say: allow high frequencies to pass, cutting out all frequencies below the one you specify, or pass all the lows below a specified frequency. Usually, you can adjust the Q or slope of the filter, taming its subtlety versus aggressiveness of frequency reduction. These special filters are usually integrated into any quality parametric. Graphic EQs are less used since they offer no control over their set Q value, often don't have high- or low-pass filters built-in, and have traditionally sounded less pristine than parametrics. They are good training wheels, but try instead to get comfortable with parametrics as soon as possible.

Better EQ plug-ins operate at a minimum of 32 or 64 bit internal resolution for better accuracy. What's most important about an EQ is how it handles – Do you find it easy to get around? Does it sound as you expect when you turn the knobs?

# Exercise: Learning frequencies

A great way to learn about frequencies is to practice on full mixes of your favorite songs. Import a song into a blank session and run it through a good parametric.

🎧 Boost or cut one frequency range at a time, say by 3dB, and listen to what happens when you bypass the plug-in. What happens to the vocal, drums, bass, etc.?

🎧 Better yet, have a friend 'quiz' you while you guess what frequency, boost, or cut, and even Q your friend has dialed in. How close was your guess?

🎧 It takes years to get comfortable 'knowing' frequencies, and the learning never stops.

When shaping the frequency spectrum of your mix with EQ:

🎧 Consider the genre and intended distribution of your film. If you're making a picture that you know will only be played on small speakers, you need not be concerned with dialing in lots of low end. In fact, reducing the bass content of the mix will create headroom for the rest of the frequency spectrum.

🎧 When listening to your mix on a full range speaker system, be sure all frequencies are represented and no particular frequency range is distractingly strong. Most films, with the exception of animations, documentaries, and some shows made for TV, will have times where the sound effects or music offer good, healthy bass extension. Be sure it is coming through as you'd expect.

🎧 Also, listen for the high-end sizzle of the treble frequencies. Is it there, or is there a dullness to the mix (or to certain elements)? If the fidelity of your sound effects isn't up to snuff, consider replacing them with sounds from a higher quality library. Or the dialogue might not be cutting through because of an unusual recording technique, or some filter you put on the dialogue track at some point in its travels. Just to check, revert to an old, raw version of a clip of dialogue and see if it sounds clearer. If so, replace and re cleanup that piece of dialogue.

🎧 Listen for sound effects and Foley that are supposed to be there but are not cutting through the mix. Sometimes a little midrange boost (EQ) is needed for these sounds, and sometimes it's a sign that something else is too loud, or that there is too much going on in general. Treat these problems carefully, trying out new sound effects instead. Or, equalize music, drones, and ambiences to make room for the things that aren't coming through. Dipping (with a wide Q) the crucial 1kHz-4kHz range can make room for dialogue and SFX to come through your drones and music. But remember that EQ is a Band-Aid that sometimes sticks and sometimes falls off. Better to start with high-quality samples and well-mixed music whenever possible.

## Mastering music

Mastering is a term we're borrowing from music production, meaning preparing the two-track (the left and right channels of a stereo mix) for broadcast and duplication. Mastering engineers clean up recordings and ensure that the frequency and dynamic ranges are consistent throughout the track and as compared to other records in the genre. Most tracks on professional labels have been mastered but some independent artists' music may or may not have been through this all important stage.

Music mastering engineers have their work cut out for them. Although a music track has been mixed, it still needs to conform to broadcast standards in terms of frequencies and dynamics. And the 'special sauce' that a good mastering engineer imparts to an almost finished record is different in every case. Assume that music is already at its highest and best resolution when it comes from the mastering engineer. However, due to age of a recording or need to conform it to picture, sometimes slight adjustments are needed.

If a music track you've chosen sounds 'small,' unprofessional, or otherwise lo-fidelity, recommend to the artist they get their music mastered by a professional, or perform some careful adjustments to it yourself.

### *Molding music to the story*

🎧 Obtaining the highest fidelity version of the track is always Job 1. Don't settle for an MP3 or other compressed formats: their origins, frequency response, and distortion levels unknown. The problem you are hearing in the music might be due to not having the highest-fidelity version of the master.

🎧 If you're employing music across several eras, understand that the tracks are supposed to sound different. A 1920s bop, a Beatles tune, and a Britney Spears song were recorded and mastered to different dynamic range and frequency spectrum standards. Just adjust their levels by ear. Your ear (in a fairly accurate room, at the right listening level) is the best determinate of loudness levels. Height of the waveform, 'normalizing,' and level meters do not reveal actual loudness. A waveform of a big band jazz record may look small but contain so much midrange that it sounds much louder than it looks. Use your ears, not your eyes.

🎧 Where you want to make some adjustments, choose the best parametric EQ with a 'musical' response, such as those by URS, Universal Audio, Voxengo, or Waves. The famous vintage Pultec EQs had wide, gentle curves for very musical-sounding mastering adjustments. Bring up low-end fullness with a gentle low-shelf gain of a few dB, to around 200 Hz. Tame the high-end hiss of an older record by reducing a few dB with a high-shelving filter, at say, 12kHz.

🎧 A trick for helping your dialogue pop while keeping background music (or busy ambience tracks) sounding big and full, is to cut the upper midrange (in the 3-4KHz region) of the music track by a couple of dB. Reducing just the frequencies that make speech intelligible effectively creates a sonic 'hole' for your dialogue to come through, while leaving the low end fullness of the music and the high end sparkle at full volume. It does put the music through another plug-in, slightly reducing its quality, so be gentle: use a high-quality equalizer with low Q values (0.2-0.6).

🎧 Another technique for keeping dialogue front and center in surround mixes is just that: keep it in the center channel, and pan the music to the L and R sides. Taking the music out of the center channel creates a sonic hole for the dialogue. But a little music in the center channel will allow people on both sides of the theater to hear both the left and right sides of a music mix, so keep some music in the center.

🎧 Since the music's purpose is to serve the story, don't underestimate the creative ways in which it can be incorporated into the picture. Maybe a nice, high-fidelity version of a tune you want for your gritty, gangster-ridden, drug-dealing drama doesn't have quite enough 'edge.' You could incorporate it into the scene so that it's coming out of a boom-box or television, on-screen or off. You could *add* some distortion, frequency-limiting, or other effect to compromise its sound. You could play it loud, or consider mixing it into the scene with some reverb as a low-level background whisper for a haunting effect. There are no limits to how you can work music into a scene. Just be sure it supports the story that's already being told through visuals, dialogue, and other elements.

## The soundstage: Creating an effective sonic panorama

Panning refers to placing a sound at a specific point of the soundstage by controlling how much of it comes out of any of the various playback speakers. Both mono and stereo sounds can be panned. This allows us to create a full, interesting soundstage, not just place a sound to reflect its position on screen. Although panning is open to a bit of interpretation, most notably with surround setups, most of the time there are common panning practices that get used to create an effective soundstage.

The panorama you are probably mixing toward is either stereo or 5.1 surround. If you're mixing in surround, you'll need to take the time to make a stereo mix as well, since broadcasters generally want a fall-back stereo mix with the surround. Check if your sequencer allows you to switch back and forth between monitoring in both modes so you can effectively be working on both mixes at the same time.

In terms of panning, multichannel (surround) mixing obviously has more options than stereo. The flip side of this is that there is more responsibility with six channels – and less mixing standards – so experiments with panning and levels can result in effects that leave listeners rather divided in opinion. Surround demands a bit more knowledge of what 'works' but in a way is easier to work with in terms of keeping things out of the way of each other.

When it comes to filling up a soundstage, there are two sides to the story: the material's original source format (mono, stereo, or surround) and what the engineer does with it. It takes special microphones and recording techniques to record in stereo or surround and we want to preserve these original intentions. Since sounds recorded in stereo often have an inherent, built-in depth, they often don't need any additional panning unless they don't follow the on-screen action. It's usually best to leave them as they are.

On the other hand, sounds can be flipped around or placed wherever you want, if desired. Mono sounds, whether dialogue or Foley, most often get panned up the middle (between the left and right front speakers) in order to create a solid, consistent sound across the whole theater (or living room). However, they can be placed anywhere, if desired. For example, following an actor's footsteps by panning them across the front speakers can be an interesting technique. Anything that must be easily heard by the whole audience (such as dialogue) is best panned up the middle, anchoring itself in the center channel.

When should dialogue be panned to follow the actor's position in the frame? Probably only for special effect. Dialogue that moves around the room distracts from the story and becomes hard to hear from every seat in a theater. However, used occasionally for special effect, a shift of pan position can effectively draw the viewer in.

Re-recording Mixers have a default mindset of: mono dialogue – panned center – with ambiences, SFX, and music in the stereo and surround speakers as desired. From there, special treatments like panned dialogue or Foley can be placed along the soundstage at times for creative effect. Let's take inventory of our soundtrack elements and their usual panorama presentation, then once you've learned the rules you'll be free to break them.

### *What sounds are usually in mono and get panned front and center?*

Anything recorded from a mono sound source, or anything that requires consistency across the whole room.

- 🎧 **Dialogue.** Even in the occasional instance when we pan dialogue left or right, dialogue is still a mono signal source. It comes from a single, mono microphone so there is no use converting it to stereo. It usually is thought of as the anchor of the mix, claiming the center channel of a surround mix for itself while also appearing in the left and right mains.

- 🎧 **ADR.** Likewise, ADR follows the same rule, as we try to make replacement dialogue sound as close to the production dialogue as possible.

- 🎧 **Room tone.** RT most often gets recorded with a mono shotgun microphone is the low-level background noise behind the dialogue and should match the production dialogue track.

- 🎧 **Foley.** Foley can be mono or stereo depending on the source. In either case, Foley usually gets spread across the front stereo mains.

- 🎧 **Narration.** Again, this is a mono mic source from a mono instrument (the voice) and works best where everyone can hear it, in the center channel.

### What should be placed in the stereo or surround fields?

Anything that benefits from a full, wide aural presentation. Any sound at risk of getting in the way of an important center-channel element (like the dialogue). Anytime you want to envelop the viewer in sound or create a larger depth of field with the sound.

- **Ambiences.** We use ambience tracks to create a background environment. In the real world these environments surround us, so we imitate this in the mix.

- **Sound effects.** Stereo sound effects are usually preferred, but it depends on the effect. You can put some of the SFX material in the surrounds, to taste, where you want it to come from the side of the room. There are also commercial effects libraries and ambiences recorded in surround, making for easy mixing if you're creating a surround-based feature.

- **Foley.** Foley from sound libraries is often provided in stereo, which gives it realism and helps it sit in the mix. But, in the case where, say, footsteps added in post need to match those in the production track, converting them to mono might help.

- **Narration.** Placing narration in the left and right mains, as well as center channel, distinguishes it from dialogue, and lends it a more 'voice of God' effect.

### What tracks might get placed anywhere?

- **Music.** Modern music almost always arrives in stereo, other times it may have been mixed in mono. In any case, it is up to the Re-recording Mixer to pan it in such a way as to best avoid other mix elements, while letting most seats in the theater be able to hear both the left and right channels. This may range from assigning music mostly to the left-right mains (with very little in the center), or to the surrounds, or putting the music in every speaker, depending on how busy the mix is at that point. Of course, it should never get in the way of dialogue and the rest of the elements telling the important parts of the story.

- **Sound effects.** Major SFX are usually recorded with stereo microphones. (Think of a car passing by, or a big, wide explosion.) Sometimes you'll find mono sound effects; these can simply be placed on mono SFX tracks and still be routed to the stereo SFX group bus. A gunshot in mono with the right reverb mixed in can be as effective as a stereo gunshot recording. Whether you want that sound to avoid the center channel (for surround mixing) is the most important question.

🎧 Any **special effects** (like those described in the last chapter) that don't fit in the categories above. Of course, now that you know the basics, creative sound effects are completely up to you.

### What should be placed in the LFE (low-frequency effects) channel?

The LFE channel is a "bass runoff" channel that really should only come into play during the loudest explosions or music. Many films' LFE tracks are, in fact, appropriately empty. As the filmmaker, you know the genre you are working toward, and thus how appropriate an ominous subwoofer presence might be at points in your film. The rule is, be willing to lose whatever is in the LFE channel, because it often doesn't translate to a playback environment.

🎧 **Sound effects.** For those instances when you really want to blow the audience away and the mains are already working overtime, dialing a little low-end enhancement can really get things shaking.

🎧 **Music.** Modern dance music, hiphop, and other bangin' beats can come alive with a touch of bass directed toward the LFE channel.

## LIVING IN SURROUND

You may have your hands full with creating a two channel (stereo) mix. Although multichannel sound has been with us since the 1940s, digital technology in the last 20 years has made surround sound ubiquitous. The challenge for engineers doing multichannel, or surround, mixing has been how to package the audio in a way that is compatible with the ubiquitous 2-channel format. After all, surround sound asks that anywhere from 4 to 11 channels of audio be packed into some type of media that originally had room for only two. Dolby labs, DTS (Digital

Theater Sound) and Sony, each with somewhat different solutions, have found ways of cramming six or more channels into the space of two.

There are two basic methods of surround 'packaging': *matrix* and *discrete encoding*. A matrix system doesn't actually contain more than two channels: it interprets and 'creates' a makeshift sort of surround mix from the engineer's surround stereo mix. It uses phase (timing) effects and other tricks to artificially manufacture pseudo-surrounds and an interpretation of a center channel upon playback.

Discrete encoding, however, packages the 4 to 11 channels into some format that preserves the all of the original channels. Dolby E is unique in that it converts everything to a proprietary digital format. Since it's digital, it can be wrapped up into packets much like internet data over a computer network. Analog audio, on the other hand, needs to represent as a continuous waveform and thus cannot interleave multiple channels of audio.

There are many multichannel formats out there, and new ones constantly being developed for new media technologies. Here are just a few of the current formats:

|  | Format | Type | Description |
|---|---|---|---|
| **Cinema:** | Dolby Digital 5.1 | Discrete | Most popular format. Uses a lossy compression scheme to fit 6 channels in the space of two on to the film stock. |
|  | DTS Digital Surround | Discrete | Technically offers higher audio quality than Dolby Digital. |
|  | SDDS (Sony Dynamic Digital Sound) | Discrete | Waning format found mostly in large cinemas. |

In addition, many of these formats, Dolby Digital, Dolby E, and the latest DTS in particular, have become somewhat 'intelligent.' They can't do your dishes but they do contain special 'metadata.' This

| Format | | Type | Description |
|---|---|---|---|
| **TV/DVD:** | Dolby E | Discrete | 5.1 format for video/TV, optimized for editing and fast multichannel encoding. |
| | Dolby TrueHD | Discrete | 24 bit lossless DVD format, HD ready. |
| | Dolby Pro Logic II | Matrixed | Pseudo-5.1 from a stereo mix |

additional non audio information gets decoded upon playback to automatically play a mono, stereo, or multichannel mix according to the user's equipment setup. It can also auto adjust program volume to even out levels of say, music versus DVD versus TV programming. This is possible because the format contains not only metadata but also multichannel, stereo, and mono mixes of the same program material inherent in the format.

Sometimes DVD players and audio hardware isn't so intelligent, however. Without clear industry standards, and with equipment manufactures making progressively cheaper and cheaper players, sometimes surround mixes get folded down to a stereo mix. The rear channel audio can get added to the front stereo mains, throwing off the balance of ambience, dialogue, sound effects, and music. This occurs mostly with films on DVD that do not have a stereo mix because they only included a surround mix. Unfortunately, these are just a few of the problems still plaguing an industry still in need of clear standards for broadcast and cinema sound.

It's important to stay on top of your mix. Panning is something of a science and an art, and it's up to you to keep your mix elements from interfering with each other. An effective mix, except when reaching for some unique effect, pans its elements in certain customary ways. Predictable panning usually allows the strongest and clearest delivery of the film's story. Panning is too disruptive of a mixing element to be used casually, and the effect can be tiring for the listener when over-used. But carefully managed, it can used to create a full soundscape that envelopes the viewer in the world of the film. Here are some more techniques for shaping your soundstage:

- 🎧 When you need the left channel of a stereo clip to come out of the right speaker and the right channel out of the left, perform an offline process called something like 'stereo flip.' It swaps the left and right channels and is particularly effective when you need to reverse vehicle fly bys that are going by in the opposite direction of the action.

- 🎧 Be willing to reduce a stereo sound to mono. If that car fly-by in the background is distracting from the dialogue, mix it to mono and manually pan it across the soundstage. It will call less attention to itself and keep the listener focused on the story. When you want to reduce a stereo clip to mono, there are several approaches: duplicate the left channel (discarding the right), dupe the right channel, or mixdown (merge) the two together.

- 🎧 As we've mentioned before, consider places in the picture where dialogue or other traditionally centered sounds might be panned off center. An example might be at the end of a scene where a

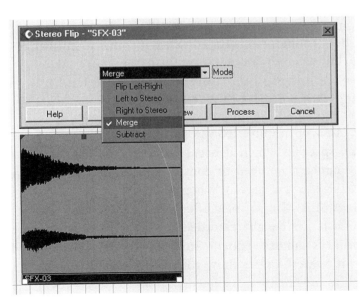

Mix to mono: Steinberg's Cubase offers several options for converting stereo clips to mono.

character walks off the right side of the screen. Panning her voice gradually to the right follows her action, adding an unexpected ending to the scene. See Chapter 13, Special Effects, for details.

- When mixing music, you could pull it *entirely* out of the center channel to avoid the dialogue, but be aware that the only people in the theater who will hear both left and right main channels are those in the center seats! Most of the audience needs *some* music in the center channel in order to hear both left and right channels of the music.

- Use the surrounds effectively, but don't overuse them. They are great for ambiences more than anything else. Possibly music, too, as well as certain sound effects. How do your favorite films of the genre in which you are working use their surrounds? How strong are the ambiences, in what kinds of scenes do they envelope the listener? When is music upfront and when does it lay back into the surrounds?

- Don't over-pan. Making insignificant sounds follow their on-screen position is not only a lot of work, the effect on the viewer is just tiring. Again, follow the story. Does the story want a sound to come from the side? Then by all means, use the surrounds.

For DVD/broadcast mixing, remember that everyone's home surround system is set up a little differently, so many people will only hear an approximation of what you're trying to get across. There is a lot of room for experiment when it comes to multichannel mixing, but when in doubt, err on the conservative side.

## Everything in its right place: Reverb

Reverberation tacks on minute reflections to a sound based on the acoustics of the space in which it occurred. Everyone has heard its effects but as engineers we need to control and create this effect to bring realism to signals that need it. When should reverb be used? The studio recordings of ADR and Foley often need some added realism. Stock sound effects are usually recorded dry as well, though some sounds like gunshots will have enough ambience of their own already. You can put a little reverb on anything you feel sounds too dry for the on-screen location in which it is depicted.

Special effects like explosions, door slams, characters in extremely large spaces, scene transitions, and other creative effects are great places to experiment with long and unusual reverb tails, but be careful not to muddy-up or wash out the mix.

When it comes to narration, reverb isn't customarily used. Narration purposely remains one step removed from the film by remaining ultra dry, taking on none of the ambience of the diegetic space. Post engineers generally do not bother with reverb on voiceovers for TV animation; feature animations, however, usually get more custom dialogue shaping.

### Add reverb for realism and effect

🎧 Create as many aux send tracks for the number of different spaces (locations in the film) that you need to artificially emulate with reverb. Insert a reverb plug-in on each aux channel. Be aware of the computer's resources, as reverbs can put a heavy load on the processor. If you need a plug-in, try a 'convolution' reverb and any of the thousands of great-sounding, free downloadable presets (called 'impulses') online.

🎧 Select a preset for each reverb that best approximates the space you need to create. (Making custom presets and learning the inner workings of a reverb algorithm is something with which you might also want to experiment.) You'll likely need various kinds of rooms, halls, vehicles, and other unique acoustic spaces.

🎧 On each track that contains audio clips in need of reverb, assign one of its FX sends to the aux channel with the appropriate reverb. Send a portion of the signal to the aux track and decide whether the chosen preset is working for you. Audition several reverb presets and let your ear decide which preset sounds most authentic for the scene's location.

🎧 Assuming you are monitoring at a calibrated level, adjust the track's send level to taste. It's easy to overdo it when working with reverbs. In most cases you are just trying to add the slightest bit of ambience to a sound for a bit of authenticity. Check reverbs on good headphones, where they get somewhat exaggerated, to be sure you're not dialing in too much.

🎧 You may want to organize, say, your Foley effects clips based on what reverbs they need. Placing all of the footsteps that need a living room ambience on the same track allows easy effects routing. Another approach is to vary the send level on the audio track by clip or by scene using automation.

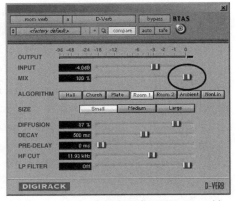

Set the reverb's wet-dry mix to the 100% wet position so the aux channel puts out only the reverb and none of the dry signal going in to it.

You can further shape your reverb tails with plug-ins placed after the reverb on the aux channel. Follow your reverbs with an EQ to shape the high or low frequencies, or a chorus for a warbled or washy effect. The possibilities for creative effects are endless. Keep in mind, however, that it's very easy to add too much or go overboard with effects, so once again, err on the conservative side until you've had a chance to check your work.

## The master channel

The master bus is literally the sum total of all your hard work. All of your signals get added together here and because of that the master channel is an easy way to make drastic changes to an entire mix, intentionally or unintentionally. For example, an equalizer plug-in on the master channel will change the sound of your dialogue, ambience tracks, music...*everything* in your mix. Rarely would you want to do such a thing. You have much more control shaping the *stems* – the four or five group channels – than by taking a machete to the whole mix. As mentioned before, less is more, and we only want to put sounds through plug-ins when necessary. Here are the more common uses for master channel effects on the master bus:

🎧 A quality limiter (such as the Waves 'C4', the Roger Nichols Digital 'Finis,' or other mastering grade limiter) can ensure that your mix never hits digital zero, but left neglected it can squash the dynamics of the soundtrack. See the beginning of this chapter for more info on limiters.

🎧 A *spectrum analyzer* is probably the most useful plug-in for the master bus. It doesn't change the sound, it just shows a pretty picture of the frequency levels in real-time. It's a series of meters broken down by all frequencies in the mix, showing what's going on in the bass, middle, and treble regions. You may want to put one on the master bus insert chain for easy visual reference. There are plenty of freeware and shareware analyzer plugs available. Roger Nichols Digital offers a free version of their 'Inspector' plug-in at www.rogernicholsdigital.com. Or try www.voxengo.com for their 'Span' plug-in.

## Metering

One of filmmakers' and editors' most common concerns involves the "correct" levels of dialogue, music, sound effects, and loudness of the overall mix. While there is no substitute for experience with such an elusive art, there are tools and techniques to help a new engineer get a mix into balance. Let's begin by understanding how volume is measured and displayed in the first place – with meters. Loudness in digital audio is measured in decibels full scale (dBFS), which is the metering scale used by all digital audio. *Full scale* refers to the convenient fact that digital audio, regardless of the content of the signal, has an absolute cutoff point at which all bets are off – and all bits are on. Once all of its 16 or 24 bits are storing data, no more volume is available and the waveform clips. This maximum loudness level that an audio file can achieve is called 0dBFS, or *digital zero*. This is why you see only negative numbers on the dBFS scale – they are measured in reference to a zero maximum.

The computer makes no excuses about returning nasty distortion when your 'overs' hit digital zero. Hitting the red in *any* piece of *digital* equipment, be it a video camera, audio interface, plug-in, etc., is simply wrong and always distorts your precious signal.

Plug-ins that emulate VU meters usually allow the user to calibrate their 'zero' mark to a corresponding level on the dBFS scale.

So the first step is never to hit 0dBFS – our ceiling – but we still need to determine the overall levels of the soundtrack elements, especially the dialogue. And from there, how much louder should the sound effects be? Or the music? Unfortunately, fast-acting peak meters don't indicate the *overall* level of a sound. For this we need to bring in another type of meter.

Re-recording Mixers have at their disposal a different type of meter called a *VU meter*. It features an analog needle lazily sweeping the signal and it tells you something different about the sound than the peak meter. Perhaps you have a plug-in or outboard mixer that features VU meters. If you do, you're ahead of the game. VU meters are calibrated with a very specific slow response such that they *ignore* fast transients, showing us instead an *average* signal level. A perfect complement to the fast-acting, LED-based peak meter.

VU meters were designed for the analog age, but still have a vital purpose today. Analog recording equipment has the luxury of *soft clipping* – overloading a tape machine produces a light

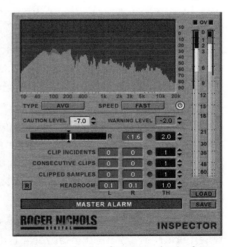

The 'Inspector' series of metering plug-ins from Roger Nichols Digital display both peak and RMS levels side-by-side, though the RMS indicators are rather thin. This free version features a frequency spectrogram as well. (screenshot courtesy of rogernicholsdigital.com).

distortion that isn't harsh on the ears. Plus, there is at least 14dB of headroom built-in *beyond* the 'zero' mark of a VU meter. The 'analog zero' point (0dB on the VU scale) has traditionally been a convenient *average* reference level for dialogue – nice and easy to read on a VU meter.

At this point our concerns are two fold: at the very least we need to stay away from digital zero (0dBFS), and we need to have an idea of the *average* levels of our mix elements. So we need both meters, for different purposes. All that is left to do is to get them to agree with each other. This is part of the calibration you performed while setting up an accurate listening environment.

The film world counts backward to -20dBFS to build an industry standard of 20dB of headroom on the digital scale before clipping. This -20dBFS mark should be set to correspond to 0dB on the VU meter. When you look at a digital sound meter, begin to think of -20dBFS as your 'zero VU' or mid-point reference. This doesn't mean that your dialogue will necessarily always sit at 0VU (or -20dBFS). We'll talk more about this in a bit.

Many post film engineers also tend to think of -6dBFS as an absolute maximum sound level for most *anything* in the mix. That means that the LEDs for the uppermost 6dB on your full scale meter wouldn't ever see daylight. Anything louder than this, they figure, had better have a good reason to be *that* loud – and probably only for a very short time. Your ears will probably tell you the same thing, if you're listening at the right level. However, we'll see in the next section that the overall loudness of a mix depends on many factors, especially where and how it's going to be played.

## Mixing and levels

Now that we know the difference between peak and average metering, we just need some kind of reference for dialogue and the rest should follow. We all have to have someplace to call home, and for a film mix it is usually the dialogue track. In this section, you'll learn that there isn't an exact science to setting mix levels, and it depends a lot on the material and the broadcast or distribution medium. Here are the key ingredients needed for setting proper mix levels:

- An acoustically-treated listening environment and, most importantly, a calibrated listening level. The success of your mix will depend largely on how carefully you set up your listening environment back in Chapter 5.

- A peak meter that measures on the dBFS scale. This is built into your audio software.

- A VU meter or a digital RMS (averaging) meter, in the form of a plug-in or as part of your hardware setup. Try the free 'Inspector' plug-in at www.rogernicholsdigital.com or the Bomb Factory 'Essential Meter Bridge' VU meter included with ProTools. These meters should be calibrated so that 0dB VU = -20dBFS.

- A clear understanding of your file format deliverables, whether providing your mix to a cinema, mastering studio, duplication house, or broadcaster.

- Preferably, access to another studio or home theater – or even a cinema – to check your mix.

### Set levels and pull the mix together

- **Prepare** everything. It's best not to assemble the mix until all editing is completed. Also, get to the point where you're happy with any special effects processing you experimented with in the last chapter.

- As you begin assembling your scenes, remember to always **follow the story**. Ask yourself, what is going to bring out the drama of this scene? Is the dialogue telling it, is it driven more by sound effects, or something else? Is the viewer hanging on the narrator's every word, or is narration a less significant element in the story? What does this tell you about how strong, how bright, how soft, or how loud certain mix elements should be?

  Consider the genre you are working toward and how you want to represent the film within it. Is it a mood piece intended to relax or a thriller intended to shock? Is it an innovatively-done documentary that is trying to boldly make a case for an issue? Comparatively speaking, what kind of mixing techniques seem to best bring out the story in similar films?

- **Weed out** extraneous sounds in busy and confusing scenes. Ask yourself – for every sound in the film – does it have a purpose? Every sound event should be consciously chosen and carefully placed. Watch for confusing passages of sonic clutter. Less is usually more.

  Adjust timing of non-sync events to make elements 'weave' around each other instead of directly overlapping (layering) them and having to reduce their volumes to keep from overloading.

- Tweak individual clip levels, draw fades, perform offline gain changes, draw volume automation, and adjust overall track volume as needed to **set levels**. Use every method possible to shape your mix, zooming in where necessary to make precise adjustments. Carefully program volume rides so that sound levels change smoothly while bringing out what you want to call attention to in the scene.

  Getting music and ambience tracks to play well together can be particularly difficult. Music can mask the ambience track, which in turn, if too loud, sounds unnatural. Get them to gel with some gentle, opposing EQ curves (e.g., boost 2kHz in the music, cut 2kHz in the ambience), panning, or volume rides throughout the scene. Carefully tweak fade-ins and fade-outs for precise entrances and exits of music and ambience tracks. Consider moving music or ambiences into or out of the surround channels as necessary to open up the mix.

- Most films are **dialogue**-driven, which means the level of dialogue should be consistent not only throughout the picture but amongst others in its genre. The average level of normal speech in a film is a bit arbitrary and determined in part by the actors' collective performances. Professional Re-recording Mixers will tell you that there really isn't a hard and fast rule for dialogue levels. For cinema or DVD release, you could start by aiming for an average dialogue level between -3dB and 0dB on the VU scale, or -23dBFS to 20dBFS using RMS metering on the digital scale. Remember that it's an average meter that we use to indicate overall volume, not a fast-jumping peak meter. These numbers may not be readable on a fast-moving peak meter.

Dialogue levels are relative to the story being told, in what genre it is being told, and for what intended distribution it is made. When it comes to television, there are all kinds of programs on many different types of networks. In general, though, television dialogue will run 6-9dB hotter than that of cinema or DVD, which is why you might find yourself turning up the volume every time you put a DVD in the player. For example, a sitcom's dialogue might be 8dB louder overall than that for a movie on DVD, but it depends on the type of movie. A TV commercial will probably take that level up a couple more notches. But a made-for-TV movie would be closer to film dialogue levels than TV dialogue. Because there are so many different kinds of programming, there is always some interpretation required.

So TV dialogue is louder than DVD or cinema, and isn't louder better? Maybe, but let's consider the rest of the mix. If the dialogue is so high in the mix, there is less *headroom* for other mix elements. For DVD and cinema we intentionally sit the dialogue *lower* in the mix (than in broadcast TV mixes) in order to leave room for the SFX and music to make more of an impact. This means your music and sound effects can be twice as loud…and louder is better, right?

Turn on the TV, flip through some channels and listen to the different *levels* of dialogue of documentaries versus feature films versus animated shows versus TV commercials versus Oprah. Get a feel for whether the dialogue is averaging higher than the levels we've been talking about, or perhaps even a bit lower. Then decide where *your* average dialogue level should be – in decibels on the VU scale – in order to compete well with programming in your genre.

Remember that people use their voices at a wide range of volumes. Maintain your chosen a*verage speaking level* across the whole picture, and allow the actors' performances to use their natural dynamic range above and below this level. Let the dialogue track "breathe" – resist the urge to compress unless your intended media calls for it. Do be sure every word is getting across, however, and not masked by another element of the mix.

🎧 Carefully sculpt what's going on the **low side** of the mix's dynamic range. Keep in mind your intended medium. Modern living room setups and cinemas with digital playback equipment have a lower noise floor than their older counterparts. The increased dynamic range means quieter mix elements will still be heard in the sound-treated room of the cinema. This might not be the case when mixing for TV, unless you're aiming for a cable- or satellite-TV audience with modern digital audio setups.

Most non-digital-playback cinemas start to literally 'lose it' (losing your low-level Foley and ambiences in the noise floor) somewhere between -30dBFS and -40dBFS. Newer digital cinemas can go much lower; that is, when the audience is quiet. Television has a reduced dynamic range overall, so a made-for-TV program may need to keep elements like ambiences and room tone a bit higher.

Perhaps you want to intentionally mix for the lowest common denominator, say for web delivery, and sacrifice dynamic range to be sure that everything is easily heard. This is a fine decision and will affect the low side of your mix's volume levels more than its high side. You just need to know how low is too low.

🎧 Watch the **high side** of the meter as well. As your ears will tell you (if you are monitoring at the correct sound pressure level, which you must!) the range from say, -6dBFS to 0dBFS is *frighteningly* loud. It's hard to say exactly because the fidelity or quality of a sound will in part determine how loud you can turn it up without it becoming harsh or painful. Both a huge explosion and the swell of music in a love scene could be mixed equally loud, just consider how much impact you are trying to have versus the dialogue track. Do you want people to enjoy the full dynamic range of the picture or be running for their remote controls?

Set the level of your sound effects according to the loudest effects in your mix, and tailor the rest back from that point. There is much discrepancy amongst engineers, but good rule of thumb for cinema is that the loudest sound effect in the picture should briefly hit around -6dBFS, and average around 12dB or higher than the dialogue. TV commercials or other loud programming will run hotter overall. Again, there is no substitute for getting sensitive to the mix levels of the genre in which you are working.

- 🎧 **Dynamic range** creates excitement in the soundtrack, but how much range you want depends partly on the film's style. Consider *relative* levels between tracks for key scenes. For a narrative film, the sound effects may be among the loudest elements of the mix, and some ambiences or Foley may be among the softest. An industrial video might pull in the reigns quite a bit more, having a much more limited dynamic range so as to be easily heard in lesser-equipped playback environments. Everything is usually considered in relation to the chosen dialogue level.

  Sitting the dialogue on the low side will make the loudest elements – the sound effects or music – appear louder and more exciting. This is an option if your broadcast medium has the dynamic range to support it (such as with DVD or cinema). Or perhaps your medium demands a mix with a comparably more limited range of volume; it's up to you. Listen at the correct level, use your ears, and be sympathetic to the viewer.

- 🎧 When considering how much of what to mix into the **surrounds**, see the previous section on panning for some tips. The surrounds widen the spatial field. Thus, using them more in outdoor scenes is a natural fit. But the surrounds should never take the focus or trump the left-right mains. As for volume levels with surrounds, your ears will tell you when an ambience is competing too much with the dialogue, or sound effects in the surrounds are too distracting. Proper room setup, comparisons to other films, and opinions of others are still the answers here. Use kid gloves with the surrounds, unless you're sure of what you're doing.

- 🎧 As for the **LFE** (subwoofer) channel, theatrical mixing uses it only for sparse accents. Action films and hip-hop documentaries notwithstanding, movies played in a cinema have the benefit of playback speakers with a full-frequency range and thus only need the LFE channel when they really want to move and shake an audience. DVD releases and TV broadcast, however, cannot count on this. Let's revisit a concept called *bass management*.

  Anthony Grimani, who coined the term 'bass management,' says that the LFE channel should only be used as a 'runoff' for low-frequency sounds that would otherwise overload the mains. In other words, it is not an all-purpose subwoofer channel – it is an extension that is used for extra headroom below the 80Hz mark.

What *bass management* does is take everything below a certain frequency and put it into a generalized subwoofer. So if a listener's main speakers can't go low enough, their own bass management circuitry will route the sound to the sub. As necessary as bass management is, you can't count on hearing a fully 'accurate' representation of your mix through such a system. On the other hand, truly full-range speakers would require a lot of space (there would be dual 12" drivers per cabinet) and air conditioning (they would require serious amplification).

When mixing, use the LFE channel for what it is – a low-frequency *extension*, not an all-purpose bass-producing machine. This means, as an engineer, you want it to come into play only when there is so much bass content that it would overload the mains. In many films, this means never. Your surround encoding algorithms should take care of this for you.

🎧 Added Foley is often mixed too loud. It really depends on the intended playback environment, but most of it should blend at an expected volume, not call attention to itself. As you are setting clip volume levels try to blend them naturally but subtly into the rest of the soundtrack, and err on the quieter side when not sure. Watch other films to get a reference for Foley levels, and check your work on headphones, which generally bring softer sounds more into the foreground.

🎧 Consider your intended broadcast or **playback medium** for the picture. As an example, think of the extremes of animated TV shows as well as TV commercials – both are usually very 'hot' mixes with little dynamic range – versus their opposite: a modern sound effects-laden film with a range of high-fidelity effects, music, and dialogue at all hearable levels. Each is mixed for a specific broadcast medium and would sound inappropriate for the other's. What you're trying to establish here is the *relative* level of, say, SFX to dialogue, and this depends a lot on your intended broadcast medium.

Here's an idea: Import soundtracks from similar films that you respect onto reference tracks in your session. Turn off your movie's visual display and compare scenes by ear. Watch your RMS meter and get a feel for levels during dialogue-only shots. Listen for similarities and differences of relative mix levels, dialogue clarity, reverb usage, and overall dynamic range. Take notes, and then make adjustments to your film according to what you learn.

## Checking the mix

One of the most elusive parts of preparing a soundtrack is ensuring it sounds great in a variety of playback environments. While an engineer never knows exactly how clear, balanced, tinny, muddy or harsh her work is going to sound in another room, she always checks her mixes on at least two or three different systems to get some type of perspective. Use all of the resources you can to check yours; it's always an enlightening experience. Make it a point to check a temporary mix of your work on as many of the following types of playback systems as possible:

- 🎧 **Studio monitors.** On full range studio monitors with a subwoofer in an acoustically treated studio, you should be able to hear most everything you would want to hear in a large theater, only smaller.

- 🎧 **Headphones.** Good, full range studio headphones should give you a full frequency range of highs to lows. Each adds its own color to the sound but all generally hype the details of the mix, making your low-level environments and reverbs sound somewhat louder than they will on loudspeakers. Knowing this, be sure your dialogue and music sounds clear, clean and natural, and your lower level sounds are easily heard, if a bit too present, on headphones.

- **Small speakers.** The popular Auratones and Yamaha NS -10M speakers (found in music studios), a small television, or another source that sounds 'midrangey' or 'tinny' should deliver the dialogue with extra clarity, while bassy sound effects and drones will be missing or under represented.

- **A public address (PA) system in a big room.**
  Keep in mind that a large, highly reflective room such as a hall with high ceilings and wood floors will muddy up a mix, making dialogue unintelligible. There may also be out-of-control low-end during bass heavy passages, further masking the dialogue. Conversely, a large, *acoustically treated* room such as the control room at a music studio or an actual cinema should offer clarity, depth, fullness and punch, moving you emotionally and representing the film closer to your intentions than on any other playback system.

- **Any system that you know well.** Maybe you know exactly what movies or TV shows are supposed to sound like on, say, your iPod. In that case, make a temporary mix of a portion of your film and see how well the dialogue, backgrounds, effects, and music comes through on the iPod. In what ways is yours comparable, and in what ways is it different?

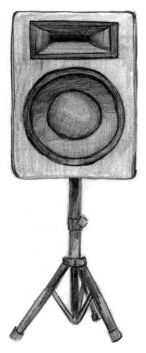

# HOW DO THEY *REALLY* GET THAT 'CINEMA SOUND'?

It comes from a good solid preparation of the stems or mix, engineered in an acoustically treated room by an engineer with sensitive and experienced ears listening at a calibrated level. Still, a real movie theater is a large room with very different sonic characteristics than a small studio. So how do we get our mixes to translate?

Just as professional music goes through a final mastering stage after it's mixed, films with larger budgets have the benefit of something called print mastering. While music gets final enhancements and tweaking by a mastering engineer, a soundtrack gets prepared for its delivery media by an experienced engineer on a dubbing stage – a studio large enough for the director and others to see and hear how it will translate to a cinema. However, there are all shapes and sizes of movie theaters with little standardization for room acoustics and speaker setup (despite Tomlinson Holman's advances in the THX calibration system). Experience is what you're paying for here.

So what exactly happens during print mastering? Your final mix gets turned into a duplication master. The frequency and dynamic ranges are modified – not for aesthetic effect, but simply to fit it onto 35mm film stock. EQ and levels also get adjusted for best translation to a typical large theater's frequency response (particularly the high-end 'Academy curve' rolloff that they exhibit). Surround encoding is performed, which may reduce the quality of the mix (read: lossy compression) in order to conform your mix to the decreased dynamic and frequency ranges of an optical soundtrack on 35mm magnetic film stock. For DTS encoding, the mix gets output to digital files and transferred to CD for synchronized playback with the film projector. In print mastering, the soundtrack can be matrixed to 2-channel (stereo) format and be made into a M&E

as well. Once print mastering is complete, translation to most theaters is ensured.

If you're going for theatrical release, you'll want to get a professional involved sooner than later. By the time it's ready to print master, your mix needs to have been carefully reviewed by a professional Re-recording Engineer. Print mastering does not necessarily mean changing the quality or nature of the original mix, but it will get it ready for performance and delivery.

Beyond improving your room acoustics, choice of monitors, and setup and monitor positioning (see Chapter 5 for a full treatment of each of those), there are a few overlooked techniques that new sound engineers can do to improve their mixes:

- 🎧 There are no hard and fast levels for the elements of a film or TV mix. Audio levels are subjective because every type of signal has a different frequency makeup. Instead, engineers use their ears and experience. The best thing you can do to ensure proper levels is to keep referencing your work to professional films you admire. This is a golden rule of mixing in both the music and film worlds: compare yours to everybody else's. Listen for clarity of your dialogue: is it easy to understand or does it sound comparatively low, muddy, tinny, dry, etc.? Listen to the level of their background ambiences for similar scenes: do you want yours at a similar level, more subtle, or maybe a bit louder? It's up to you and your ears. Again, calibrating your listening environment is the key to being able to make these decisions with maximum clarity.

- 🎧 Remember to calibrate your room to monitor at 85dB SPL (82dB SPL if mixing for TV broadcast). It's the only way to even begin to assure that the relative levels of the elements of your mix will come out in the proper proportions. And even modest room acoustical treatments will help bring out the clarity of your mixes more than you may think.

- 🎧 Another thing that people don't take the time to do is ask the opinion of friends whose ears they respect. Make a temporary mix, have a listening party, and get some honest feedback from some friendly movie lovers.

🎧 Lastly, there is no substitute for time. Depending on your schedule, it's always enlightening to return to mixing after taking a day or a night off. When your ears are fresh, problems pop out: you realize things like the dialogue sounds thin, the ambiences are too loud, or a music track sounds grainy and needs a better quality transfer.

When you do come back to mixing after some time away, try to watch the entire picture in one sitting, pausing the playback while taking notes on what needs to be corrected. You'll save time, energy, and perspective if you resist the temptation to correct every problem as you hear it, which encourages distractions and takes away from your holistic view of the film. Aiming for consistency throughout the duration of the picture means watching the picture straight through as much as possible.

## Chapter 15

# Home Stretch:
# Output, Layback, and Archiving

In this chapter you'll see your audio session crystallize into a mono, stereo, or 5.1 surround mix and be laid back to picture in the video sequencer. We'll also give some tips on backing up your project.

Mix outputs are tailored to the intended distribution or broadcast of the mix. Reducing a mix to mono rarely has any benefit, but it could be useful for certain distribution methods. For example, a short film that will only be distributed via the web could be mixed in mono to keep the file size down. In this case, the only benefit of 'upgrading' the mix to stereo would be for compatibility with a delivery medium, if necessary. Consider your website's or broadcaster's file format needs and output accordingly.

## Exporting the final mix

Performing an audio export or mixdown is your ticket to rendering a single waveform of what you hear in playback. Before making any kind of mix export:

- Spot-check the session for problem areas (by ear and by eye).

- Set your left and right locator points – you probably want these to line up to the start and end points of the video file.

- Be sure all tracks and stems that are supposed to be online are not muted or disabled.

- Some sequencers (like Cu-base and Nuendo) let you choose options such as split or interleaved files. Split creates individual exports and interleaved creates one combined file. One or the other might be appropriate depen-ding if you are mixing to stereo or surround, or on your desired delivery format.

When you're ready to proceed, consider which of the following types of exports you need to make:

- To make a single (mono or stereo) file from your mono or stereo mix, simply select 'File – Export Audio Mixdown…' or something similar. Specify a location for the file, the proper sample rate and bit depth if prompted, and away you go. For stereo mixes of simple projects, this may be the only export you need to make. This creates a mix of every track in the project that is not muted or disabled.

- Make *stem* exports instead of a full mix down whenever you need to keep any of the mix elements (such as the music) separate, or you want to bring a rough mix to another studio for further tweaking.

## STEMS: LEAVING YOUR OPTIONS OPEN

Not sure how loud to mix in the music track overall? Worried about getting a license for that last music track, or not sure if you'll want to change a music choice in the future? Solo the music group and create a stem export – the full length of the picture – of just the MUSIC group. Then mute that group and create another export of the rest of the mix. Layered together, the two combine into a complete mix when re-mixed.

You can also output and port over individual stems of every mix element to a dubbing stage to create a print master for theatrical release, giving the post house more control over making a better cinema-quality mix. As you can see, there are several reasons for making stem mixes.

The downside is that stems take longer to export than a final mix. Soloing each group channel while you export each stem results in perhaps four to six stereo files, a manageable number of files. With surround mixes, however, this gets a bit out of hand – six channels for each of six stems would result in 36 individual exports, leaving a lot of room for error, and perhaps very little drive space!

- A M&E (music and effects) mix contains everything besides the dialogue, ADR, and narration. It is used as a background track for dubbing the film into other languages. Create this mix now, or keep the session in backup to create a M&E when the time comes for it.

- In some cases you may need to make a mixdown of the picture without the music, in cases where you are awaiting rights clearance or where music choices may change. Just mute the music group and create your audio export as normal. You can then solo the music group and create another export of just the music. Combined later, they will yield the same result as the final mix.

🎧 If you're working in surround, create your surround outputs. Each one is a mono channel. Solo the individual output channel you are exporting, one at a time, as you create full-length exports.

Unless you're feeding your own surround-encoding plug-ins or hardware (in which case, you'll have read its manual and know the proper order of output channels, etc.) create the exports in the following order:

1. Left channel

2. Center channel

3. Right channel

4. Ls (left surround)

5. Rs (right surround)

6. LFE (low-frequency effects)

If you're delivering a 5.1 mix, you'll also need to include a fold-down stereo mix (Lt/Rt – left total and right total) as a fall-back to which home or theater equipment can auto-switch over in case of a problem with the surround setup. Consult your surround encoder's manual for the appropriate procedure.

## SESSION PORTING

When transporting your session or mix over to a system in a different studio it's important to have a playback reference level between systems. This helps ensure expected playback and equipment levels in the new room. The standard way to do this is to include the same 30-second, 1kHz sine wave tone at -20dBFS (or 0VU) on a track at the beginning of your session (or at the front of the audio mixdown). You can find this tone at www.abluesky.com/

asp/catalogue/download.asp?prodcode=blueskytestfiles with the other test tones we used in previous chapters.

Upon playing your mix in the new studio, calibrate the software and hardware levels to -20BFS and 0dB, respectively. Now the meters will behave as you expect. Then calibrate the new room's listening level to 85 (or 82) dB SPL with the same pink noise you used for your room. Then your masterpiece will play back at the proper level, too.

## Laying the sound back into the video

It's time to verify that your audio export(s) were done properly and are to your liking. Import the mixdown into the NLE and line it up. It should start at the original point you exported the QuickTime (or other) movie file. Zoom in close and use the 2-beep to help you get it aligned, if need be. If for some reason it doesn't sync up, check that the mix's sample rate matches the video project.

You can also use clipboard 'Add' feature in QuickTime Pro to perform a quick layback to your project video instead, if you find that to be faster or easier. Consult the QuickTime help for instructions.

If you choose to go back, tweak the sound, and make new exports, watch the entire picture and keep a list of all the changes you want to make. Also it can be helpful to give yourself some time between sessions, if you have the luxury. Both time and other people can be great sources of inspiration and perspective when it comes to finalizing your oeuvre. Offer popcorn to any critical eye and ear that might be willing to give you some technical and aesthetic feedback on your picture.

## Backing up, going forward

Audio post-session data can get quite large. You'll want to choose a backup medium with room for not just the audio, but the video too, as a reference of the exact cut (or video version) to which you mixed the sound.

Furthermore, media formats change. Choose a backup format that you feel is here to stay for a long time. Perhaps you have some older, lower-capacity hard drives that you've outgrown but that still work just fine. These are great candidates for backup media. The capacity of DVDs has increased to the point where short films' audio sessions often fit on to one or two discs. Be aware that DVD and similar media is heat sensitive, and that one scratch in the wrong place might render a disc unusable. With proper care, however, they are a good second or third backup choice. For other options, check your favorite computer equipment retailer.

Make at least two complete backups of the session and an additional version of the final audio mix or stems. Use different kinds of media for each backup, in case one becomes damaged in storage, and store them in a cool, dry place. What should you include in the backup?

- 🎧 The audio session and all associated audio files, edit files, and any plug-in presets. Normally, the sequencer copies audio files to the project folder, so you may be able to simply backup this folder. When in doubt, be sure to locate and organize all audio clips before making the backups.

- 🎧 The video file to which you cut the audio mix.

- 🎧 Stem outputs (if they were performed).

- 🎧 Final mix outputs (stereo and surround).

- 🎧 Be sure to hold on to your audio software itself and the installation files of any plug-ins you used in the project, in case future versions of the software refuse to open older session files.

PC users would do well to perform a full defragmentation of their audio hard drive after having removed the project from the drive. Freeing up space and organizing your drives gets you mentally and physically ready for the next project!

# Chapter 16

# Post Mortem:
# Looking Ahead

## Tips for location recording

If you've made it through the whole process of creating a sound-track in post, you've no doubt made some mental notes on what to do, or what not to do, next time in production. Here is some 'sound' direction for your next shoot. Some we've touched on in the earlier chapters and some are new ideas. For more ideas on improving your production sound, check the author's website at www.whatsound.net/.

- Focus solely on getting the best quality *dialogue* you can and keep out as much non-dialogue as possible. Keeping the elements discrete allows the post engineer independent control over levels. Separation of each sonic element is one of the secrets to creating a dream mix.

- Quiet the location as much as possible. This means, wherever possible, snuffing out camera and lens motors, generators, heaters, fans, A/C, gum-chewing PAs, background traffic, and so on. While you may not be able to stop traffic, keep sound recording in mind in pre-production when deciding your locations. Staging that shoot-out in the desert instead of the city might get you great sounding dialogue – real, live, emotional performances that wouldn't be possible in the city – and won't be nearly as convincing if re-recorded in the studio.

- Shoot crucial dialogue scenes in enclosed, controllable locations. A soundstage might be a bit out of budget, but consider any quiet alternatives you have access to: the apartments, houses, office spaces, bridge clubs, etc., of people you know. If it doesn't matter to the scene, shoot critical dialogue scenes after hours, when surroundings are quieter. Dialogue restoration is time consuming, expensive, and never results in the quality of a good location recording.

- Consider your choice of microphones. Listen to the background noise when you're scouting or on set. Use lavalieres in noisy locations (or on documentary shoots). Take the time to properly fasten lavs to avoid clothing rustle. Instruct the actors to go through their blocking and give a test listen before shooting.

- Reverb, echo, and ambience are virtually impossible to remove in post. Treat the off camera walls and other hard surfaces of your location with acoustic absorbers, or at least heavy blankets. Insist that the sound mixer put this kind of preparation into every scene for which you need quality dialogue. Build portable absorbers as described in the chapter on Acoustics for your next location shoot. In addition, sound equipment houses will include large blankets with your rental order if you ask. Get the location sounding as much like a 'dead' or 'dry' recording booth as possible. Additional ambience can always be added in post, but not removed. Obviously for exterior and urban locations, this may be difficult or impractical.

🎧 Booties. Yes, booties for off camera actors' feet. Or just have them walk lightly in their socks. Add all the footsteps in post rather than having some bleed into the dialogue track and then trying to match up library footsteps to the natural ones.

🎧 Remind actors to quietly fake off-camera movements like car starts, pulling the emergency brake, punches, bodyfalls, kissing, eating, drinking…anything action that makes a sound but can Foleyed in post. You will have more control over tone quality, placement, and levels if the talent isn't cluttering up the dialogue track with non-dialogue sounds.

🎧 Always instruct crowds/restaurants/offices/club scenes to be as silent as possible, faking all talking and making silent movements, and then overdub the ambiences in post.

🎧 Know when to say when: For scenes with very little dialogue, MOS scenes, or in particularly noisy locations, treat the production soundtrack as a scratch track. If you're shooting digital, record it right into the camera but don't worry about making it perfect. Just get a typical boom capture of the action – placed as close as possible to the action in the usual way – and plan on re-recording those scenes in the studio. Mark in pre-production the scenes you can shoot without dialogue and prepare the sound crew to make only these scratch tracks. This assumes that you can count on your actors to perform ADR as needed.

🎧 Encourage the Sound Mixer to go off on her own and record wild-sound between scenes or when camera or wardrobe is busy setting up other shots. It's like SFX re-recording….actually more like pre-recording. With a quiet environment, decent gear, and good ears you can get recordings that will stand up to stock library sounds. They will be cheap, and yours, and unique to your film. See the sound effects chapter for the full procedure of recording SFX.

## Make time for sound

🎧 Prepare your entire crew in pre-production. Let them know that sound is an important part of your picture and getting that sound requires the support of every crew member. When it's time to be quiet for a recording, they need to take it seriously.

🎧 Having a dedicated Sound Mixer, Assistant Mixer, and Boom Operator – like professional shoots do – is the best chance you have to getting high quality, usable sound for every scene. And yet sometimes people assume that one person can cover all three bases. Anyone who understands the need for quality dialogue, wild sound, room tone, and location sound effects knows that this is rarely possible.

For narrative films especially, a one or two person sound department makes things difficult. With a two person department (Boom Op and Sound Mixer), at least one PA should be knowledgeable of and available for assistant sound recording, running cables, etc. It only takes one experience of post-audio production to realize the effort required just to capture usable dialogue, never mind additional sound. Think of it as saving time and money in post.

🎧 Often the sound department's workload gets staggered versus the rest of the crew; for example, they might take lunch while shooting MOS scenes. Instead, location sound personnel need to use every opportunity to capture extra sounds useful in post. Get your money's worth: keep your sound department working by having them gather sound effects, ambiences, wild sound, and extra dialogue between scenes. Of course this is only possible with the help of a director who will take the time to quiet the set in the down time, such as before load-in or during breaks.

🎧 We could continue this list with more juicy production tips but a group of industry pros has beaten us to it. Check out http://www. recordingarts-forum.com/TheOpenLetter.html for some solid advice on making your next shoot go smoothly.

Remember to have fun when recording, editing, and mixing your picture. One great thing about digital post-production is that almost everything is 'undo'able, so it pays to experiment! Happy mixing!

# Glossary

**2-pop (or 2-beep)** – a short (one-frame) reference tone (1kHz at a volume of -20dBFS is standard) used for line-up and sync purposes among audio and video tracks.

**AC3** – Dolby Laboratory's proprietary compression system (codec) that takes a full-frequency and full-dynamic-range 5.1 surround mix and compresses it into the space allotted for sound on an optical film stock.

**Attenuate** – to reduce the volume output of.

**Audio interface** – like a soundcard, the hardware device that passes and converts audio from the computer to the outside world. Usually it converts analog signals to digital and vice-versa.

**AudioSuite processing** – Digidesign's ProTools' term for offline processing of audio clips.

**Automation** – recordable volume, panorama, and other parameters of an audio track that upon playback.

**Balanced/unbalanced** – balanced cables and connections create a lower noise analog connection than their unbalanced counterparts. They do this by redundantly duplicating the signal line (in reverse polarity, on an extra wire or connector lug) while the gear with which they interface performs a noise reduction trick called common mode rejection. They employ XLR or 1/4" TRS connectors. Unbalanced signals, such as guitar, CD player, and all headphone output signals have only two connectors – signal and ground – and as such have no way to reduce any noise interference that appears on their lines.

**Boom pole** – a telescoping extension rod to which (usually) a shotgun mic is attached during on set production recordings.

**Clipping** – overloading a gain stage of an amplifier, producing analog or digital distortion, usually indicated by a red LED on a piece of equipment.

**dBFS** – decibels full scale (or full code) – the metering scale for digital audio gear. 0dBFS is the maximum voltage level possible before clipping.

**dBu** – the decibel scale used in measuring the voltage level (amplitude) of professional analog audio signals. One dBu = .775 volts.

**dBV** – the decibel scale used in measuring the voltage level (amplitude) of consumer or prosumer grade analog audio signals. One dBu = 1 volt.

**Diegesis** – the 'world of the film (or plot).' The time and space in which the actors on screen are playing.

**Driver** – software program usually in form of a DLL file (on a PC) that allows control and interaction with a piece of hardware

**Dynamics, dynamic range** – the range of amplitudes (volumes) of a sound event, mix, or of human hearing itself, from the lowest audible sound to the loudest sound pressure level able to be captured or reproduced.

**Foley** – the everyday sounds of footsteps, clothing movement, car doors, creaky floors, etc., that are spotted to character actions in post.

**Frequency spectrum** – the range of pitch from the lowest rumble to the highest hearable tone. In humans this range is generally considered to span from 20Hz to 20kHz, though the practical range is less.

**Hertz (Hz)** – pitch, measured in cycles (wave periods) per second. The threshold of human hearing, a low rumble that most speakers cannot reproduce, has 20 wave periods per second (20Hz). Every doubling of this number amounts to one octave, such that the scale is logarithmic, not linear. 100Hz is one octave below 200Hz. However, 10,000Hz (or 10kHz) is one octave below 20kHz, which incidentally is considered the upper limit of human hearing. Apparently cats can hear up to 65kHz, which might explain why they dart their heads around so often at seemingly nothing at all.

**Lavaliere microphone** – a miniature microphone usually clipped under clothing or in the hair that, while often problematic in action sequences, are a 'hands free' approach to mic'ing an actor or interviewee.

**Limiter** – a 'brick wall' compressor that keeps all volume levels below a specified ceiling.

**M&E** – a music and effects mix is an additional mixdown of the soundtrack for international dialogue-dubbing purposes. It should contain everything except dialogue and narration.

**Mastering** – the final editing (EQ, compression, harmonic enhancement, clean up, etc.) stage in which recorded music is prepared for broadcast and distribution.

**Monitors** – studio-grade speakers designed to more accurately represent the signal source than consumer or hi-fi speakers. Powered monitors have built-in amplifiers and can take a direct audio signal input (from say, a mixer or soundcard). Passive monitors are smaller and lighter and require an amplifier and speaker cables.

**NLE – Non linear (video) editing platform** – the software and hardware environment used to edit digital video.

**Noise** – the subjective, unwanted sound in a recording.

**Offline processing** – destructive (permanent) application of a plug-in while playback is not running, opposite of real-time processing using inserts or aux tracks. Destructive is a bit of a misnomer since the audio sequencer creates a new version of the processed clip, usually leaving the old one on disk or in the audio pool (or bin, or region list).

**Over** – a moment of digital overload. The content of a digital over is total harmonic distortion for its duration, indicated by a red light in the audio sequencer, plug-in, or driver's metering display.

**Pan** – to place sound events in a mix so that they playback from a specific point between a properly set up loudspeaker array. The Greek god of shepherds known for his sexual prowess and his flute (probably unrelated).

**Panorama** – the imaginary soundstage created between properly set up loudspeakers in a listening environment.

**Plosive** – a strong burst of air from hard consonants (P, D, T, etc.) that overloads a microphone element. Employing a pop filter can reduce the effect, as can angling the mic off-axis (at a non-90 degree angle to the mouth) can help allow the air to pass by the mic diaphragm without overloading it.

**Print mastering** – the process by which a stereo or multichannel film mix is final tweaked in a studio capable of applying the 'Academy EQ curve' and performing other preparations necessary for playback in large theaters.

**Q** – equalizers don't affect just the frequency that is dialed in, and the measure of the range of adjacent frequencies that are being affected is the Q (Quality). Lower numbers are a more gentle slope and affect a wider range of octaves around the specified frequency. Higher numbers imply a more surgical cut (i.e., affecting more of just the chosen frequency).

**Reverberation (reverb)** – the contribution of the acoustical space in which a sound occurs. Often misstated as 'echo,' which is made up of distinct reflections of sound off the hard surfaces of a space. Sounds with little to no reverb, like most narration, are called 'dry' while sounds with a lot of reverb, such as a gunshot in a gym, are described as 'wet.'

**Room tone** – the subtle din of constant, random noise unique to a space. Without room tone, silent portions of a film sound dead and sterile.

**Shotgun (line) microphone** – a microphone with a very directional pickup pattern that favors sound sources from its extreme front (and rejects those from its rear and, to some extent, its sides). Longer shotguns are more directional than shorter ones, though they can suffer from a somewhat more phasey sound. Recognized as the most neutral and desirable sound source for most location recording.

**Sibilance** – a vocal whistling produced by mouth structure sometimes heard when a person speaks or sings the letter S. The offending frequencies live anywhere between 4kHz and 10kHz and should be attenuated by the mix engineer.

**Signal** – the subjective, desirable portion of a sound recording

**Signal-to-noise ratio** – the decibel range of the loudest sound event down to the threshold of equipment or recorded noise.

**SMPTE timecode** – assigned by a chosen frame rate (24fps and 29.97fps are common in digital video), SMPTE is a standardized numeric label imposed on audio, video, or film media using a sequential number for each frame. In audio post, it provides a more relevant reference for lining up audio events to picture than a ruler or timestamp based on samples, milliseconds, or bars and beats.

**Soundcard** – a budget audio interface. See Audio Interface.

**Spot** – to spot is simply to place an event on the timeline at a specific moment, usually in relation to a video event

**Stems** – discrete 'group' outputs of the dialogue, sound effects, music, etc., that combine to make up the final mix.

**Toslink** – 2-channel digital audio over an optical (a.k.a. ADAT lightpipe) cable. Optical cables can also be used for 8-channels of digital audio, this is determined by the gear itself or in its audio driver.

**Transient** – the initial attack or rising edge of a sound event that often defines much of its uniqueness. Usually contains much high frequency content and the loudest part of the sonic event, such as with the initial hit of a stick on a drum.

**Two-track** – a stereo (left and right channel) mix of a recorded work.

**Unity gain** – zero dB of gain or attenuation in a gain stage. The volume coming in is the same as the volume going out.

**Wild sound** – recordings of specific non-sync events on set. Examples: engine revs, gunshots, misc. Foley.

# Index

## A

AAF. *See also Advanced Authoring Format*
absorption materials 73
AC3 301
acoustical diffusers 65, 73
acoustical sealant 71
acoustical treatment 64, 69, 71
action 6, 10, 16, 25, 26, 27, 28, 30, 31, 32, 33, 81, 86, 89, 163, 170, 171, 172, 174, 177, 178, 179, 184, 191, 192, 199, 216, 217, 218, 252, 267, 273, 274, 284, 299, 303
AD 43, 44, 182
Adobe Premiere 41, 43, 97
ADR mixers 6
ADR recordist 6
ADR supervisor 6
Advanced Authoring Format 3, 89
AES/EBU 45, 48, 49, 50
airspace 71
ambience track 27, 28, 173, 194, 196, 199, 206, 207, 212, 214, 281
analog audio cable 50
analog signals 44, 46, 301
animation 10, 20, 32, 39, 84, 170, 171, 192, 275
art house cinema 192
attenuate 247, 248, 301
audio driver 40, 79, 80, 81, 82, 113, 117, 305
audio engineer 25, 45, 84, 85, 87, 88, 101, 132
audio fades 91, 94
audio interface 37, 41, 43, 44, 46, 63, 79, 112, 113, 141,

277, 301, 305
audio post ii, 4, 7, 12, 14, 16, 20, 21, 22, 24, 25, 26, 28, 30, 32, 34, 36, 38, 40, 42, 44, 46, 48, 50, 52, 54, 56, 58, 60, 62, 64, 66, 68, 70, 72, 74, 76, 78, 80, 82, 84, 86, 88, 90, 92, 94, 96, 98, 100, 102, 104, 106, 108, 110, 112, 116, 195, 295, 305
audio sequencer 3, 37, 38, 39, 40, 41, 44, 59, 86, 87, 88, 89, 90, 91, 92, 94, 95, 96, 97, 98, 99, 100, 101, 102, 104, 106, 112, 113, 115, 118, 119, 120, 121, 122, 125, 130, 182, 303
audio software 36, 280, 296
aux inputs 109
aux send 108, 253, 254, 275
aux sends 106, 108
auxiliary channel 108
Avid Xpress 41

## B

balanced cables 46, 50, 51, 53, 301
bass build up 69, 71
bass drones 31, 181, 200
bass management 81, 284, 285
bass traps 65, 74, 75, 82
bit depth 47, 113, 114, 115, 117, 122, 292,
Bomb Factory Essential Meter Bridge 80
boom 72, 75, 90, 94, 105, 106, 129, 131, 149, 150, 156, 174, 190, 195, 214, 266, 299, 300, 301
buffer size 40, 113, 117

## C

cable ties 51
calibration 64, 69, 76, 279, 288
center channel 56, 65, 68, 81, 111, 116, 257, 266, 268, 269, 270, 271, 274, 294
clapper 84
click and crackle removal 148
clipped peak restoration 148
clipping 23, 24, 159, 257, 260, 278, 279, 301, 302
codecs 95, 116
comedy 32, 192
composer 30, 33, 41, 222, 232, 233, 234, 235, 236
compression 4, 34, 39, 95, 97, 125, 129, 143, 152, 244, 249, 257, 259, 271, 288, 301, 303
compressor 107, 151, 244, 258, 259, 303
copyright law 219
crosscut 212
crossfade. *See also non linear video editor*
crossfades 39, 40, 91, 92, 119, 128, 147, 151, 168, 184, 203, 206, 207, 209, 210, 211, 237, 238, 242, 249, 256, 257
crossover 27, 81, 82
custom scores 233

## D

DA 43, 44, 86
DAW 37, 38, 47, 59, 86, 87, 88, 89, 91, 92, 94, 100, 101, 106, 112, 125, 239, 244, 248

de-buzz 133
de-click 133
de-crackle 133
de-hiss 133
de-hum 133
de-pop 133
decibel 3, 65, 76, 302, 305
decoding 34
density 12, 248
Dialogue Editor 129, 131, 132, 145
dialogue editors 5, 6, 129, 203
dialogue matching 34
dialogue supervisor 5
dialogue tracks 7, 110, 123, 128, 129, 130, 133, 145, 172, 173, 196, 200, 211
diegesis 302
diegetic 33, 171, 187, 250, 275
diffuser 74
digital audio 2, 7, 37, 38, 45, 46, 48, 49, 50, 53, 100, 112, 114, 277, 283, 302, 305
digital audio interface 37
digital audio signals 45
digital audio workstation 37, 38, 100
digital technology 5, 41, 270
digital zero 260, 277, 279
direct box 46
discrete surround 111
display format 115, 117
distortion 7, 23, 24, 46, 47, 114, 128, 137, 138, 184, 244, 245, 265, 266, 277, 279, 301, 303
documentaries 25, 27, 31, 131, 211, 217, 263, 282, 284
doubling 242, 251, 302
drama 10, 15, 27, 32, 181, 192, 197, 252, 266, 280
dream sequence 248
driver 40, 48, 79, 80, 81, 82, 112, 113, 115, 116, 117, 118, 245, 302, 303, 305
drones 31, 32, 73, 154, 172, 181, 182, 184, 197, 199, 200, 203, 204, 210, 212, 242, 252, 253, 264, 287
duck 32, 207

dynamic range 20, 47, 101, 114, 129, 237, 244, 257, 258, 260, 265, 282, 283, 284, 285, 286, 302

**E**

edit groups 109
editors 5, 6, 20, 95, 129, 130, 143, 152, 203, 218, 236, 237, 239, 244, 258, 277
electromagnetic interference 56
EMI 56
encapsulated OMF 93
encoding 34, 95, 96, 129, 219, 271, 272, 285, 288, 294
EQ 4, 33, 34, 59, 64, 78, 79, 106, 108, 110, 113, 123, 125, 138, 139, 140, 143, 145, 146, 147, 149, 150, 155, 166, 185, 212, 213, 238, 244, 249, 251, 254, 257, 261-265, 276, 281, 288, 303, 304
equalization 33, 39, 58, 129, 184, 237, 244, 254, 260
ergonomics 61

**F**

filmic 5, 15, 33
filmmaker 1, 2, 10, 11, 14, 21, 30, 31, 36, 41, 42, 69, 85, 116, 222, 223, 224, 225, 231, 232, 233, 235, 244
Final Cut Pro 41, 88, 89, 92, 96
Fletcher Munson 77
foley artist 6, 25, 177, 188, 190
foley artists 6, 177, 178
foley mixer 6
foley supervisor 6
Jack Foley 7, 177
frame rate 87, 103, 114, 115, 116, 119, 120, 122, 305
frequency spectrum 77, 78, 101, 244, 245, 247, 260, 263, 265, 302
full scale 277, 279, 302

**G**

gain changes 108, 281
generator 87
gold pins 51

**H**

handles 92, 93, 94, 119, 144, 145, 203, 205, 218, 227, 262
headphone level 45
hertz 302
high pass filter 149, 156, 244, 249, 252
high pass filters 262
high side 283
horror 31, 172, 177, 192, 197
HPF. *See also high pass filter*

**I**

I/O setup 113
impedance 46, 49, 155
input meter 159
insert effects 106, 108, 110
inserts 106, 107, 108, 249, 251, 303
instrument level 44, 45, 49
isolation transformers 53, 55, 141

**J**

jacks 50

**K**

keyboard patch 242

**L**

latency 113, 114
lavaliere mic 90, 105
Lavaliere mics 130, 250

layering 25, 28, 100, 173, 174, 185, 192, 199, 202, 281

layers 3, 7, 17, 21, 26, 27, 28, 31, 35, 173, 182, 184, 185, 193, 196, 197, 199, 200, 204, 253

level meter 78

LFE 81, 82, 111, 116, 174, 284, 285, 294

lighting dimmers 53

limiter 111, 123, 259, 260, 276, 303

line level 44, 45, 46, 49, 50

long form noise 137

low pass filters 262

low side 283, 284

LPF. *See also low pass filters*

lyrics 31, 242

## M

M&E 36, 110, 172, 288, 293, 303

mass 71

master bus 109, 110, 111, 118, 122, 123, 124, 256, 260, 276, 277

master effects 106

master license 220, 221

mastering 123, 259, 264, 265, 276, 280, 288, 289, 303, 304

Material eXchange Format (MXF) 89

matrix 271

Media Composer 41

metering 34, 277, 279, 281, 302, 303

microphone level 45, 49

midrange 34, 73, 76, 77, 78, 99, 157, 185, 259, 260, 264, 265

mix groups 110

mixdown 34, 81, 110, 114, 118, 120, 125, 273, 292, 293, 294, 295, 303

modulation 248, 249

mono tracks 130, 159

mood 13, 33, 215, 280

multichannel mix 36, 272

music acquisition 31

music licensing 219, 221, 227, 230, 231

music spotting 32

music video 199

musical loop 241

## N

NLE 38, 39, 41, 83, 87, 89, 90, 91, 94, 96, 100, 105, 106, 107, 117, 119, 120, 121, 256, 295, 303

noise drones 182, 200

noise reduction 28, 58, 59, 107, 125, 144, 145, 148, 198, 202, 211, 212, 213, 301

noiseprint 144

non linear video editor 38

## O

off axis 150, 165, 304

offline processing 41, 106, 107, 125, 184, 253, 254, 301, 303

OMF. *See also Open Media Framework*

Open Media Framework 3, 89, 92

optical (ADAT lightpipe) 48

outboard mixer 79, 278

## P

Pan law 80, 115, 117

panning 34, 112, 250, 251, 266, 267, 272, 274, 281, 284

panorama 266, 268, 301, 304

parametric 59, 138, 140, 166, 212, 261, 262, 263, 265

parametric equalizer 59, 140, 261

pitch shift 252

plosive 24, 147, 304

plosives 128, 132, 135, 146, 163, 165, 249

pool 47, 69, 100, 102, 104, 119, 121, 122, 125, 254, 303

post audio engineer 25

production libraries 229

production sound mixers 25

project 11, 45, 47, 48, 49, 60, 61, 85, 86, 87, 88, 89, 90, 94, 97, 103, 104, 106, 112, 114, 115, 116, 117, 119, 120, 121, 122, 123, 124, 162, 184, 227, 236, 291, 292, 295, 296

ProTools 42, 60, 105, 107, 109, 110, 118, 123, 124, 147, 148, 280, 301

public domain 225, 226, 228

## Q

Q value 247, 262

QuickTime 60, 87, 95, 96, 97, 116, 119, 120, 121, 234, 295

## R

random diffusion 71

re-recording mixers 6, 278, 281

reality genre 31, 34, 194

reflection 73

Reverb 4, 33, 34, 59, 109, 123, 127, 134, 156, 157, 162, 190, 191, 201, 245, 246, 247, 248, 249, 251, 252-254, 257, 266, 270, 274, 275, 276, 286, 298, 304

reverse 210, 212, 231, 252, 273, 301

RMS 76, 280, 281, 286

rockwool 74

room tone 5, 28, 29, 35, 36, 86, 129, 142, 155, 173, 193, 194, 195, 196, 199, 200, 201, 202, 203, 204, 205, 206, 211, 212, 214, 268, 283, 300, 304

royalty free 31, 225, 226, 228, 229

# S

S/PDIF 45, 47, 48, 49, 53
sample rate 40, 47, 86, 93, 94, 97, 103, 113, 114, 116, 117, 118, 120, 121, 122, 292, 295
scene transitions 85, 181, 192, 275
science fiction 32, 188, 197
SFX editor 6
SFX supervisor 6
shotgun 50, 130, 131, 150, 155, 156, 162, 189, 191, 214, 250, 268, 301, 304
sibilance 24, 106, 128, 132, 146, 147, 249, 305
signal flow 37, 106, 107
signal to noise ratio 142, 143, 305
silent film 217
sine wave 52, 76, 79, 80, 294
slate 84, 85
SMPTE timecode 23, 87, 305
soft clipping 278
sonic layer 3, 127, 195
sonic layers 17, 21, 184
Sony Vegas 41, 43
sound absorption panels 73
sound coupling 67
sound designer 6, 41, 171, 195
sound effects mixer 6
sound mixer 6, 25, 84, 130, 131, 142, 198, 201, 203, 214, 298, 299, 300
sound proofing 248
sound restoration 59, 133, 211
sound ripples 71
sound smear 71
sound treating 248
sound waves 71, 74
soundboard 71
soundcard 37, 50, 78, 103, 113, 114, 157, 158, 301, 303, 305
Soundminer 176, 180, 182
soundscape 9, 273
Space 4, 5, 12, 13, 33, 38, 58, 60, 69, 89, 93, 142, 173, 175, 187, 199, 217, 245, 271, 274, 275, 285, 293, 296, 301, 302, 304
special treatment 34
spectrum analyzer 123, 277
SPL meter 78, 79, 80, 81, 82
spline 209
standing waves 71, 74
stem exports 293
stems 118, 123, 260, 276, 288, 292, 293, 296, 305
stock libraries 20, 25, 30, 170, 177, 195, 199, 214, 242, 245
stock library 28, 33, 34, 170, 173, 192, 197, 198, 203, 299
strain relief 50, 51
studio monitors 37, 56, 57, 63, 64, 65, 67, 72, 75, 150, 158, 286
subwoofer 56, 65, 69, 80, 81, 82, 174, 284, 285, 286
supervising sound editor 5
surround mix 36, 112, 268, 271, 272, 291, 301
surrounds 56, 112, 257, 269, 271, 274, 284
suspense 10, 31, 73, 181, 200, 218
sweet spot 67
sync license 220, 221, 226, 233
syncing dialogue 161

# T

tempo 33, 234
The Home Stretch 4, 6, 191
timbre 33, 101, 128, 129, 130, 150, 155, 190, 256, 259, 261
time stretch 252
time stretching 40, 180, 184, 192
timecode reader 87, 88
timing 161, 167, 168, 191, 209, 216, 218, 219, 237, 246, 271, 281
Toslink 45, 48, 305
transient 305

transients 259, 278
tweeter 67
two track 264, 305

# U

unbalanced cables 46, 53
unclean ground 55
unity gain 46, 79, 305

# V

video editing 3, 14, 20, 21, 38, 40, 41, 100, 105, 118
video editor 2, 38, 83, 84, 85, 87
video sequence. *See also non linear video editor*
video sequencing program 2
vinyl restoration 148
VO. *See also voiceover*
voiceover 4, 17, 21, 84, 100, 122, 162, 163, 165, 168, 171, 201
VU meter 278, 279, 280

# W

washouts 257
waveform 40, 47, 81, 106, 117, 120, 134, 135, 136, 137, 138, 160, 161, 184, 237, 238, 239, 260, 265, 271, 277, 292
Waves Restoration Bundle 147
wild dialogue 86
wild sound 25, 86, 299, 300, 305
word clock 45, 48
word length 47, 94, 114, 115, 117